D1132150

331
WHAT IS ART?
AND
ESSAYS ON ART

Oxford University Press, Ely House, London W. 1

GLASGOW   NEW YORK   TORONTO   MELBOURNE   WELLINGTON
CAPE TOWN   IBADAN   NAIROBI   DAR ES SALAAM   LUSAKA   ADDIS ABABA
DELHI   BOMBAY   CALCUTTA   MADRAS   KARACHI   LAHORE   DACCA
KUALA LUMPUR   SINGAPORE   HONG KONG   TOKYO

WHAT IS ART?
AND
ESSAYS ON ART
BY
LEO TOLSTÓY

Translated with an Introduction by
AYLMER MAUDE

LONDON
OXFORD UNIVERSITY PRESS
NEW YORK   TORONTO

LEO TOLSTOY

Born, Yásnaya Polyána, Túla
    28 August (old style) = 9 September, n.s., 1828
Died, Astapovo, Riazan
    7 November (old style) = 20 November, n.s. 1910

ISBN 0 19 250331 6

What is Art? *first appeared in* 1898; *the other essays in the
years given in the Contents. In* The World's Classics *the
Maude translation was first published in* 1930, *and reprinted
in* 1938, 1942, 1946, 1950, 1955, 1959, 1962, 1969,
and 1975

*Printed in Great Britain
at the University Press, Oxford
by Vivian Ridler
Printer to the University*

INTRODUCTION

TOLSTÓY was intensely interested at different times in many different subjects but was always interested in art. To no other topic did he recur so often and over so long a period of years. He tells us that it took him fifteen years to elucidate the ideas expressed in *What is Art?* the most important of the dozen essays he wrote on the subject; and he considered it the best arranged and best thought-out of all his philosophical works.

To expect that we—differing from him in race, upbringing, and time—should agree with him in all his likes and dislikes of particular artists, and works, and ideals, is to demand too much; nor did he attach importance to the particular examples he gave, for he remarks that: 'My old, inured habits may cause me to err, and I may mistake for absolute merit the impression a work produced on me in my youth.'

But it is of interest to see what general theory of art satisfied the author of *War and Peace*, *Anna Karénina*, and *Twenty-three Tales*, who was also one of Russia's greatest dramatists, besides being keenly interested in music and all the other arts.

In extracting the essence of his book let us follow the lines he indicated in an essay on an important classic which has aroused much discussion and been very variously interpreted. He advises us to: 'Read it, putting aside all foregone conclusions; read it with the sole desire to understand what is there said. But just because it is an important book read it considerately, reasonably, and with discernment, and not haphazard or mechanically as though all the words were of equal weight.

'To understand any book one must choose out the parts that are quite clear, dividing them from what is obscure or confused, and from what is clear we must form our idea of the drift and spirit of the whole work. Then on the basis of what we have understood we may proceed to make out what is confused or not quite intelligible. That is how all kinds of books should be read. . . . To understand, we must first of all separate what is quite simple and intelligible from what is confused and unintelligible, and must afterwards read this clear and intelligible part several times over, trying fully to understand it. Then, helped by the comprehension of the general meaning, we can try to explain to ourselves the drift of the parts which seemed involved and obscure. . . . Very likely in selecting what is, from what is not, fully comprehensible, people will not all choose the same passages. What is comprehensible to one may seem obscure to another. But all will certainly agree in what is most important, and these are things which will be found quite intelligible to every one. It is just this—just what is fully comprehensible to all men—that constitutes the essence of the teaching.'

Reading Tolstóy's essays on art in that spirit, what is the marrow one can extract from them?

First, his explanation that art is: 'an activity by means of which one man, having experienced a feeling, intentionally transmits it to others.' This, Bernard Shaw says, 'is the simple truth: the moment it is uttered, whoever is really conversant with art recognizes in it the voice of the master'.

Tolstóy once remarked to me in conversation, that the sign of any great philosophy is that it generalizes a wide range of important ideas so that it can be explained to an intelligent boy of twelve in a quarter of an hour. Let us apply that test to his own philosophy of art, confining ourselves to the simplest examples.

If a boy out for a walk sees a bull coming towards him and is terrified, and if on reaching home he tells the story of how the bull coming towards him lowered its head and looked fierce, and of how he hurried away, stumbled, recovered his balance, climbed over a stile, and was happy to escape—and if he tells the story so that his parents are infected by his emotion and feel what he has gone through—he has achieved a work of art. So also if he did not see any bull, but only imagined how he would feel if he met one, and then recalling that feeling, imagined and told the tale so that his parents shared the feelings he had experienced, that too would be a work of art.

Or again: if a man passing through a crowded room treads on a lady's toe and causes her to shriek with pain so that her feeling is communicated to others—that is *not* a work of art, because her transmission of feeling is spontaneous and instinctive at the very moment she herself experiences it. But if the man passes her again *without* stepping on her toe, and it occurs to her to pretend that he has, and in order to cause others to share the sense of discomfort she had experienced she recalls it, and by voice and gesture expresses it, pretending that he has hurt her again, that might be a work of art. It would depend on how she used her voice and her gesture. If she used them so that they infected others with her feeling, it would be art; but if voice or gesture failed to respond to her intention, the attempt would miss fire and would not be art.

The second point is even simpler. It is the difference between the *form* and the *feeling* of a work of art.

Take the action of music. Tolstóy says of one of the many feelings art deals with:

'Sometimes people who are together, if not hostile to one another are at least estranged in mood and feeling, till perhaps a story, a performance, a picture, or even a building, but oftenest of all music, unites them all as by an electric flash, and in place of their former isolation or even enmity they are all conscious of union and mutual love. Each is glad that another feels what he feels, glad of the communion established not only between him and all those present, but also with all now living who will yet share the same impression, and more than that, he feels the mysterious gladness of the communion which reaching beyond the grave unites us with all men of the past who have been moved by the same feelings and with all men of the future who will yet be touched by them.'

But what are the conditions, what is the *form* of the art, which can accomplish this? Tolstóy quotes the remark of Bryulóv, a Russian painter, that 'Art begins where the *wee bit* begins', and adds: 'The remark is true of all arts, but its justice is particularly noticeable in the performance of music. That musical execution should be artistic, should be art, that is, should carry infection, three chief conditions must be observed. There are many others needed for musical perfection: the transition from one sound to another must be

interrupted or continuous; the sound must increase
or diminish steadily; it must blend with one and not
with another sound; the sound must have this or that
timbre, and much besides—but take the three chief
conditions: the pitch, the time, and the strength of
the sound. Musical execution is only then art, only
then infects, when the sound is neither higher nor
lower than it should be, that is, when exactly the
infinitely small centre of the required note is taken;
when that note is continued exactly as long as is
needed; and when the strength of the sound is neither
more nor less than is required. The slightest deviation
of pitch in either direction, the slightest increase or
decrease in time, or the slightest strengthening or
weakening of the sound beyond what is needed, destroys the perfection and consequently the infectiousness of the work. So that the feeling of infection
by the art of music, which seems so simple and so
easily obtained, is a thing we receive only when
the performer finds those infinitely minute degrees which are necessary to perfection in music.
It is the same in all arts: a wee bit lighter, a wee
bit darker, a wee bit higher or lower, to the right or
the left—in painting; a wee bit weaker or stronger in
intonation, a wee bit sooner or later—in dramatic art;
a wee bit omitted, over-emphasized, or exaggerated
—in poetry, and there is no contagion. Infection
is only obtained when an artist finds those infinitely minute degrees of which the work of
art consists, and only to the extent to which he
finds them. And it is quite impossible to teach
people by external means to find these minute
degrees: they can only be found when a man yields

to his feeling. No instruction can make a dancer catch just the tact of the music, or a singer or fiddler take exactly the infinitely minute centre of his note, or a sketcher draw of all possible lines the only right one, or a poet find the only right arrangement of the only suitable words. All this is found by feeling. And therefore schools may teach what is necessary in order to produce something resembling art, but not art itself.'

Unless the form be adequate, no story, or song, or tune, or picture, or statue, or dance, or play, or ornament, or building, can convey its creator's feeling to its audience or spectators. Whether a thing is a work of art or not depends on its form. If a feeling, beneficial or harmful, is diffused by the infectiousness of its form, it is a work of art, and whether its creator was or was not prompted by feelings of social, political, religious, or ethical importance does not alter that fact.

The idea that the feelings conveyed must not be important feelings is a delusion that grew up because people engaged on the propaganda of certain views often have not been actuated by genuine feeling, or have lacked artistic power of expression; so that many critics have been deluded into supposing that a genuine feeling connected with a great movement could not be expressed by art. The grain of truth hidden in such opinions is, that no motive, however excellent or however important, will replace the essentials of a genuine work of art: real feeling and adequate form.

But though without the right *form* no work of art can exist, it is a fact that, when we have genuine works of art, it makes a great difference whether the feelings they spread abroad are such as to benefit or to injure mankind. That is Tolstóy's third main point.

To say that it does not matter, would be to declare that art dwells in a water-tight compartment and has no vital relation to human life. But as the artist himself is a human being and cannot well cut himself in two, whatever makes life in general better or worse must relate to him—unless indeed he be the kind of specialist of whom Tolstóy says: 'These people grow savage over their specialized and stupefying occupations and become one-sided and self-complacent specialists, dull to all the serious phenomena of life, and skilful only at rapidly twisting their legs, their tongues, or their fingers.'

This brings us to the fourth and last of the main planks of his theory of art, namely, the justification of the importance we attach to it. Were art merely a matter of dexterity and technical skill it would be comparable to billiards, cricket, or professional chessplaying. But we rightly attribute to it a far greater importance; for it is art that shapes, forms, and develops man's feelings by the general diffusion and contagion of those that artists express. And as our feelings influence our thoughts, our beliefs, our activities, and the whole of our lives, there is much sound sense in the remark quoted by Fletcher of Saltoun that, 'If a man were permitted to make all the ballads' [which in Fletcher's time stood for music, poetry, and the whole of art] 'he would not care who should make the laws of a nation.' For, indeed, the lawgiver would be but wax in the artist's hands.

That is why art may and should be 'an organ co-

equally important with science for the life and progress of mankind'.

The need of distinguishing the form of a work—on
which its powers of infection depend—from the feelings it conveys (the real 'subject-matter' of a work
of art) was to Tolstóy so obvious that though he expressed it, he does not specially emphasize or insist on
it but merely states it incidentally. Some readers
have overlooked this essential point, and that no
one may suspect me of having invented it (I would
gladly claim it as my own were I entitled to do so)
let me draw attention to the passages in which he
states it.

In Chapter XII he says: 'Infection is only
obtained when an artist finds those infinitely
minute degrees of which a work of art consists,
and only to the extent to which he finds them.'

In Chapter XIV he says: 'If a man is infected by the author's condition of soul, if he
feels this emotion and this union with others,
then the object which has effected this is art. . . .
And not only is infection a sure sign of art, but
the degree of infection is also the sole measure of
excellence in art.

'*The stronger the infection the better is the art*, as art,
speaking now apart from its subject-matter, that
is, not considering the quality of the feelings it
transmits.'

These passages taken together are a plain statement that what constitutes a work of art is its
excellence of form, and that on that its power
to transmit feeling depends. Tolstóy puts this assertion in a distinct chapter from that in which he deals

with the 'subject-matter' of art, that is to say, with the quality of the feelings art transmits, and argues that those feelings which make for the betterment of human life are preferable to those which make life worse, and should be encouraged if we wish the world to improve.

Gray evidently anticipated Tolstóy's perception when he said that art could

> 'heap the shrine of luxury and pride
> With incense kindled at the Muses' flame'.

Tolstóy co-ordinated, amplified, and elucidated the ideas Fletcher and Gray had previously expressed, and he has so combined them as to present for the first time in literature a reasonable, convincing, and complete theory of the relation of art to other human activities and to life in general.

It should be unnecessary to explain that when Tolstóy says that an artist 'hands on to others feelings he has lived through' he means what he says. Were an explanation of the word 'feelings' needed, it would be found in the paragraph immediately preceding his definition of art, which says: 'The feelings with which the artist infects others may be most various —very strong or very weak, very important or very insignificant, very bad or very good: feelings of love of one's country, self-devotion and submission to fate or to God expressed in a drama, raptures of lovers described in a novel, feelings of voluptuousness expressed in a picture, courage expressed in a triumphal march, merriment evoked by a dance, humour evoked by a funny story, the feeling of quietness transmitted by an evening landscape or by a lullaby, or the

feeling of admiration evoked by a beautiful arabesque
—it is all art.'

While writing this Introduction I have, however,
opened a book by Mr. Hugh I'Anson Faussett in
which some thirty pages are devoted to the discussion
of Tolstóy's views on art, and I find in it the extraordinary statement that Tolstóy tries to define the word
'feeling' by the phrase 'flowing from their religious
perception'. As every reader may see for himself,
those words are taken from a subsequent page, where
Tolstóy is not defining art at all, but is saying that
people have always attached special importance to
that part of the activity of art which flows 'from their
religious perception'. This need not, however, trouble
those who take the theory as Tolstóy states it and
not as the critic interprets it.

How far Tolstóy went beyond the understanding of
art current when he wrote the book at the end of the
nineteenth century is indicated by the fact that its
first reviewers were quite unable to understand what
he was saying, and even now, thirty years later, some
of our ablest critics—as in the instance just cited—
seem unable to believe that he meant what he clearly
and emphatically said, and still feel impelled to
attribute to him preposterous theories, as though
when he spoke on the subject he knew most about—
that of art—Tolstóy became a semi-imbecile whose
raving they are quite competent to correct. The
attitude calls to mind the Russian saying about 'the
sick who send the hale to bed'. As the years pass
Tolstóy's masterpiece becomes better understood, the
confusion caused by the critics dies down, the facts and
people concerned are seen in better proportion, and

the value of an understanding of the part that art plays in human life becomes more generally recognized.

The question of the interaction of art and life is no doubt complex, and when anybody holding strong convictions, as Tolstóy did, expresses his sympathies or antipathies for certain feelings—let us say, for those favourable to pacificism or to militarism—he must encounter opposition from people whose feelings run counter to his own; and so, if the theory of art as outlined above is not clearly grasped, people may think they are differing about art when they are really differing about ethics.

It is certain that a Roman Catholic, an Evangelical, a Unitarian, an Atheist, and a worshipper of Venus, Bacchus, Mars, Moloch, Mammon, or Mumbo-Jumbo, each ardent in his peculiar faith, cannot all approve of the same feelings; but whatever feelings men have may be strengthened or weakened by artistic expression.

To think sanely we must separate the two complex problems, and take them one at a time, not allowing the importance of morals to prevent us from understanding the nature and influence of art.

It has so long been common to regard morals as an obstacle to art, that the fact is not readily grasped (especially by those who are concerned mainly with art for the sake of pleasure) that art can promote any kind of feeling, and may therefore ally itself with any religious or irreligious tendency you please. The Puritans disliked art because they realized that the beauty of cathedrals and of church music helped to preserve the influence of an established religion they disapproved of, and they therefore diligently chipped the noses off the church statues. It took them a long time to realize that in oratory, as well as in satire, in prose, in verse, and in hymns, art could afford them valuable aid. Only by art can the influence of art be successfully countered, and there is nothing in Tolstóy's theory that a reasonable man need reject, whether he agrees or disagrees with Tolstóy's ethics and consequently with the instances he quotes of works he considers good 'in the subject-matter', that is to say, good in the quality of the *feelings conveyed*.

I have here dealt with *What is Art?* because it is by far the most important and complete of Tolstóy's writings on the subject. The other essays are chiefly of value as preliminary steps to the theory there propounded or as supplementary applications of it.

In *Schoolboys and Art* we have a glimpse of the experience which proved to Tolstóy that peasant children can appreciate art, and can also—as stories written by some of them showed—create works of art themselves once the mechanical difficulties are removed from their path; and that convinced him also that the first requisite of artistic appreciation is the possession of 'that simple feeling familiar to the plainest man and even to a child, that sense of infection with another's feeling—compelling us to rejoice in another's gladness, to sorrow at another's grief, and to mingle souls with another—which is the very essence of art'. That is why he affirms that a peasant, a child, or even a savage, may be susceptible to the influence of art, while a sophisticated man who has lost 'that simple feeling' may, though highly educated, be immune to art.

On Truth in Art is a simple explanation, for children, of the fact that an invented or even fantastic story may be artistically true and convey a true feeling.

The short *Introduction to Amiel's Journal* does not deal with what is generally considered to be 'artistic' work, but—apart from the fact that the *Journal* is literature of 'elegance, and (in passages) apparent choiceness of phrasing'—its inclusion in this book may be justified by Tolstóy's statement that the different kinds of literature—philosophic, hortatory, and artistic,— merge into one another.

The *Introduction to Seménov's Peasant Stories*, though those stories are not known in English, is valuable because it comes near to Tolstóy's final view of art and helps the reader to understand the view expressed in *What is Art?*

The *Introduction to the Works of Guy de Maupassant* is, next to *What is Art?*, the most valuable essay in the book. It would indeed be hard to find a more penetrating and appreciative essay on any modern writer.

On Art, written only a couple of years before *What is Art?*, marks the stage in Tolstóy's progress towards an elucidation of the problem, immediately preceding its achievement. Much in it comes very near the mark, but it contains some propositions which he afterwards discarded, and is a much barer, more purely intellectual, treatment of the matter, and is therefore less attractive. The writer does not let himself go, nor display his personal sympathies and antipathies in the attractive fashion of *What is Art?*

Tolstóy's Preface to *What is Art?* is an emphatic protest against the mutilation of his work by the Russian censor, but incidentally it is an almost unique instance of a great writer's preferring a translation of his work to the original as it was published in his own language.

The absence of copyright in Tolstóy's work has long led to a scramble among publishers, so that no less than forty-nine of them have published one or more of his works in England or America, and it became quite a puzzle for readers or booksellers to know which versions to consider reliable. The indication given in this Preface by Tolstóy has, however, considerably helped to obtain recognition for the Tolstóy translations now appearing in the 'World's Classics' series.

The article on von Polenz's novel *Der Büttnerbauer* is excellent, apart from what it says on that particular work, in its treatment of the function of criticism and of the fact that the really great literature of the past is being constantly pushed aside by a flood of works 'of no artistic merit, printed and circulated by millions under the guise of artistic productions'.

The *Afterword to Chékhov's story, 'Darling'* is a happy example of readiness to appreciate excellence in other writers—in this case in Tolstóy's personal friend A. P. Chékhov. Incidentally the article expresses his disagreement with the women's movement prevalent when he wrote. But that need not concern us here for it does not touch the question of art. As the story *Darling* was not written by Tolstóy it is not included in this book. A translation of it is included in the larger, illustrated volume, *Tolstóy on Art*, which contains other matter not included here.

It only remains to mention that six of the pictures alluded to in *What is Art?* are also reproduced in *Tolstóy on Art*, and that the bulk of what has been said of *What is Art?* in this Introduction appeared first in an article in the musical monthly, *The Sackbut*, and is here reproduced by kind consent of Miss Ursula Greville, the editor of that periodical. Of the influence of music on Tolstóy, and his particular likes and dislikes in that domain, we may read in his eldest son's article on the subject in *Family Views of Tolstóy*.

AYLMER MAUDE.

GREAT BADDOW,
CHELMSFORD.

CONTENTS

PART I

SCHOOLBOYS AND ART

The following account of Tolstóy's walk with some boys from his school at Yásnaya Polyána shows how Tolstóy found himself faced by the question: what is art? put to him by a ten-year-old peasant boy. It then seemed to him that 'we said all that can be said about utility and plastic and moral beauty'; but another thirty-seven years had to pass before, in *What is Art?*, he succeeded in elucidating the whole problem to his satisfaction.

THE classes generally finish about eight or nine o'clock (unless carpentering keeps the elder boys somewhat later), and the whole band run shouting into the yard, and there, calling to one another, begin to separate, making for different parts of the village. Occasionally they arrange to coast down-hill to the village in a large sledge that stands outside the gate. They tie up the shafts, throw themselves into it, and squealing, disappear from sight in a cloud of snow, leaving here and there on their path black patches of children who have tumbled out. In the open air, out of school (for all its freedom), new relations are established between pupil and teacher: freer, simpler, and more trustful—those very relations which seem to us the ideal that School should aim at.

Not long ago we read Gógol's story *Vii*[1] in the highest class. The final scenes affected them greatly and excited their imagination. Some of them played the witch, and kept alluding to the last chapters. . . .

---

[1] The *Vii* is an Earth-Spirit, and Gógol's tale is gruesome.

Out of doors it was a moonless winter night with clouds in the sky, not cold. We stopped at the cross-roads. The elder boys, in their third year at school, stopped near me asking me to accompany them farther. The younger ones looked at us and rushed off down-hill. They had begun to learn with a new master, and between them and me there is not the same confidence as between the older boys and myself.

'Well, let us go to the wood' (a small wood about one hundred and twenty yards from the house), said one of them. The most insistent was Fédka, a boy of ten, with a tender, receptive, poetic yet daring nature. Danger seems to form the chief condition of pleasure for him. In summer it always frightened me to see how he, with two other boys, would swim out into the very middle of the pond, which is nearly a hundred and twenty yards wide, and would now and then dis-appear in the hot reflection of the summer sun and swim under water; and how he would then turn on his back, causing fountains of water to rise, and calling with his high-pitched voice to his comrades on the bank to see what a fine fellow he was.

He now knew there were wolves in the wood, and so he wanted to go there. All agreed; and the four of us went to the wood. Another boy, a lad of twelve, physically and morally strong, whom I will call Sëmka, went on in front and kept calling and 'ah-ou-ing' with his ringing voice to some one at a distance. Prónka, a sickly, mild, and very gifted lad from a poor family (sickly probably chiefly from lack of food), walked by my side. Fédka walked between me and Sëmka, talking all the time in a particularly gentle voice: now relating how he had herded horses in summer, now saying there was nothing to be afraid of, and now asking, 'Suppose one should jump out?' and insisting on my giving some reply. We did not go into the wood: that would have been too dreadful; but even where we were, near the wood, it was darker, the road was scarcely visible, and the lights of the village were hidden from view. Sëmka stopped and listened: 'Stop, you fellows! What is this?' said he suddenly.

We were silent and, though we heard nothing, things seemed to grow more gruesome.

'What shall we do if it leaps out . . . and comes at us?' asked Fédka.

We began to talk about Caucasian robbers. They remembered a Caucasian tale I had told them long ago, and I again told them of 'braves,' of Cossacks, and of Hadji Murad.[1] Sëmka went on in front, treading boldly in his big boots, his broad back swaying regularly. Prónka tried to walk by my side, but Fédka pushed him off the path, and Prónka—who, probably on account of his poverty, always submitted —only ran up alongside at the most interesting passages, sinking in the snow up to his knees.

Every one who knows anything of Russian peasant children knows that they are not accustomed to, and cannot bear, any caresses, affectionate words, kisses, hand-touchings, and so forth. I have seen a lady in a peasant school, wishing to pet a boy, say: 'Come, I will give you a kiss, dear!' and actually kiss him; and the boy was ashamed and offended, and could not understand why he had been so treated. Boys of five are already above such caresses—they are no longer babies. I was therefore particularly struck when Fédka, walking beside me, at the most terrible part of the story suddenly touched me lightly with his sleeve, and then clasped two of my fingers in his hand and kept hold of them. As soon as I stopped speaking, Fédka demanded that I should go on, and did this in such a beseeching and agitated voice that it was impossible not to comply with his wish.

[1] A daring leader of the hill-tribes, who was prominent when Tolstóy was serving in the Caucasus.

'Now then, don't get in the way!' he said once angrily to Prónka, who had run in front of us. He was so carried away as even to be cruel; so agitated yet happy was he, holding on to my fingers, that he could let no one dare to interrupt his pleasure.

'More! More! It is fine!' said he.

We had passed the wood and were approaching the village from the other end.

'Let's go on,' said all the boys when the lights became visible. 'Let us take another turn!'

We went on in silence, sinking here and there in the snow which was not hardened by much traffic. A white darkness seemed to sway before our eyes; the clouds hung low, as though something had heaped them upon us. There was no end to the whiteness amid which we alone crunched along the snow. The wind sounded through the bare tops of the aspens, but where we were, behind the woods, it was calm.

I finished my story by telling how a 'brave', surrounded by his enemies, sang his death-song and threw himself on his dagger. All were silent.

'Why did he sing a song when he was surrounded?' asked Sëmka.

'Weren't you told?—he was preparing for death!' replied Fédka aggrieved.

'I think he said a prayer,' added Prónka.

All agreed. Fédka suddenly stopped.

'How was it, you told us, your Aunt had her throat cut?' he asked. (He had not yet had enough horrors.) 'Tell us! Tell us!'

I again told them that terrible story of the murder of Countess Tolstóy,[1] and they stood silently about me watching my face.

'The fellow got caught!' said Sëmka.

'He was afraid to go away in the night while she

[1] Some details of this crime are given in 'Why do Men Stupefy Themselves?' one of Tolstóy's *Essays*.

was lying with her throat cut!' said Fédka; 'I should have run away!' and he gathered my two fingers yet more closely in his hand.

We stopped in the thicket beyond the threshing-floor at the very end of the village. Sëmka picked up a dry stick from the snow and began striking it against the frosty trunk of a lime tree. Hoar frost fell from the branches on to our caps, and the noise of the blows resounded in the stillness of the wood.

'Lëv Nikoláevich,' said Fédka to me (I thought he was again going to speak about the Countess), 'why does one learn singing? I often think, why, really, does one?'

What made him jump from the terror of the murder to this question, heaven only knows; yet by the tone of his voice, the seriousness with which he demanded an answer, and the attentive silence of the other two, one felt that there was some vital and legitimate connexion between this question and our preceding talk. Whether the connexion lay in some response to my suggestion that crime might be explained by lack of education (I had spoken of that), or whether he was testing himself—transferring himself into the mind of the murderer and remembering his own favourite occupation (he has a wonderful voice and immense musical talent), or whether the connexion lay in the fact that he felt that now was the time for sincere conversation, and all the problems demanding solution rose in his mind—at any rate his question surprised none of us.

'And what is drawing for? And why write well?' said I, not knowing at all how to explain to him what art is for.

'What is drawing for?' repeated he thoughtfully. He was really asking, What is Art for? And I neither dared nor could explain.

'What is drawing for?' said Sëmka. 'Why, you

draw anything, and can then make it from the drawing.'

'No, that is designing,' said Fédka. 'But why draw figures?'

Sëmka's matter-of-fact mind was not perplexed.

'What is a stick for, and what is a lime tree for?' said he, still striking the tree.

'Yes, what is a lime tree for?' said I.

'To make rafters of,' replied Sëmka.

'But what is it for in summer, when not yet cut down?'

'It's no use then.'

'No, really,' insisted Fédka; 'why does a lime tree grow?'

And we began to speak of the fact that not everything exists for use but that there is also beauty, and that Art is beauty; and we understood one another, and Fédka quite understood why the lime tree grows and what singing is for.

Prónka agreed with us, but he thought rather of moral beauty: goodness.

Sëmka's big brain understood, but did not acknowledge, beauty apart from usefulness. He was in doubt (as often happens to men with great reasoning power): feeling Art to be a force, but not feeling in his soul the need of that force. He, like them, wished to get at Art by his reason, and tried to kindle that fire in himself.

'We'll sing *Who hath* to-morrow. I remember my part,' said he. (He has a correct ear, but no taste or refinement in singing.) Fédka, however, fully understood that the lime tree is good when in leaf: good to look at in summer, and that that is enough.

Prónka understood that it is a pity to cut it down, because it, too, has life:

'Why, when we take the sap of a lime it's like taking blood.'

Sëmka, though he did not say so, evidently thought that there was little use in a lime when it was sappy.

It feels strange to repeat what we then said, but it seems to me that we said all that can be said about utility, and plastic and moral beauty.

We went on to the village. Fédka still clung to my hand; now, it seemed to me, from gratitude. We were all nearer one another that night than we had been for a long time. Prónka walked beside us along the broad village street.

'See, there is still a light in Masánov's house,' said he. 'As I was going to school this morning, Gavrúka was coming from the pub, as dru-u-nk as could be! His horse all in a lather and he beating it! I am always sorry for such things. Really, why should it be beaten?'

'And the other day, coming from Túla, my daddy gave his horse the reins,' said Sëmka; 'and it took him into a snowdrift, and there he slept—quite drunk.'

'And Gavrúka kept on beating his horse over the eyes, and I felt so sorry,' repeated Prónka again. 'Why should he beat it? He got down and just flogged it.'

Sëmka suddenly stopped.

'Our folk are already asleep,' said he, looking in at the window of his crooked, dirty hut. 'Won't you walk a little longer?'

'No.'

'Go-o-od-bye, Lëv Nikoláevich!' he shouted suddenly, and tearing himself away from us as it were with an effort, he ran to the house, lifted the latch, and disappeared.

'So you will take each of us home? First one and then the other?' said Fédka.

We went on. There was a light in Prónka's hut, and we looked in at the window. His mother, a tall and handsome but toil-worn woman, with black eyebrows and eyes, sat at the table, peeling potatoes. In the middle of the hut hung a cradle. Prónka's brother, the mathematician from our second class, was standing at the table, eating potatoes with salt. It was a black, tiny, and dirty hut.

'What a plague you are!' shouted the mother at Prónka. 'Where have you been?'

Prónka glanced at the window with a meek, sickly smile. His mother guessed that he had not come alone, and her face immediately assumed an artificial expression that was unpleasant.

Only Fédka was left.

'The travelling tailors are at our house, that is why there's a light there,' said he in the softened voice that had come to him that evening. 'Good-bye, Lëv Nikoláevich!' he added, softly and tenderly, and began to knock with the ring attached to the closed door. 'Let me in!' his high-pitched voice rang out amid the winter stillness of the village. It was long before they opened the door for him. I looked in at the window. The hut was a large one. The father was playing cards with a tailor, and some copper coins lay on the table. The wife, Fédka's stepmother, was sitting near the torch-stand, looking eagerly at the money. The young tailor, a cunning drunkard, was holding his cards on the table, bending them and looking triumphantly at his opponent. Fédka's father, the collar of his shirt unbuttoned, his brow wrinkled with mental exertion and vexation, changed one card for another, and waved his horny hand in perplexity above them.

'Let me in!'

The woman rose and went to the door.

'Good-bye!' repeated Fédka, once again. 'Let us always have walks like this!'

1861

PART II

ON TRUTH IN ART

Preface to a Miscellany, 'The Flower Garden,' for Children.

'O generation of vipers, how can ye, being evil, speak good things? for out of the abundance of the heart the mouth speaketh. The good man out of his good treasure bringeth forth good things: and the evil man out of his evil treasure bringeth forth evil things. And I say unto you, that every idle word that men shall speak, they shall give account thereof in the day of judgment. For by thy words thou shalt be justified, and by thy words thou shalt be condemned.' (Matt. xii, 34–37).

IN this book, besides tales in which true occurrences are narrated, there are also stories, traditions, proverbs, legends, fables, and fairy tales, that have been composed and written for man's benefit.

We have chosen such as we consider to be in accord with Christ's teaching, and therefore regard as good and truthful.

Many people, especially children, when reading a story, fairy-tale, legend, or fable, ask first of all: 'Is it true?' and if they see that what is described could not have happened, they often say: 'Oh, this is mere fancy, it isn't true.'

Those who judge so, judge amiss.

Truth will be known not by him who knows only what has been, is, and really happens, but by him who recognizes what should be according to the will of God.

He does not write the truth who describes only what has happened and what this or that man has done, but he who shows what people do that is right—

that is, in accord with God's will; and what people do wrong—that is, contrary to God's will.

Truth is a path. Christ said, 'I am the way, the truth, and the life.'

And so he who looks down at his feet will not know the truth, but he who discerns by the sun which way to go.

Verbal compositions are good and necessary, not when they describe what has happened, but when they show what ought to be; not when they tell what people have done, but when they set a value on what is good and evil—when they show men the narrow path of God's will, which leads to life.

And in order to show that path one must not describe merely what happens in the world. The world abides in evil and is full of offence. If one is to describe the world as it is, one will describe much evil and the truth will be lacking. In order that there may be truth in what one describes, it is necessary to write not about what is, but about what should be; to write not the truth of what is, but of the kingdom of God which is drawing nigh unto us but is not as yet. That is why there are mountains of books in which we are told what really has happened or might have happened, yet they are all false if those who write them do not themselves know what is good and what is evil, and do not know and do not show the one path which leads to the kingdom of God. And there are fairy-tales, parables, fables, legends, in which marvellous things are described which never happened or ever could happen, and these legends, fairy-tales, and fables, are true, because they show wherein the will of God has always been, and is, and will be: they show the truth of the kingdom of God.

There may be a book, and there are indeed many novels and stories, that describe how a man lives for his passions, suffers, torments others, endures danger and want, schemes, struggles with others, escapes from his poverty, and at last is united with the object of his love and becomes distinguished, rich, and happy. Such a book, even if everything described in it really happened, and though there were in it nothing improbable, would nevertheless be false and untrue, because a man who lives for himself and his passions, however beautiful his wife may be and however distinguished and rich he becomes, cannot be happy.

And there may be a legend of how Christ and his apostles walked on earth and went to a rich man, and the rich man would not receive him, and they went to a poor widow, and she received him. And then he commanded a barrel full of gold to roll to the rich man and sent a wolf to the poor widow to eat up her last calf, and it might prove a blessing for the widow and be bad for the rich man.

Such a story is totally improbable, because nothing of what is described ever happened or could happen; but it may all be true because in it is shown what always should be—what is good and what is evil, and what a man should strive after in order to do the will of God.

No matter what wonders are described, or what animals may talk in human language, what flying carpets may carry people from place to place, the legends, parables, or fairy-tales will be true, if there is in them the truth of the kingdom of God. And if that truth is lacking, then everything described, however well attested, will be false, because it lacks the truth of the kingdom of God. Christ himself spoke in parables, and his parables have remained eternally true. He only added, 'Take heed how ye hear.'

1887

PART III

INTRODUCTION TO AMIEL'S 'JOURNAL'

ABOUT eighteen months ago I chanced for the first time to read Amiel's book, *Fragments d'un journal intime*. I was struck by the significance and profundity of its contents, the beauty of its presentation, and above all by the sincerity of that book.

While reading it I marked the passages which specially struck me. My daughter¹ undertook to translate these passages, and in this way these extracts from *Fragments d'un journal intime* were produced: that is to say, they are extracts from the whole many-volumed diary Amiel wrote day by day during thirty years, much of which remained unprinted.

Henri Amiel was born at Geneva in 1821, and was early left an orphan. Having completed a course of higher education at Geneva, Amiel went abroad and spent some years at the universities of Heidelberg and Berlin. Returning in 1849 to his native land he, a young man of 28, obtained a professorship at the Geneva Academy, first of Esthetics and afterwards of Philosophy, which he held till his death.

Amiel's whole life was passed at Geneva, where he died, in 1881, in no way distinguished from the large number of those ordinary professors who, mechanically compiling their lectures from the latest books on their special subject, pass them on in an equally mechanical way to their hearers, or from the yet greater number of writers of verse lacking in substance, who supply these wares, which though no one needs them are still

¹ That is, Márya Lvóvna, Tolstóy's second daughter, who was devoted both to her father and to his teachings.

sold by tens of thousands in the periodicals that are published.

Amiel had not the slightest success either in the academic or literary field. When he was already approaching old age he wrote of himself as follows:

'What have I been able to extract from the gifts bestowed upon me, and from the special circumstances of my half-a-century of life? What have I drawn from my soil? Is all my scribbling collected together—my correspondence, *these thousands of sincere pages*, my lectures, my articles, my verses, my various memoranda—anything but a collection of dry leaves? To whom and for what have I been of use? And will my name live for even a day after me, and will it have any meaning for any one? An insignificant, empty life! *Vie nulle!*'

Two well-known French authors have written on Amiel and his *Journal* since his death—his friend, the well-known critic, E. Scherer, and the philosopher Caro. It is interesting to note the sympathetic but rather patronizing tone in which both these writers refer to Amiel, regretting that he lacked the qualities necessary for the production of real works. Yet the real works of these two writers—the critical works of Scherer and the philosophical works of Caro—will hardly long outlive their authors, while the accidental, unreal work of Amiel, his *Journal*, will always remain a living book, needed by men and fruitfully affecting them.

For a writer is precious and necessary for us only to the extent to which he reveals to us the inner labour of his soul—supposing, of course, that his work is new and has not been done before. Whatever he may write—a play, a learned work, a story, a philosophic treatise, lyric verse, a criticism, a satire—what is precious to us in an author's work is only that inner labour of his soul, and not the architectural structure

B

in which usually, and I think perhaps always, distorting it, he packs his thoughts and feelings.

All that Amiel poured into a ready mould: his lectures, treatises, poems, are dead; but his *Journal*, where without thinking of the form he only talked to himself, is full of life, wisdom, instruction, consolation, and will ever remain one of those best of all books which have been left to us accidentally by such men as Marcus Aurelius, Pascal, and Epictetus.

Pascal says: 'There are only three kinds of people: those who, having found God, serve Him; those who, not having found Him, are engaged in seeking Him; and those who, though they have not found Him, do not seek Him.

'The first are sensible and happy; the last are senseless and unhappy; the second are unhappy, but sensible.'

I think that the contrast Pascal makes between the first and the second groups, between those who, as he says in another place, having found God, serve Him with their whole heart, and those who, not having found Him, seek Him with their whole heart, is not only not so great as he thought, but does not exist at all. I think that those who with their whole heart and with suffering (*en gémissant*, as Pascal says) seek God, are already serving Him. They are serving Him because by the suffering they endure in their search they are laying, and revealing to others, the road to God, as Pascal himself did in his *Pensées*, and as Amiel did all his life in his *Journal*.

Amiel's whole life, as presented to us in this *Journal*, is full of this suffering and whole-hearted search for God. And the contemplation of this search is the more instructive because it never ceases to be a search, never becomes settled, and never passes into a consciousness of having attained the truth, or into a teaching. Amiel is not saying either to himself or to others, 'I now know the truth—hear me!' On the contrary it seems to him, as is natural to one who is sincerely seeking truth, that the more he knows the more he needs to know, and he unceasingly does all he can to learn more and more of truth, and is therefore constantly aware of his ignorance. He is continually speculating on what Christianity and the condition of a Christian should be, never for a moment pausing on the thought that Christianity is the very thing that he is professing, and that he is himself realizing the condition of a Christian. And yet the whole *Journal* is full of expressions of the most profound Christian understanding and feeling. And these expressions affect the reader with special force by their very unconsciousness and sincerity. He is talking to himself, not thinking that he is overheard, neither attempting to appear convinced of what he is not convinced of, nor hiding his sufferings and his search.

It is as if one were present without a man's knowledge at the most secret, profound, impassioned, inner working of his soul, usually hidden from an outsider's view.

And therefore while one may find many more shapely and elegant expressions of religious feeling than Amiel's, it is difficult to find any more intimate or more heart-searching. Nor long before his death, knowing that his illness might any day end in strangulation, he wrote:

'When you no longer dream that you have at your disposal tens of years, a year, or a month, when you already reckon in tens of hours, and the coming night brings with it the menace of the unknown, obviously you renounce art, science, politics, and are content to talk with yourself, and that is possible up to the very end. This inner conversation is the only thing left to him who is sentenced to death but whose execution is delayed. He (this condemned man) concentrates within himself. He no longer emits rays, but only talks with his own soul. He no longer acts, but contemplates ... Like a hare he returns to his lair, and that lair is his conscience, his thought. As long as he can hold a pen and has a moment of solitude he concentrates before that echo of himself and holds converse with God.

'This is however not a moral investigation, not a repentance, not an appeal; it is only an "Amen" of submission.

' "My child, give me thine heart."

'Renunciation and agreement are less difficult for me than for others, because I want nothing. I should only like not to suffer. Christ in the Garden of Gethsemane prayed for that same thing. Let us say with him: "Nevertheless, not my will, but thine, be done!" and let us wait.'

Such was he on the eve of his death. He is not less sincere and serious throughout his *Journal*, in spite of the elegance, and (in passages) apparent choiceness of phrasing, which had become a habit with him. In the course of the whole thirty years of his *Journal* he felt what we all so carefully forget—that we are all sentenced to death and our execution is only deferred. And that is why this book is so sincere, serious, and profitable.

1893

PART IV

INTRODUCTION TO S. T. SEMËNOV'S PEASANT STORIES

I LONG ago laid down for myself the rule of judging every artistic production from three aspects, first from the side of its content; in how far is what the artist reveals from a new side important and necessary for man—for any production is, I think, a work of art only if it reveals a new side of life: secondly, in how far is the form of the work good, beautiful, and in accord with its contents: and thirdly, to what extent is the relation of the artist to his subject sincere, that is, in how far does he believe in what he presents to us. This last quality always seems to me the most important in artistic work. It gives its force to a work of art and makes it infectious, that is, it evokes in the spectator, the hearer, or the reader, those feelings which the artist himself experiences.

And Semënov possesses that quality in the highest degree.

There is a well-known story of Flaubert's which Turgénev has translated, *La légende de Julien l'hospitalier*; the last episode, intended to be the most touching in the story, is one in which Julien lies down in the same bed with a leper and warms him with his own body. This leper is Christ, who carries Julien off to heaven with him. All this is told with great mastery, but I always remain perfectly cold when I read that story. I feel that the author himself would not have done, and would not even have wished to do, what his hero does, and therefore I myself do not wish to do it and do not experience any agitation when reading of this amazing exploit.

But when Semënov describes the simplest story it always touches me. A village youth comes to Moscow to get a place, and helped by a coachman from his part of the country who is living with a rich merchant, he gets a job as the yard-porter's assistant. This place had previously been held by an old man. The merchant, by his coachman's advice, had discharged the old man and taken the lad in his place. The lad comes in the evening to begin his service, and standing in the yard hears the old man complain, in the porter's lodge, that through no fault of his he has been dismissed merely to give place to a younger man. The lad suddenly feels pity for the old man and is ashamed to have pushed him out. He considers the matter, hesitates, and finally decides to give up the situation which he needs so much and would have been so glad to take.

All this is told in such a way that every time I read it I feel that the author would not only have wished to, but certainly would, have acted in that way under similar circumstances; his feelings infect me and I feel pleased, and it seems to me that I too should have done, or have been ready to do, something good.

Sincerity is Semënov's chief merit. But besides that his content is always important: important because it relates to the most important class in Russia, the peasantry, whom Semënov knows as only a peasant can know them who himself lives in the laborious village; and the content of his stories is also important because, in them all, the chief interest is not in external events or in the peculiarity of the life, but in the way men approach or fall away from the ideal of Christian truth which is present clearly and firmly in the author's soul and supplies him with a safe standard and appraisement of the quality and importance of human actions. The form of the stories fully corresponds to their content: it is serious and simple, the details are always correct, and there are no false notes. What is particularly good is the language—often quite original in its expressions but always natural and strikingly strong and picturesque—in which the characters in the story speak.

1894

PART V

INTRODUCTION TO THE WORKS OF GUY DE MAUPASSANT

(This article was written by Tolstóy to serve as preface to a Russian edition of a selection of Guy de Maupassant's stories.)

IT was, I think, in 1881 that Turgénev while visiting me took out of his portmanteau a small French book entitled *La Maison Tellier*, and gave it to me.

'Read it some time,' said he in an off-hand way just as, a year before, he had given me a number of *Russian Wealth* that contained an article by Gárshin, who was then only beginning to write. Evidently on this occasion, as in Gárshin's case, he was afraid of influencing me one way or the other, and wished to know my own unbiassed opinion.

'It is by a young French writer,' said he. 'Have a look at it. It isn't bad. He knows you and esteems you highly,' he added, as if wishing to propitiate him. 'As a man he reminds me of Druzhínin. He is, like Druzhínin, an excellent son, an admirable friend, *un homme d'un commerce sûr*,[1] and besides that he associates with the working people, guides them, and helps them. Even in his relations with women he reminds me of Druzhínin.' And Turgénev told me something astonishing, incredible, of Maupassant's conduct in that respect.

That time (1881) was for me a period of most ardent inner reconstruction of my whole outlook on life, and in this reconstruction the activity called the fine arts, to which I had formerly devoted all my powers, had

[1] A reliable man.

not only lost the importance I formerly attributed to it, but had become simply obnoxious to me on account of the unnatural position it had hitherto occupied in my life, as it generally does in the estimation of the people of the well-to-do classes.

And therefore such works as the one Turgénev was recommending to me did not then interest me in the least. But to please him I read the book he had handed me.

From the first story, *La Maison Tellier*, despite the indecency and insignificance of the subject, I could not help recognizing that the author had what is called talent.

He possessed that particular gift called talent, which consists in the capacity to direct intense concentrated attention, according to the author's tastes, on this or that subject, in consequence of which the man endowed with this capacity sees in the things to which he directs his attention some new aspect which others have overlooked; and this gift of seeing what others have not seen Maupassant evidently possessed. But judging by the little volume I read, he unfortunately lacked the chief of the three conditions, besides talent, essential to a true work of art. These are: (1) a correct, that is, a moral relation of the author to his subject; (2) clearness of expression, or beauty of form, —the two are identical; and (3) sincerity, that is, a sincere feeling of love or hatred of what the artist depicts. Of these three, Maupassant possessed only the two last and was quite lacking in the first. He had not a correct, that is a moral, relation to the subjects depicted.

Judging by what I read I was convinced that Maupassant possessed talent, that is to say, the gift of attention revealing in the objects and facts of life with which he deals qualities others have not perceived. He was also master of a beautiful style, expressing what he wanted to say clearly, simply, and with charm. He was also master of that condition of true artistic production without which a work of art does not produce its effect, namely, sincerity; that is, he did not pretend that he loved or hated, but really loved or hated what he described. But unfortunately, lacking the first and perhaps the chief condition of good artistic production, a correct moral relation to what he described—that is to say, a knowledge of the difference between good and evil—he loved and described things that should not have been loved and described. Thus in this little volume, the author described with great detail and fondness how women seduce men, and men women; and in *La femme de Paul* he even describes certain obscenities difficult to understand. And he presents the country labouring folk not merely with indifference but even with contempt, as though they were animals.

This unconsciousness of the difference between good and evil is particularly striking in the story, *Une partie de campagne*, in which is given, as a very pleasant and amusing joke, a detailed description of how two men rowing with bare arms in a boat, tempt and afterwards seduce at the same time, one of them an elderly mother and the other a young girl, her daughter.

The sympathy of the author is evidently all the time so much on the side of these two wretches that he not merely ignores, but simply does not see, what must have been felt by the seduced mother and the maid (her daughter), by the father, and by a young man who is evidently engaged to the daughter; and therefore not merely is an objectionable description of a revolting crime presented in the form of an amusing jest, but the occurrence itself is described falsely, for what is given is only one side, and that the most insignificant—namely, the pleasure received by the rascals.

In that same little volume there is a story, *Histoire d'une fille de ferme*, which Turgénev particularly recommended to me and which particularly displeased me, again by this incorrect relation of the author to his subject. He evidently sees in all the working folk he describes mere animals, who rise to nothing more than sexual and maternal love, so that his descriptions give one an incomplete and artificial impression.

Lack of understanding of the life and interests of working people and the presentation of them as semi-brutes moved only by sensuality, spite, and greed, is one of the chief and most important defects of most recent French writers, including Maupassant, who not only in this but in all his other stories where he refers to the people, always describes them as coarse, dull animals at whom one can only laugh. Of course the French writers should know the nature of their own people better than I do; but despite the fact that I am a Russian and have not lived among the French peasants, I nevertheless affirm that in so representing their people the French authors are wrong, and that the French labourers cannot be such as they represent them to be. If France—such as we know her, with her truly great men and the great contributions those great men have made to science, art, citizenship, and the moral development of mankind—if this France exists, then that working class which has maintained and maintains on its shoulders this France with its great men, must consist not of brutes but of people with great spiritual qualities; and I therefore do not believe what I read in novels such as *La terre* [1] and in Maupassant's stories; just as I should not believe it if I were told of the existence of a beautiful house stand-ing without foundations. It may very well be that these high qualities of the people are not such as are described to us in *La petite Fadette* and *La Mare aux diables*,[2] but I am firmly convinced that these qualities exist, and a writer who portrays the people only as

[1] By Zola.   [2] Stories by Georges Sand.

Maupassant does, describing with sympathy only the *hanches* and *gorges*[1] of the Breton servant-girls, and describing with detestation and ridicule the life of the labouring men, commits a great artistic mistake, because he describes his subject only from one, and that the least interesting, physical, side and leaves quite out of sight another, and the most important, spiritual, side wherein the essence of the matter lies.

On the whole, the perusal of the little book handed me by Turgénev left me quite indifferent to the young writer.

So repugnant to me were the stories, *Une partie de campagne*, *La femme de Paul*, *L'histoire d'une fille de ferme*, that I did not then notice the beautiful story, *Le papa de Simon*, and the story, excellent in its description of the night, *Sur l'eau*.

'Are there not in our time, when so many people want to write, plenty of men of talent who do not know to what to apply this gift or who boldly apply it to what should not, and need not, be described?' thought I. And so I said to Turgénev, and thereupon forgot about Maupassant.

The first thing of his that fell into my hands after that was *Une Vie*, which some one advised me to read. That book at once compelled me to change my opinion of Maupassant, and since then I have read with interest everything signed by him. *Une Vie* is excellent, not only incomparably the best of his novels, but perhaps the best French novel since Hugo's *Les Misérables*. Here, besides remarkable talent—that special strenuous attention applied to the subject, by which the author perceives quite new features in the life he describes—are united in almost equal degree all three qualities of a true work of art: first, a correct, that is a moral, relation of the author to his subject; secondly, beauty of form; and thirdly, sincerity, that is, love of

[1] Hips and throats.

what the author describes. Here the meaning of life no longer presents itself to the author as consisting in the adventures of various male and female libertines; here the subject, as the title indicates, is life—the life of a ruined, innocent, amiable woman, predisposed to all that is good, but ruined by precisely the same coarse animal sensuality which in his former stories the author presented as if it were the central feature of life, dominant over all else. And in this book the author's whole sympathy is on the side of what is good.

The form, which was beautiful in the first stories, is here brought to such a pitch of perfection as, in my opinion, has been attained by no other French writer of prose. And above all, the author here really loves, and deeply loves, the good family he describes; and he really hates that coarse debauchee who destroys the happiness and peace of this charming family and, in particular, ruins the life of the heroine.

That is why all the events and characters of this novel are so life-like and memorable. The weak, kindly, debilitated mother; the upright, weak, attractive father; the daughter, still more attractive in her simplicity, artlessness, and sympathy with all that is good; their mutual relations, their first journey, their servants and neighbours; the calculating, grossly sensual, mean, petty, insolent suitor, who as usual deceives the innocent girl by the customary empty idealization of the foulest instincts; the marriage, Corsica with the beautiful descriptions of nature, and then village life, the husband's coarse faithlessness, his seizure of power over the property, his quarrel with his father-in-law, the yielding of the good people and the victory of insolence; the relations with the neighbours—all this is life itself in its complexity and variety. And not only is all this vividly and finely described, but the sincere pathetic tone of it all involuntarily infects the reader. One feels that the author loves this woman, and loves her not for her external form but for her soul, for the goodness there is in her; that he pities her and suffers on her account, and this feeling is involuntarily communicated to the reader. And the questions: Why, for what end, is this fine creature ruined? Ought it indeed to be so? arise of themselves in the reader's soul and compel him to reflect on the meaning of human life.

Despite the false notes which occur in the novel, such as the minute description of the young girl's skin, or the impossible and unnecessary details of how, by the advice of an abbé, the forsaken wife again became a mother—details which destroy all the charm of the heroine's purity—and despite the melodramatic and unnatural story of the injured husband's revenge; notwithstanding these blemishes, the novel not only seemed to me excellent, but I saw behind it no longer a talented chatterer and jester who neither knew nor wished to know right from wrong—as from his first little book Maupassant had appeared to me to be—but a serious man penetrating deeply into life and already beginning to see his way in it.

The next novel of Maupassant's that I read was *Bel-Ami*.

Bel-Ami is a very dirty book. The author evidently gives himself a free hand in describing what attracts him, and at times seems to lose his main negative attitude towards his hero and to pass over to his side: but on the whole *Bel-Ami*, like *Une Vie*, has at its base a serious idea and sentiment. In *Une Vie*, the fundamental idea is perplexity in face of the cruel senselessness of the suffering life of an excellent woman ruined by a man's coarse sensuality; whereas here it is not only perplexity, but indignation, at the prosperity and success of a coarse, sensual brute who by that very sensuality makes his career and attains a high position in society; and indignation also at the depravity of the whole sphere in which the hero attains his success. In the former novel the author seems to ask: 'For what, and why, was a fine creature ruined? Why did it happen?' Here in the latter novel he seems to answer: all that is pure and good has perished and is perishing in our society, because that society is depraved, senseless, and horrible.

The last scene in the novel—the marriage in a fashionable church of the triumphant scoundrel, decorated with the Legion of Honour, to the pure girl, the daughter of an elderly and formerly irreproachable mother whom he had seduced; a wedding blessed by a bishop and regarded as something good and proper by everybody—expresses this idea with extraordinary force. In this novel, despite the fact that it is encumbered with dirty details (in which it is to be regretted that the author seems to find pleasure) the same serious questions are presented to life.

Read the conversation of the old poet with Duroy when after dinner, if I remember rightly, they are leaving the Walters. The old poet bares life to his young companion and shows it as it is, with its eternal and inevitable concomitant and end—death.

'She has hold of me already, *la gueuse*,'[1] says he of death. 'She has already shaken out my teeth, torn out my hair, crippled my limbs, and is now ready to swallow me. I am already in her power. She is only playing with me as a cat does with a mouse, knowing that I cannot escape. Fame? Riches? What is the use of them since they cannot buy a woman's love? For it is only a woman's love that makes life worth living, and that too death takes away. It takes that away, and then one's health, strength, and life itself. It is the same for every one, and there is nothing else.'

Such is the meaning of what the old poet says. But Duroy, the successful lover of all the women who

[1] The old hag.

please him, is so full of sensual energy and strength
that he hears and does not hear, understands and does
not understand, the old poet's words. He hears and
understands, but the source of sensual life throbs in
him so strongly that this unquestionable truth, fore-
telling the same end for him, does not disturb him.

This inner contradiction, besides its satirical value,
gives the novel its chief significance. The same idea
gleams in the fine scenes of the death of the consump-
tive journalist. The author sets himself the question:
What is this life? How solve the contradiction between
the love of life and the knowledge of inevitable death?
He seems to seek, pauses, and decides neither one way
nor the other. And therefore the moral relation to
life in this novel continues to be correct.

But in the novels that follow, this moral relation to
life grows confused. The appraisement of the phenomena of life begins to waver, to grow obscure, and
in the last novels it is quite perverted.

In *Mont-Oriol* Maupassant seems to unite the motives
of his two previous novels and repeats himself to order.
Despite the fine descriptions of the fashionable water-
ing-place and of the medical activity in it, which is
executed with delicate taste, we have here the same
bull-like Paul, just as empty and despicable as the
husband in *Une Vie*; and the same deceived, frank,
meek, weak, lonely—always lonely—good woman,
and the same impassive triumph of pettiness and
triviality as in *Bel-Ami*.

The thought is the same, but the author's moral
relation to what he describes is already much lower,
lower especially than in *Une Vie*. The author's inner
estimate of right and wrong begins to get confused.
Notwithstanding his abstract wish to be impartially
objective, the scoundrel Paul evidently has all his
sympathy, and therefore the love story of this Paul and
his attempts at, and success in, seduction produce a dis-

cordant impression. The reader does not know what the author intends: is it to show the whole emptiness and vileness of Paul (who turns indifferently away from and insults a woman merely because her waist has been spoilt by her pregnancy with his child); or, on the contrary, is it to show how pleasant and easy it is to live as this Paul lives?

In the next novels, *Pierre et Jean*, *Fort comme la mort*, and *Notre cœur*, the author's moral attitude towards his characters becomes still more confused, and in the last-named is quite lost. All these novels bear the stamp of indifference, haste, unreality, and, above all, again that same absence of a correct moral relation to life which was present in his first writings. This began from the time when Maupassant's reputation as a fashionable author had become established and he became liable to the temptation, so terrible in our day, to which every celebrated writer is subject, especially one so attractive as Maupassant. In the first place the success of his first novels, the praise of the press, and the flattery of society, especially of women; in the second the ever increasing amount of remuneration (never however keeping up with his continually increasing wants); in the third the pertinacity of editors outbidding one another, flattering, begging, and no longer judging the merits of the works the author offers, but enthusiastically accepting everything signed by a name now established with the public—all these temptations are so great that they evidently turn his head, and he succumbs to them; and though he continues to elaborate the form of his work as well as or sometimes even better than before, and even though he is fond of what he describes, yet he no longer loves it because it is good or moral and lovable to all, or hates it because it is evil and hateful to all, but only because one things pleases and another thing happens to displease him.

On all Maupassant's novels, beginning with *Bel-Ami*, there lies this stamp of haste and still more of artificiality. From that time Maupassant no longer did what he had done in his first two novels. He did not take as his basis certain moral demands, and on that ground describe the actions of his characters, but wrote as all hack novelists do, that is, he devised the most interesting and pathetic, or most up-to-date, persons and situations, and made a novel out of them, adorning it with whatever observations he had opportunity to make which fitted into the framework of the story, quite indifferent as to how the incidents described were related to the demands of morality. Such are *Pierre et Jean*, *Fort comme la mort*, and *Notre cœur*.

Accustomed as we are to read in French novels of how families live in threes, always with a lover known to every one except the husband, it still remains quite unintelligible to us how it happens that all husbands are always fools, *cocus et ridicules*,[1] but all lovers (who themselves in the end marry and become husbands) are not only not *cocus et ridicules*, but are heroic. And still less comprehensible is it how all women can be depraved, and yet all mothers saintly.

And on these unnatural and unlikely, and above all profoundly immoral, propositions *Pierre et Jean* and *Fort comme la mort* are built, and therefore the sufferings of the characters so situated affect us but little. The mother of Pierre and Jean, who can live her whole life deceiving her husband, evokes little sympathy when she is obliged to confess her sin to her son, and still less when she justifies herself by asserting that she could not but avail herself of the chance of happiness which presented itself. Still less can we sympathize with the gentleman who, in *Fort comme la mort*, having all his life deceived his friend and debauched his friend's wife, now only regrets that having grown old

[1] Deceived and ridiculous.

he cannot seduce his mistress's daughter. The last novel, *Notre cœur*, has even no kernel at all beyond the description of various kinds of sex-love. The satiated emotions of an idle debauchee are described, who does not know what he wants, and who first lives with a woman yet more depraved than himself—a mentally depraved woman, who lacks even the excuse of sensuality—then leaves her and lives with a servant-girl, and then again rejoins the former, and, it seems, lives with them both. If in *Pierre et Jean* and *Fort comme la mort* there are still some touching scenes, this last novel excites only disgust.

The question in Maupassant's first novel, *Une Vie*, consists in this: here is a human being, good, wise, pleasing, predisposed to all that is good, and this creature is for some reason offered up as a sacrifice first to a coarse, small-minded, stupid animal of a husband without having given anything to the world. Why is this? The author puts that question and as it were gives no answer, but his whole novel, all his feeling of pity for her and abhorrence of what has ruined her, serves as answer. If there is a man who has understood her suffering and expressed it, then it is redeemed, as Job put it to his friends when they said that no one would know of his sufferings. When suffering is recognized and understood, it is redeemed; and here the author has recognized and understood and shown men this suffering, and the suffering is redeemed, for once it is understood by men it will sooner or later be done away with.

In the next novel, *Bel-Ami*, the question no longer is, Why do good persons suffer? but Why do wealth and fame go to the unworthy? What are wealth and fame? How are they obtained? And as before, these questions carry with them their own answers, which consist in the repudiation of all that the crowd of men so highly prize. The subject of this second novel is still serious, but the moral relation of the author to the subject he describes already weakens considerably, and whereas in the first novel blots and sensuality which spoil it only appear here and there, in *Bel-Ami* these blots have increased, and many chapters are filled with dirt alone, which seems to please the author.

In the next book, *Mont-Oriol*, the questions: Why, and to what end, does the amiable woman suffer and the savage male secure success and happiness? are no longer put; but it seems tacitly admitted that it should be so, and hardly any moral demands are felt. But without the least necessity, uncalled for by any artistic consideration, dirty, sensual descriptions are presented. As an example of this violation of artistic taste, resulting from the author's incorrect relation to his subject, the detailed description in this novel of the heroine in her bath is specially striking. This description is quite unnecessary and is in no way connected either with the external or the inner purpose of the novel: 'Bubbles appear on her pink skin.'

'Well, what of that?' asks the reader.

'Nothing more,' replies the author. 'I describe it because I like such descriptions.'

In the next novels, *Pierre et Jean* and *Fort comme la mort*, no moral demand at all is perceptible. Both novels are built on debauchery, deceit, and falsehood, which bring the actors to tragic situations.

In the last novel, *Notre cœur*, the position of the actors is most monstrous, wild, and immoral; they no longer struggle with anything, but only seek satisfaction for their vanity, sensuality, and sexual desires, and the author appears quite to sympathize with their aims. The only deduction one can draw from this last novel is that the greatest pleasure in life consists in sexual intercourse, and that therefore one must secure that happiness in the pleasantest way.

Yet more striking is this immoral relation to life in

the half-novel, *Yvette*. The subject, which is horrible in its immorality, is as follows: A charming girl, innocent in soul and depraved only in the manners she has learned in her mother's dissolute circle, leads a libertine into error. He falls in love with her, but imagining that this girl knowingly chatters the obscene nonsense she has picked up in her mother's society and repeats parrot-like without understanding—imagining that she is already depraved—he coarsely offers her an immoral union. This proposal horrifies and offends her (for she loves him); it opens her eyes to her own position and to that of her mother, and she suffers profoundly. This deeply touching scene is admirably described: the collision between a beautiful innocent soul and the depravity of the world. And with that it might end; but the author, without either external or inner necessity, continues to write and makes this man penetrate by night to the girl and seduce her. Evidently in the first part of the story the author was on the girl's side, but in the later part he has suddenly gone over to the debauchee, and the one impression destroys the other—the whole novel crumbles and falls to pieces like ill-kneaded bread.

In all his novels after *Bel-Ami* (I am not now speaking of the short stories, which constitute his chief merit and glory—of them later) Maupassant evidently submitted to the theory which ruled not only in his circle in Paris, but which now rules everywhere among artists: that for a work of art it is not only unnecessary to have any clear conception of what is right and wrong, but that on the contrary an artist should completely ignore all moral questions, there being even a certain artistic merit in so doing. According to this theory the artist may or should depict what is true to life, what really is, what is beautiful and therefore pleases him, or even what may be useful as material for 'science'; but that to care about what is moral or immoral, right or wrong, is not an artist's business.

I remember a celebrated painter showing me one of his pictures representing a religious procession. It was all excellently painted, but no relation of the artist to his subject was perceptible.

'And do you regard these ceremonies as good and consider that they should be performed, or not?' I asked him.

With some condescension to my naïveté, he told me that he did not know about that and did not want to know it; his business was to represent *life*.

'But at any rate you sympathize with this?'

'I cannot say I do.'

'Well then do you dislike these ceremonies?'

'Neither the one thing nor the other,' with a smile of compassion at my silliness, replied this modern, highly cultured, artist who depicted life without understanding its purpose and neither loving nor hating its phenomena.

And so unfortunately thought Maupassant.

In his preface to *Pierre et Jean* he says that people say to a writer, 'Consolez-moi, amusez-moi, attristez-moi, attendrissez-moi, faites-moi rêver, faites-moi rire, faites-moi frémir, faites-moi pleurer, faites-moi penser. Seuls quelques esprits d'élite demandent à l'artiste: faites-moi quelque chose de beau dans la forme qui vous conviendra le mieux d'après votre tempérament.'[1]

Responding to this demand of the *élite* Maupassant wrote his novels, naïvely imagining that what was considered beautiful in his circle was that beauty which art should serve.

---

[1] 'Console me, amuse me, sadden me, touch my heart, make me dream, make me laugh, make me tremble, make me weep, make me think. Only a few chosen spirits bid the artist compose something beautiful, in the form that best suits his temperament.'

And in the circle in which Maupassant moved, the beauty which should be served by art was, and is, chiefly woman—young, pretty, and for the most part naked—and sexual connexion with her. It was so considered not only by all Maupassant's comrades in art—painters, sculptors, novelists, and poets—but also by philosophers, the teachers of the rising generation. Thus the famous Renan, in his work, *Marc-Aurèle*, p. 555, when blaming Christianity for not understanding feminine beauty, plainly says:

'Le défaut du christianisme apparaît bien ici. Il est trop uniquement moral; la beauté, chez lui, est tout-à-fait sacrifiée. Or, aux yeux d'une philosophie complète, la beauté, loin d'être un avantage superficiel, un danger, un inconvénient, est un don de Dieu, comme la vertu. Elle vaut la vertu; la femme belle exprime aussi bien une face du but divin, une des fins de Dieu, que l'homme de génie ou la femme vertueuse. Elle le sent et de là sa fierté. Elle sent instinctivement le trésor infini qu'elle porte en son corps; elle sait bien que, sans esprit, sans talent, sans grande vertu, elle compte entre les premières manifestations de Dieu. Et pourquoi lui interdire de mettre en valeur le don qui lui a été fait, de sertir le diamant qui lui est échu? La femme, en se parant, accomplit un devoir; elle pratique un art, art exquis, en un sens le plus charmant des arts. Ne nous laissons pas égarer par le sourire que certains mots provoquent chez LES GENS FRIVOLES. On décerne le palme du génie à l'artiste grec qui a su résoudre le plus délicat des problèmes, orner le corps humain, c'est à dire orner la perfection même, et l'on ne veut voir qu'une affaire de chiffons dans l'essai de collaborer à la plus belle œuvre de Dieu, à la beauté de la femme! La toilette de la femme, avec tous ses raffinements, est du grand art à sa manière. Les siècles et les pays qui savent y réussir sont les grands siècles, les grands pays, et le christianisme montra, par l'exclusion dont il frappa ce genre de recherches, que l'idéal social qu'il concevait ne deviendrait le cadre d'une société complète que bien plus tard, quand la révolte des gens du monde aurait brisé le joug étroit imposé primitivement à la secte par un piétisme exalté.'¹

(So that in the opinion of this leader of the young generation, only now have Paris milliners and coiffeurs

¹ The defect of Christianity is clearly seen in this. It is too exclusively moral; it quite sacrifices beauty. But in the eyes of a complete philosophy beauty, far from being a superficial advantage, a danger, an inconvenience, is a gift of God, like virtue. It is worth as much as virtue; the beautiful woman expresses an aspect of the divine purpose, one of God's aims, as well as a man of genius does, or a virtuous woman. She feels this, and hence her pride. She is instinctively conscious of the infinite treasure she possesses in her body; she is well aware that without intellect, without talent, without great virtue, she counts among the chief manifestations of God. And why forbid her to make the most of the gift bestowed upon her, or to give the diamond allotted to her its due setting? By adorning herself woman accomplishes a duty; she practises an art, an exquisite art, in a sense the most charming of arts. Do not let us be misled by the smile which certain words provoke in the *frivolous*. We award the palm of genius to the Greek artist who succeeded in solving the most delicate of problems, that of adorning the human body, that is to say, adorning perfection itself, and yet some people wish to see nothing more than an affair of *chiffons* in the attempt to collaborate with the finest work of God—woman's beauty! Woman's toilette with all its refinements is a great art in its own way. The epochs and countries which can succeed in this are the great epochs and great countries, and Christianity, by the embargo it laid on this kind of research, showed that the social ideal it had conceived would only become the framework of a complete society at a much later period, when the revolt of men of the world had broken the narrow yoke originally imposed on the sect by a fanatical pietism.

corrected the mistake committed by Christianity, and re-established beauty in the true and lofty position due to it.)

In order that there should be no doubt as to how one is to understand beauty, the same celebrated writer, historian, and savant, wrote the drama, *L'Abbesse de Jouarre*, in which he showed that to have sexual intercourse with a woman is a service of this beauty, that is to say, is an elevated and good action. In that drama, which is striking by its lack of talent and especially by the coarseness of the conversations between d'Arcy and the abbesse, in which the first words make it evident what sort of love that gentleman is discussing with the supposedly innocent and highly moral maiden, who is not in the least offended thereby—in that drama it is shown that the most highly moral people, at the approach of death to which they are condemned, a few hours before it arrives, can do nothing more beautiful than yield to their animal passions.

So that in the circle in which Maupassant grew up and was educated, the representation of feminine beauty and sex-love was and is regarded quite seriously, as a matter long ago determined and recognized by the wisest and most learned men, as the true object of the highest art— *Le grand art*.

And it is this theory, dreadful in its folly, to which Maupassant submitted when he became a fashionable writer; and, as was to be expected, this false ideal led him in his novels into a series of mistakes and to ever weaker and weaker production.

In this the fundamental difference between the demands of the novel and of the short story is seen. A novel has for its aim, even for external aim, the description of a whole human life or of many human lives, and therefore its writer should have a clear and firm conception of what is good and bad in life, and

this Maupassant lacked; indeed, according to the
theory he held, that is just what should be avoided.
Had he been a novelist like some talentless writers of
sensual novels, he would, being without talent, have
quietly described what was evil as good, and his novels
would have had unity and would have been interesting to people who shared his view. But Maupassant
had talent, that is to say, he saw things in their
essentials and therefore involuntarily discerned the
truth. He involuntarily saw the evil in what he wished
to consider good. That is why, in all his novels except
the first, his sympathies continually waver, now pre-
senting the evil as good and now admitting that the
evil is evil and the good good, but continually shifting
from the one standpoint to the other. And this
destroys the very basis of any artistic impression—the
framework on which it is built. People of little artistic
sensibility often think that a work of art possesses
unity when the same people act in it throughout, or
when it is all constructed on one plot, or describes the
life of one man. That is a mistake. It only appears
so to a superficial observer. The cement which binds
any artistic production into one whole and therefore
produces the illusion of being a reflection of life, is not
the unity of persons or situations, but the unity of the
author's independent moral relation to his subject.
In reality, when we read or look at the artistic production of a new author the fundamental question
that arises in our soul is always of this kind: 'Well,
what sort of a man are you? Wherein are you different
from all the people I know, and what can you tell me
that is new about how we must look at this life of
ours?' Whatever the artist depicts—saints, robbers,
kings, or lackeys—we seek and see only the artist's
own soul. If he is an established writer with whom we
are already familiar, the question no longer is, 'What
sort of a man are you?' but, 'Well, what more can you

tell me that is new?' or, 'From what new side will you now illumine life for me?' And therefore a writer who has not a clear, definite, and just, view of the universe, and especially a man who considers that this is not even wanted, cannot produce a work of art. He may write much and admirably, but a work of art will not result.

So it was with Maupassant in his novels. In his first two novels, and particularly in the first, *Une Vie*, there was a clear, definite, and new, relation to life, and it was an artistic production; but as soon as, submitting to the fashionable theory, he decided that this relation of the author to life was quite unnecessary and began to write merely in order to *faire quelque chose de beau* (to produce something beautiful), his novels ceased to be works of art. In *Une Vie* and *Bel-Ami* the author knows whom he should love and whom he should hate, and the reader agrees with him and believes in him— believes in the people and events he describes. But in *Notre cœur* and *Yvette* the author does not know whom he should love and whom he should hate, and the reader does not know either. And not knowing this the reader does not believe in the events described and is not interested in them. And therefore, except the two first, or, strictly speaking, only the first one, all Maupassant's novels, as such, are weak; and if he had left us only his novels he would have been merely a striking instance of the way in which brilliant talents may perish as a result of the false environment in which the author has developed, and of those false theories of art that have been devised by people who neither love nor understand it. But fortunately Maupassant wrote short stories in which he did not subject himself to the false theory he had accepted, and wrote not *quelque chose de beau*, but what touched or revolted his moral feeling. And in these short stories—not in all, but in the best of them—we see how that moral feeling grew in the author.

And it is in this that the wonderful quality of every true artist lies, if only he does not do violence to himself under the influence of a false theory. His talent teaches its possessor and leads him forward along the path of moral development, compelling him to love what deserves love and to hate what deserves hate. An artist is an artist because he sees things not as he wishes to see them but as they really are. The man, the possessor of a talent, may make mistakes, but if only his talent is allowed free play, as Maupassant gave it free play in his short stories, it discloses, undrapes the object, and compels love of it if it deserves love, and hatred of it if it deserves hatred. With every true artist, when under the influence of his circle he begins to represent what should not be represented, there happens what happened to Balaam, who, wishing to bless, cursed what should be cursed, and wishing to curse, blessed what should be blessed: involuntarily he does not what he wishes to do but what he should do. And this happened to Maupassant.

There has hardly been another writer who so sincerely thought that all the good, all the meaning of life, lies in woman—in love—and who with such strength of passion described woman and her love from all sides; and there has hardly ever been a writer who reached such clearness and exactitude in showing all the awful phases of that very thing which had seemed to him the highest and the greatest of life's blessings. The more he penetrated into the question the more it revealed itself, and the more did the coverings fall from it and only its horrible results and yet more horrible essence remain.

Read of the idiot son, of the night with a daughter (*L'ermite*), of the sailor with his sister (*Le port*), *Le champ d'oliviers*, *La petite Roque*, of the English girl (*Miss Harriet*), *Monsieur Parent*, *L'armoire* (the girl who fell asleep in the cupboard), the wedding in *Sur l'eau*, and last expression of all, *Un cas de divorce*. Just what was said by Marcus Aurelius when devising means to destroy the attractiveness of this sin in his imagination, is what Maupassant does in most vivid artistic forms, turning one's soul inside out. He wished to extol sex-love, but the better he came to know it the more he cursed it. He cursed sex-love for the misfortunes and sufferings it bears within it, and for the disillusionments, and above all the falsification of real love, the fraud which is in it—from which the more trustingly he has yielded to the deception the more acutely man suffers.

The powerful moral development of the author in the course of his literary activity is recorded in indelible traits in these charming short stories and in his best book, *Sur l'eau.*

And not alone in this involuntary and therefore all the more powerful dethronement of sex-love is the moral growth of the author seen, but also in the more and more exalted moral demands he makes upon life.

Not alone in sex-love does he see the innate contradiction between the demands of animal and rational man; he sees it in the whole organization of the world.

He sees that the world as it is, the material world, is not only not the best of worlds, but might on the contrary be quite different—this thought is strikingly expressed in *Horla*—and that it does not satisfy the demands of reason and life. He sees that there is some other world, or at least the demand for such another world, in the soul of man.

He is tormented not only by the irrationality of the material world and its ugliness, but by its unlovingness, its discord. I do not know a more heart-rending cry of horror from one who has lost his way and is conscious of his loneliness, than the expression of this idea in that most charming story, *Solitude.*

The thing that most tormented Maupassant and to which he returns many times, is the painful condition of isolation—spiritual isolation—of man; the barrier standing between him and his fellows; a barrier, he says, the more painfully felt the nearer one's bodily connexion.

What is it torments him, and what would he have? What can destroy this barrier? What end this isolation? Love—not woman's love, which has become disgusting to him, but pure, spiritual, divine love. And that is what Maupassant seeks. Towards it, towards this saviour of life long since plainly disclosed to all men, he painfully strains from those fetters in which he feels himself bound.

He does not yet know how to name what he seeks. He does not wish to name it with his lips alone lest he should profane his holy-of-holies. But his unexpressed striving, shown in his dread of loneliness, is so sincere that it infects and attracts one more strongly than many and many a sermon about love, uttered only by the lips.

The tragedy of Maupassant's life is that in a most monstrous and immoral circle, he was escaping by the strength of his talent, by that extraordinary light which was in him, from the outlook on life held by that circle, and was already near to deliverance, was already breathing the air of freedom but—having exhausted his last strength in the struggle and not being able to make a final effort—perished without having attained freedom.

The tragedy of that ruin lies in what still afflicts the majority of the so-called cultured men of our time.

Men in general have never lived without an expression of the meaning of their life. Always and everywhere, highly-gifted men going in advance of others have appeared—the prophets, as they are called—

who have explained to men the meaning and purport of their life; and always the ordinary, average men, who had not the strength to explain that meaning for themselves, have followed the explanation of life their prophets have disclosed to them.

That meaning was explained eighteen hundred years ago by Christianity, simply, clearly, indubitably, and joyfully, as is proved by the lives of all who acknowledge it and follow the guidance of life which results from that conception.

But then people appeared who misinterpreted that meaning so that it became meaningless, and men are placed in the dilemma either of acknowledging Christianity as interpreted by Orthodoxy, Lourdes, the Pope, the dogma of the Immaculate Conception, and so forth, or of going on with life according to the teachings of Renan and his kind, that is, living without any guidance or understanding of life, following only their lusts as long as they are strong, and their habits when their lusts become feeble.

And people, ordinary people, choose the one or the other—sometimes both: first dissoluteness and then Orthodoxy; and thus whole generations live, shielding themselves with various theories invented not to disclose the truth but to hide it. And ordinary, and more especially dull, people are content.

But there are others—not many, they are rare—such as Maupassant, who with their own eyes see things as they are, see their significance, see the contradictions in life concealed from others, and vividly realize to what these contradictions must inevitably lead them—and seek to solve them in advance. They seek these solutions everywhere except where they are to be found, namely in Christianity, because Christianity appears to them outlived and discarded, repelling them by its absurdity. And vainly trying to find these solutions for themselves, they come to the con-

viction that there are no solutions, and that it is
inherent in life that one should always bear in oneself
these unsolved contradictions. And having come to
such a conclusion, if these people are feeble unener-
getic natures, they put up with such meaningless life
and are even proud of their position, accounting their
ignorance a quality and a sign of culture. But if they
are energetic, truthful, and gifted natures, such as
Maupassant was, they do not endure it, but one way
or other try to get out of this senseless life.

It is as if men thirsting in a desert sought water
everywhere except near those people who standing
round a spring pollute it and offer stinking mire
instead of the water that unceasingly flows beneath
the mire. Maupassant was in this position; he could
not believe—evidently it never even entered his head
—that the truth he sought had long ago been found
and was so near him; but neither could he believe
that man can live in such contradiction as that in
which he felt himself to be living.

Life—according to the theories in which he had been
brought up, which surrounded him and were corrobo-
rated by all the lusts of his young, and mentally and
physically strong, being—life consists in pleasure, of
which the chief is to be found in woman with her love,
and in the reproduction of this pleasure in its reflection, in the presentation of this love, and in exciting
it in others. All this might be well; but on examining
these pleasures other quite different things emerge,
alien and hostile to this love and this beauty: woman
for some reason is disfigured, becomes unpleasantly
pregnant and repulsive, gives birth to children, un-
wanted children; then come deceptions, cruelties,
moral suffering, then mere old age, and ultimately
death.

Then is this beauty indeed beauty? And why is all
this so? It would be all very well if one could arrest

life, but life goes on. And what does that mean? 'Life goes on' means that the hair falls out, turns grey, the teeth decay, and there are wrinkles and offensive breath. Even before all is finished, everything becomes dreadful, disgusting: the rouge, the powder, the sweat, the smell, and the repulsiveness, are evident. Where then is that which I serve? Where is beauty? But she is all! And if she is not, there is nothing left. There is no life!

But not merely is there no life in what seemed to be life: one begins to forsake it oneself, one becomes weaker, more stupid, one decays; others before one's eyes seize those delights in which all the good of life lay. Nor is that all. Some other possibility of life begins to glimmer in one's mind; something else, some other kind of union with men, with the whole world, one which does not admit of all these deceptions, something which cannot by any means be infringed, which is true and forever beautiful. But this cannot be. It is only the tantalizing vision of an oasis when we know that it does not exist and that there is nothing but sand everywhere.

Maupassant reached that tragic moment in life when the struggle begins between the falseness of the life about him and the truth of life of which he began to be conscious. Pangs of spiritual birth had already begun in him.

And it is the pangs of this birth that are expressed in his best work, especially in the short stories printed in this edition.

Had he been fated not to die while still suffering, but to fulfil all his possibilities, he would have left us great and illuminating works; but even what he gave us in the midst of his pain is much. Let us then be thankful to this strong and truthful man for what he has given us.

1894

PART VI

The essay *On Art* that follows was the last attempt Tolstóy made, to express his views on art before he wrote *What is Art?* *On Art* did not satisfy him, but in several respects it drew near to what he was finally to say. What he had not arrived at when he wrote it was (1) the clear-cut, working definition of art given in his later work, and (2) a clear perception of the importance and necessity of appraising separately the *form* of a work of art, which makes it infectious, and the *subject-matter of feeling* which by its connexion with life in general benefits or harms mankind.

In *On Art*, one feels that Tolstóy is still warily treading a path he has not fully explored; it was only later, in *What is Art?* that he let himself go—asserting his convictions with emphasis and exuberance.

ON ART:

What is and what is not Art; And when is Art Important, and when is it Trivial?

I

IN our life there are many insignificant or even harmful activities which enjoy a respect they do not deserve, or are tolerated merely because they are considered to be of importance. The copying of flowers, horses, and landscapes, such clumsy learning of musical pieces as is carried on in most of our so-called educated families, and the writing of feeble stories and bad verses, hundreds of which appear in the newspapers and magazines, are obviously not artistic activities; and the painting of indecent, pornographic pictures stimulating sensuality, or the composition of songs and stories of that nature, even if they have artistic qualities, is not a worthy activity deserving of respect.

And therefore, taking all the productions which are considered among us to be artistic, I think it would be useful, first, to separate what really is art from what has no right to that name; and secondly, taking what really is art, to distinguish what is important and good from what is insignificant and bad.

The question of how and where to draw the line separating Art from Non-Art, and the good and important in art from the insignificant and evil, is one of enormous importance in life.

A great many of the wrong-doings and mistakes in our life result from our calling things Art which are not Art. We accord an unmerited respect to things which not only do not deserve it, but deserve condemnation and contempt. Apart from the enormous amount of human labour spent on the preparation of articles needed for the production of art—studios, paints, canvas, marble, musical instruments, and the theatres with their scenery and appliances—even the lives of human beings are actually perverted by the one-sided labours demanded in the preparation of those who train for the arts. Hundreds of thousands if not millions of children are forced to one-sided toil, practising the so-called arts of dancing and music. Not to speak of the children of the educated classes who pay their tribute to art in the form of tormenting lessons,—children devoted to the ballet and musical professions are simply distorted in the name of Art to which they are dedicated. If it is possible to compel children of seven or eight to play an instrument, and for ten or fifteen years to continue to do so for seven or eight hours a day; if it is possible to place girls in the schools for the ballet,[1] and then to make them cut capers during the first months of their pregnancy, and

[1] The schools for training ballet-dancers, as well as the theatres where the chief ballets were performed, were State institutions in Russia.

if all this is done in the name of art, then it is certainly necessary to define, first of all, what really is art—lest under the guise of art a counterfeit should be produced—and then also to prove that art is a matter of importance to mankind.

Where then is the line dividing art, an important and necessary matter valuable to humanity, from useless occupations, commercial productions, and even from immorality? In what does the essence and importance of true art lie?

II

One theory—which its opponents call 'tendencious' —says that the essence of true art lies in the importance of the subject treated of: that for art to be art, it is necessary that its content should be something important, necessary to man, good, moral, and instructive.

According to that theory the artist—that is to say the man who possesses a certain skill—by taking the most important theme which interests society at the time, can, by clothing it in what looks like artistic form, produce a work of true art. According to that theory religious, moral, social, and political truths clothed in what seems like artistic form are artistic productions.

Another theory, which calls itself 'æsthetic,' or 'art for art's sake,' holds that the essence of true art lies in the beauty of its form; that for art to be true, it is necessary that what it presents should be beautiful.

According to that theory it is necessary for the production of art that an artist should possess technique, and should depict an object which produces in the highest degree a pleasant impression; and therefore a beautiful landscape, flowers, fruit, a nude figure, and ballets, will be works of art.

A third theory—which calls itself 'realistic'—says that the essence of art consists in the truthful, exact, presentation of reality: that for art to be true it is necessary that it should depict life as it really is.

According to that theory, it follows that works of art may be anything an artist sees or hears, all that he is able to make use of in his function of reproduction, independently of the importance of the subject or beauty of the form.

Such are the theories; and on the basis of each of them so-called works of art appear which fit the first, the second, or the third. But, apart from the fact that each of these theories contradicts the others, not one of them satisfies the chief demand, namely, to ascertain the boundary which divides art from commercial, insignificant, or even harmful productions.

In accordance with each of these theories, works can be produced unceasingly, as in any handicraft, and they may be insignificant or harmful.

As to the first theory ('tendency'), important subjects—religious, moral, social, or political—can always be found ready to hand, and therefore one can continually produce works of so-called art. Moreover, such subjects may be presented so obscurely and insincerely that works treating of the most important of them will prove insignificant and even harmful, the lofty content being degraded by insincere expression.

Similarly according to the second theory ('æsthetic') any man having learned the technique of any branch of art can incessantly produce something beautiful and pleasant, but again this beautiful and pleasant thing may be insignificant and harmful.

Just in the same way according to the third theory ('realistic'), every one who wishes to be an artist can incessantly produce objects of so-called art, because everybody is always interested in something. If the author is interested in what is insignificant and evil, then his work will be insignificant and evil.

The chief point is that, according to each of these three theories, 'works of art' can be produced incessantly, as in every handicraft, and that they actually are being so produced. So that these three dominant and discordant theories not merely fail to fix the line that separates art from non-art, but on the contrary they, more than anything else, serve to stretch the domain of art and bring within it all that is insignificant and harmful.

III

Where then is the boundary dividing art that is needful, important, and deserving of respect, from that which is unnecessary, unimportant, and deserving not of respect but of contempt—such as productions which have a plainly depraving effect? In what does true artistic activity consist?

To answer this question clearly we must first discriminate between artistic activity and another activity (usually confused with it), namely, that of handing on impressions and perceptions received from preceding generations—separating such activity as that, from the reception of new impressions: those, namely, which will thereafter be handed on from generation to generation.

The handing on of what was known to former generations, in the sphere of art as in the sphere of science, is an activity of teaching and learning. But the production of something *new* is creation—the real artistic activity.

The business of handing on knowledge—teaching— has not an independent significance, but depends entirely on the importance people attach to that which has been created—what it is they consider necessary to hand on from generation to generation.

And therefore the definition of what a creation is, will also define what it is that should be handed on. Moreover, the teacher's business is not usually considered to be artistic; the importance of artistic activity is properly attributed to creation—that is, to artistic production.[1]

What then is artistic (and scientific) creation?

Artistic (and also scientific) creation is such mental activity as brings dimly-perceived feelings (or thoughts) to such a degree of clearness that these feelings (or thoughts) are transmitted to other people.

The process of 'creation'—one common to all men and therefore known to each of us by inner experience —occurs as follows: a man surmises or dimly feels

---

[1] The most usual and widely diffused definition of art is that art is a particular activity not aiming at material utility, but affording pleasure to people; a pleasure, it is usually added, 'ennobling and elevating to the soul.'

This definition corresponds to the conception of art held by the majority of people; but it is inexact and not quite clear, and admits of very arbitrary interpretation.

It is not clear, for it fuses in one conception art as a human activity producing objects of art, and also the feelings of the recipient; and it admits of arbitrary interpretation, because it does not define wherein lies the pleasure that 'ennobles and elevates the soul.' So that one person may declare that he receives such pleasure from a certain production from which another does not receive it at all.

And therefore to define art it is necessary to define the peculiarity of that activity, both in its origin in the soul of the producer and in the peculiarity of its action on the souls of the recipients. This activity is distinguished from any other activity of craftsmanship, or trade, or even science (though it has great affinity with this last), in that it is not evoked by any material need, but supplies to both producer and recipient a special kind of so-called 'artistic satisfaction.' To explain to oneself this characteristic one must understand what impels people to this activity—that is, how artistic production originates.

something that is perfectly new to him, which he has never heard of from anybody. This something new impresses him, and in ordinary conversation he points out to others what he perceives, and to his surprise finds that what is apparent to him is quite unseen by them. They do not see or do not feel what he tells them of. This isolation, discord, disunion from others, at first disturbs him, and verifying his own perception the man tries in different ways to communicate to others what he has seen, felt, or understood; but these others still do not understand what he communicates to them, or do not understand it as he understands or feels it. And the man begins to be troubled by a doubt as to whether he imagines and dimly feels something that does not really exist, or whether others do not see and do not feel something that does exist. And to solve this doubt he directs his whole strength to the task of making his discovery so clear that there cannot be the smallest doubt, either for himself or for other people, as to the existence of that which he perceives; and as soon as this elucidation is completed and the man himself no longer doubts the existence of what he has seen, understood, or felt, others at once see, understand, and feel as he does, and it is this effort to make clear and indubitable to himself and to others what both to others and to him had been dim and obscure, that is the source from which flows the production of man's spiritual activity in general, or what we call works of art—which widen man's horizon and oblige him to see what had not been perceived before.[1]

---

[1] The division of the results of man's mental activity into scientific, philosophic, theological, hortatory, artistic, and other groups, is made for convenience of observation. But such divisions do not exist in reality; just as the divisions of the River Vólga into the Tver, Nizhnigórod, Simbírsk and Sarátov sections, are not divisions of the river itself, but divisions we make for our own convenience.

It is in this that the activity of an artist consists; and to this activity is related the feeling of the recipient. This feeling has its source in imitativeness, or rather in a capacity to be infected, and in a certain hypnotism—that is to say in the fact that the artist's stress of spirit elucidating to himself the subject that had been doubtful to him, communicates itself, through the artistic production, to the recipients. A work of art is then finished when it has been brought to such clearness that it communicates itself to others and evokes in them the same feeling that the artist experienced while creating it.

What was formerly unperceived, unfelt, and uncomprehended by them, is by intensity of feeling brought to such a degree of clearness that it becomes acceptable to all, and the production is a work of art.

The satisfaction of the intense feeling of the artist who has achieved his aim gives pleasure to him. Participation in this same stress of feeling and in its satisfaction, a yielding to this feeling, the imitation of it and infection by it (as by a yawn), the experiencing in brief moments what the artist has lived through while creating his work, is the enjoyment those who assimilate a work of art obtain.

Such in my opinion is the peculiarity that distinguishes art from any other activity.

IV

According to this division, all that imparts to mankind something new, achieved by an artist's stress of feeling and thought, is a work of art. But that this mental activity should really have the importance people attach to it, it is necessary that it should contribute what is good to humanity, for it is evident that to a new evil, to a new temptation leading people into evil, we cannot attribute the value given to art as to something that benefits mankind. The importance, the value, of art consists in widening man's outlook, in increasing the spiritual wealth that is humanity's capital.

Therefore, though a work of art must always include something new, yet the revelation of something new will not always be a work of art. That it should be a work of art, it is necessary:

(1) That the new idea, the content of the work, should be of importance to mankind.

(2) That this content should be expressed so clearly that people may understand it.

(3) That what incites the author to work at his production should be an inner need and not an external inducement.

And therefore that in which no new thing is disclosed will not be a work of art; and that which has for its content what is insignificant and therefore unimportant to man will not be a work of art however intelligibly it may be expressed, and even if the author has worked at it sincerely from an inner impulse. Nor will that be a work of art which is so expressed as to be unintelligible, however sincere may be the author's relation to it; nor that which has been produced by its author not from an inner impulse but for an external aim, however important may be its content and however intelligible its expression.

That is a work of art which discloses something new and at the same time in some degree satisfies the three conditions: content, form, and sincerity.

And here we come to the problem of how to define that lowest degree of content, beauty, and sincerity, which a production must possess to be a work of art.

To be a work of art it must, in the first place, be a thing which has for its content something hitherto unknown but of which man has need; secondly, it must show this so intelligibly that it becomes generally accessible; and thirdly, it must result from the author's need to solve an inner doubt.

A work in which all three conditions are present even to a slight degree, will be a work of art; but a production from which even one of them is absent will not be a work of art.

But it will be said that every work contains something needed by man, and every work will be to some extent intelligible, and that an author's relation to every work has some degree of sincerity. Where is the limit of needful content, intelligible expression, and sincerity of treatment? A reply to this question will be given us by a clear perception of the highest limit to which art may attain: the opposite of the highest limit will show the lowest limit, dividing all that cannot be accounted art from what is art. The highest limit of content is such as is always necessary to all men. That which is always necessary to all men is what is good or moral.[1] The lowest limit of content, consequently, will be such as is not needed by men, and is a bad and immoral content. The highest limit of expression will be such as is always intelligible to all men. What is thus intelligible is that which has nothing in it obscure,

---

[1] Half-a-century ago no explanation would have been needed of the words 'important', 'good', and 'moral', but in our time nine out of ten educated people, at these words, will ask with a triumphant air: 'What *is* important, good or moral?' assuming that these words express something conditional and not admitting of definition, and therefore I must answer this anticipated objection.

That which unites people not by violence but by love: that which serves to disclose the joy of the union of men with one another, is 'important', 'good', or 'moral'. 'Evil' and 'immoral' is that which divides them, that leads men to the suffering produced by disunion. 'Important' is that which causes people to understand and to love what they previously did not understand or love.

superfluous, or indefinite, but only what is clear, concise, and definite—what is called beautiful. Conversely, the lowest limit of expression will be such as is obscure, diffuse, and indefinite—that is to say formless. The highest limit of the artist's relation to his subject will be such as evokes in the soul of all men an impression of reality—the reality not so much of what exists, as of what goes on in the soul of the artist. This impression of reality is produced by truth only, and therefore the highest relation of an author to his subject is *sincerity*. The lowest limit, conversely, will be that in which the author's relation to his subject is not genuine but false. All works of art lie between these two limits.

A perfect work of art will be one in which the content is important and significant to all men, and therefore it will be *moral*. The expression will be quite clear, intelligible to all, and therefore *beautiful*; the author's relation to his work will be altogether sincere and heartfelt, and therefore true. Imperfect works, but still works of art, will be such productions as satisfy all three conditions though it be but in unequal degree. That alone will be no work of art, in which either the content is quite insignificant and unnecessary to man, or the expression quite unintelligible, or the relation of the author to the work quite insincere. In the degree of perfection attained in each of these respects lies the difference in quality between all true works of art. Sometimes the first predominates, sometimes the second, and sometimes the third.

All the remaining imperfect productions fall naturally, according to the three fundamental conditions of art, into three chief kinds: (1) those which stand out by the importance of their content, (2) those which stand out by their beauty of form, and (3) those which stand out by their heartfelt sincerity. These three kinds all yield approximations to perfect art, and are inevitably produced wherever there is art.

Thus among young artists heartfelt sincerity chiefly prevails, coupled with insignificance of content and more or less beauty of form. Among older artists, on the contrary, the importance of the content often predominates over beauty of form and sincerity. Among laborious artists beauty of form predominates over content and sincerity.

All works of art may be appraised by the prevalence in them of the first, the second, or the third quality, and they may all be subdivided into (1) those that have content and are beautiful, but have little sincerity; (2) those that have content, but little beauty and little sincerity; (3) those that have little content, but are beautiful and sincere, and so on, in all possible combinations and permutations.

All works of art, and in general all the mental activities of man, can be appraised on the basis of these three fundamental qualities; and they have been and are so appraised.

The differences in valuation have resulted, and do result, from the extent of the demand presented to art by certain people at a certain time in regard to these three conditions.

So for instance in classical times the demand for significance of content was much higher, and the demand for clearness and sincerity much lower than they subsequently became, especially in our time. The demand for beauty became greater in the Middle Ages, but on the other hand the demand for significance and sincerity became lower; and in our time the demand for sincerity and truthfulness has become much greater, but on the other hand the demand for beauty, and especially for significance, has been lowered.

V

The evaluation of works of art is necessarily correct when all three conditions are taken into account, and inevitably incorrect when works are valued not on the basis of all three conditions but only of one or two of them.

And yet such evaluation of works of art on the basis of only one of the three conditions is an error particularly prevalent in our time, lowering the general level of what is demanded from art to what can be reached by a mere imitation of it, and confusing the minds of critics, and of the public, and of artists themselves, as to what is really art and as to where its boundary lies —the line that divides it from craftsmanship and from mere amusement.

This confusion arises from the fact that people who lack the capacity to understand true art, judge of works of art from one side only, and according to their own characters and training observe in them the first, the second, or the third side only, imagining and assuming that this one side perceptible to them—and the significance of art based on this one condition—defines the whole of art. Some see only the importance of the content, others only the beauty of form, and others again only the artist's sincerity and therefore truthfulness. And according to what they see they define the nature of art itself, construct their theories, and praise and encourage those who, like themselves, not understanding wherein a work of art consists, turn them out like pancakes and inundate our world with foul floods of all kinds of follies and abominations which they call 'works of art.'

Such are the majority of people and, as representatives of that majority, such were the originators of the three æsthetic theories already alluded to, which meet the perceptions and demands of that majority.

All these theories are based on a misunderstanding of the whole importance of art and on severing its three fundamental conditions; and therefore these three false theories of art clash, as a result of the fact that real art has three fundamental conditions of which each of those theories accepts but one.

The first theory, of so-called 'tendencious' art, accepts as a work of art one that has for its subject something which, though it be not new, is important to all men by its moral content, independently of its beauty and spiritual depth.

The second ('art for art's sake') recognizes as a work of art only that which has beauty of form, independently of its novelty, the importance of its content, or its sincerity.

The third theory, the 'realistic,' recognizes as a work of art only that in which the author's relation to his subject is sincere, and which is therefore truthful. The last theory says that however insignificant or even foul may be the content, with a more or less beautiful form the work will be good, if the author's relation to what he depicts is sincere and therefore truthful.

VI

All these theories forget one chief thing—that neither importance, nor beauty, nor sincerity, provides the requisite for works of art, but that the basic condition of the production of such works is that the artist should be conscious of something new and important; and that therefore, just as it always has been, so it always will be, necessary for a true artist to be able to perceive something quite new and important. For the artist to see what is new, it is necessary that he should observe and think, and not occupy his life with trifles which hinder his attentive penetration into, and meditation on, life's phenomena. In order that the new things he sees may be important ones, the artist must be a morally enlightened man, and he must not live a selfish life but must share the common life of humanity.

If only he sees what is new and important he will be sure to find a form which will express it, and the sincerity which is an essential content of artistic production will be present. He must be able to express the new subject so that all may understand it. For this he must have such mastery of his craft that when working he will think as little about the rules of that craft as a man when walking thinks of the laws of motion. And in order to attain this, the artist must not look round on his work and admire it, must not make technique his aim—as one who is walking should not contemplate and admire his gait—but should be concerned only to express his subject clearly, and in such a way as to be intelligible to all.

Finally, to work at his subject not for external ends but to satisfy his inner need, the artist must rise superior to motives of avarice and vanity. He must love with his own heart and not with another's, and not pretend that he loves what others love or consider worthy of love.

And to attain all this the artist must do as Balaam did when the messengers came to him and he went apart awaiting God so as to say only what God commanded; and he must not do as that same Balaam afterwards did when, tempted by gifts, he went to the king against God's command, as was evident even to the ass on which he rode, though not perceived by him while blinded by avarice and vanity.

VII

In our time nothing of that kind is demanded. A man who wishes to follow art need not wait for some important and new perception to arise in his soul, which he can sincerely love and having loved can clothe in suitable form. In our time a man who wishes to follow art either takes a subject current at the time and praised by people who in his opinion are clever, and clothes it as best he can in what is called 'artistic form'; or he chooses a subject which gives him most opportunity to display his technical skill, and with toil and patience produces what he considers to be a work of art; or having received some chance impression he takes what caused that impression for his subject, imagining that it will yield a work of art since it happened to produce an impression on him.

And so there appear an innumerable quantity of so-called works of art which, as in every mechanical craft, can be produced without the least intermission. There are always current fashionable notions in society, and with patience a technique can always be learnt, and something or other will always seem interesting to some one. Having separated the conditions that should be united in a true work of art, people have produced so many works of pseudo-art that the public, the critics, and the pseudo-artists themselves, are left quite without any definition of what they themselves hold to be art.

The people of to-day have, as it were, said to themselves: 'Works of art are good and useful; so it is necessary to produce more of them.' It would indeed be a very good thing if there were more; but the trouble is that you can only produce to order works which are no better than works of mere craftsmanship because of their lack of the essential conditions of art.

A really artistic production cannot be made to order, for a true work of art is the revelation (by laws beyond our grasp) of a new conception of life arising in the artist's soul, which, when expressed, lights up the path along which humanity progresses.

PART VII

WHAT IS ART?

Tolstóy's Preface to the First English Edition, which Mr. Aylmer Maude had translated from the Original with Tolstóy's co-operation.

THIS book of mine, 'What is Art?' appears now for the first time in its true form. More than one edition has already been issued in Russia, but in each case it has been so mutilated by the Censor that I request all who are interested in my views on art only to judge of them by the work in its present shape. The causes which led to the publication of the book in a mutilated form—with my name attached to it—were the following: In accordance with a decision I arrived at long ago—not to submit my writings to the Censorship (which I consider to be an immoral and irrational institution), but to print them only in the shape in which they were written—I intended not to attempt to print this work in Russia. However, my good acquaintance Professor Grote, editor of a Moscow psychological magazine, having heard of the contents of my work asked me to print it in his magazine and promised me that he would get the book through the Censor's office unmutilated if I would but agree to a few very unimportant alterations, merely toning down certain expressions. I was weak enough to agree to this, and it has resulted in a book appearing under my name, from which not only have some essential thoughts been excluded, but into which the thoughts of other men—even thoughts utterly opposed to my own convictions—have been introduced.

The thing occurred in this way. First Grote softened my expressions and in some cases weakened them. For instance, he replaced the words: *always* by *sometimes*, *all* by *some*, *Church* religion by *Roman Catholic* religion, '*Mother of God*' by *Madonna*, *patriotism* by *pseudo-patriotism*, *palaces* by *palatii*,[1] etc., and I did not consider it necessary to protest. But when the book was already in type, the Censor required that whole sentences should be altered, and that instead of what I said about the evil of landed property, a remark should be substituted on the evils of a landless proletariat.[2] I agreed to this also and to some further alterations. It seemed not worth while to upset the whole affair for the sake of one sentence, and when one alteration had been agreed to it seemed not worth while to protest against a second and a third. Thus little by little expressions crept into the book which altered the sense and attributed things to me that I could not have wished to say; so that by the time the book was printed it had been deprived of some part of

[1] Tolstóy's remarks on Church religion were re-worded so as to seem to relate only to the Western Church, and his disapproval of luxurious life was made to apply not, say, to Queen Victoria or Nicholas II, but to the Cæsars or the Pharaohs.

[2] The Russian peasant was usually a member of a village commune, and had therefore a right to share in the land belonging to the village. Tolstóy disapproved of the order of society which allows less land for the support of a whole village full of people than was sometimes owned by a single landed proprietor. The Censor did not allow disapproval of this state of things to be expressed, but was prepared to admit that the laws and customs, say, of England—where a yet more extreme form of landed property existed and the men who actually labour on the land usually possessed none of it—deserved criticism.—A. M.

its integrity and sincerity. But there was consolation in the thought that the book, if it contains something good, would even in this form be of use to Russian readers whom it would otherwise not have reached. Things however turned out otherwise. *Nous comptions sans notre hôte.* After the legal term of four days had already elapsed, the book was seized and, on instructions received from Petersburg, it was handed over to the Spiritual Censor. Then Grote declined all further participation in the affair, and the Spiritual Censor proceeded to do what he liked with the book. The Spiritual Censorship is one of the most ignorant, venal, stupid, and despotic institutions in Russia. Books which disagree in any way with the recognized State religion of Russia, if once it gets hold of them are almost always totally suppressed and burnt; which is what happened to all my religious works when attempts were made to print them in Russia. Probably a similar fate would have overtaken this work also, had not the editors of the magazine employed all means to save it. The result of their efforts was that the Spiritual Censor, a priest who probably understands art and is interested in art as much as I understand or am interested in church services, but who gets a good salary for destroying whatever is likely to displease his superiors, struck out all that seemed to him to endanger his position, and substituted his thoughts for mine wherever he considered it necessary to do so. For instance, where I speak of Christ going to the Cross for the sake of the truth he professed, the Censor substituted a statement that Christ died for mankind, that is, he attributed to me an assertion of the dogma of the Redemption, which I consider to be one of the most untruthful and harmful of Church dogmas. After correcting the book in this way, the Spiritual Censor allowed it to be printed.

To protest in Russia is impossible; no newspaper would publish such a protest, and to withdraw my book from the magazine and place the editor in an awkward position with the public was also impossible.

So the matter has remained. A book has appeared under my name, containing thoughts attributed to me which are not mine.

I was persuaded to give my article to a Russian magazine in order that my thoughts, which may be useful, should become the possession of Russian readers; and the result has been that my name is affixed to a work from which it might be assumed that I quite arbitrarily assert things contrary to the general opinion without adducing my reasons: that I only consider false patriotism bad, but patriotism in general a very good feeling; that I merely deny the absurdities of the Roman Catholic Church and disbelieve in the Madonna, but that I believe in the Orthodox Eastern faith and in the 'Mother of God'; that I consider all the writings collected in the Bible to be holy books, and see the chief importance of Christ's life in the Redemption of mankind by his death.

I have narrated all this in such detail because it strikingly illustrates the indubitable truth, that all compromise with institutions of which your conscience disapproves—compromises which are usually made for the sake of the general good—instead of producing the good you expect, inevitably lead you not only to acknowledge the institution you disapprove of, but also to participate in the evil that institution produces.

I am glad to be able by this statement to do at least something to correct the error into which I was led by my compromise.

I have also to mention that besides reinstating the parts excluded by the Censor from the Russian editions, other corrections and additions of importance have been made in this edition.

29th March 1898. LEO TOLSTÓY.

NOTE: When a subscription edition of Tolstóy's works, edited by Professor Leo Wiener, was published in 1904, in U.S.A. and by G. M. Dent & Co. in London, this request of Tolstóy's to 'all who are interested in my views on art only to judge of them by the work in its present shape,' was disregarded, another version was substituted, and incidentally this preface was omitted from that edition of his works—which incorrectly claimed to be complete.

PART VIII

WHAT IS ART?

CONTENTS

APPENDICES

(This Table of Contents is compiled by the translator.)

WHAT IS ART?

CHAPTER I

Time and labour spent on art. Lives stunted in its service. Morality sacrificed to art. The rehearsal of an opera described.

TAKE up any one of our ordinary newspapers, and you will find a part devoted to the theatre and music. In almost every number you will find a description of some art-exhibition or of some particular picture, and you will always find reviews of new works of art that have appeared, of volumes of poems, of short stories, or of novels.

Promptly and in detail as soon as it has occurred an account is published of how such and such an actress or actor played this or that rôle in such and such a drama, comedy, or opera, and of the merits of the performance as well as of the contents of the new drama, comedy, or opera, with its defects and merits. With as much care and detail, or even more, we are told how such and such an artist has sung a certain piece, or has played it on the piano or violin, and what were the merits and defects of the piece and of the performance. In every large town there is sure to be at least one, if not more than one, exhibition of new pictures, the merits and defects of which are discussed in the utmost detail by critics and connoisseurs.

New novels and poems, in separate volumes or in the magazines, appear almost every day, and the newspapers consider it their duty to give their readers detailed accounts of these artistic productions.

For the support of art in Russia (where for the education of the people only a hundredth part is spent of what would be required to give every one an opportunity of instruction) the Government grants millions of rubles in subsidies to academies, conservatoires, and theatres. In France twenty million francs are assigned for art, and similar grants are made in Germany and elsewhere.

In every large town enormous buildings are erected for museums, academies, conservatoires, dramatic schools, and for performances and concerts. Hundreds of thousands of workmen—carpenters, masons, painters, joiners, paper-hangers, tailors, hairdressers, jewellers, moulders, type-setters—spend their whole lives in hard labour to satisfy the demands of art; so that hardly any other department of human activity, the military excepted, consumes so much energy as this.

Not only is enormous labour spent on this activity, but in it, as in war, the very lives of men are sacrificed. Hundreds of thousands of people devote their lives from childhood to learning to twirl their legs rapidly (dancers), or to touch notes and strings very rapidly (musicians), or to sketch with paint and represent what they see (artists), or to turn every phrase inside out and find a rhyme to every word. And these people, often very kind and clever and capable of all sorts of useful labour, grow savage over their specialized and stupefying occupations, and become one-sided and self-complacent specialists, dull to all the serious phenomena of life and skilful only at rapidly twisting their legs, their tongues, or their fingers.

But even this stunting of human life is not the worst. I remember being once at the rehearsal of one of the most ordinary of the new operas which are produced at all the opera houses of Europe and America.

I arrived when the first act had already commenced. To reach the auditorium I had to pass through the stage-entrance. By dark entrances and passages, past immense machines for changing the scenery and lighting the stage and the theatre, I was led through the vaults of an enormous building; and there in the gloom and dust I saw workmen busily engaged. One of these men—pale, haggard, in a dirty blouse, with dirty, work-worn hands and cramped fingers, evidently tired and out of humour—went past me, angrily scolding another man. Ascending by a dark stair I came out on the boards behind the scenes. Amid various poles and rings and scattered scenery, decorations and curtains, stood and moved dozens, if not hundreds, of painted and dressed-up men in costumes fitting tight to their thighs and calves, and also women, who were, as usual, as nearly nude as might be. These were all singers, or members of the chorus, or ballet-dancers, awaiting their turns. My guide led me across the stage and, by means of a bridge of boards, across the orchestra, in which perhaps a hundred musicians of all kinds, from kettle-drum to flute and harp, were seated, to the dark pit-stalls.

On an elevation, between two lamps with reflectors and in an arm-chair placed before a music-stand, sat the director of the musical part, *bâton* in hand, managing the orchestra and singers, and in general the production of the whole opera.

The performance had already commenced, and on the stage was being represented a procession of Indians who had brought home a bride. Besides men and women in costume, two other men in ordinary clothes bustled and ran about on the stage: one was the director of the dramatic part, and the other, who stepped about in soft shoes and ran from place to place with unusual agility, was the dancing-master, whose salary per month exceeded what ten labourers earn in a year.

These three directors arranged the singing, the orchestra, and the procession. The procession, as usual, was enacted by men and women in couples with tinfoil halberds on their shoulders. They all came from one place and walked round and round again and then stopped. The procession took a long time to arrange: first the Indians with halberds came on too late, then too soon; then at the right time but crowded together at the exit; then they did not crowd but arranged themselves badly at the sides of the stage,— and each time the whole performance was stopped and recommenced from the beginning. The procession is preceded by a recitative, delivered by a man dressed up like some variety of Turk, who, opening his mouth in a curious way, sings, 'Home I bring the bri-i-ide.' He sings, and waves his arm (which is of course bare) from under his mantle. The procession commences. But here the French horn, in the accompaniment of the recitative, does something wrong; and the director, with a shudder as if some catastrophe had occurred, raps with his stick on the stand. All is stopped, and the director, turning to the orchestra, attacks the French horn, scolding him in the rudest terms—as cabmen abuse one another—for taking the wrong note. And again the whole thing recommences. The Indians with their halberds again come on, treading softly in their extraordinary boots; again the singer sings, 'Home I bring the bri-i-ide.' But here the pairs get too close together. More raps with the stick, more scolding, and a recommencement. Again 'Home I bring the bri-i-ide,' again the same gesticulation with the bare arm from under the mantle and again the couples, treading softly with halberds on their shoulders, some with sad and serious faces, some talking and smiling, arrange themselves in a circle and begin to sing. All seems to be going well, but again the stick raps and the director in a distressed and angry voice begins to scold the men and women of the chorus. It appears that when singing they had omitted to raise their hands from time to time in sign of animation. 'Are you all dead, or what? What oxen you are! Are you corpses, that you can't move?' Again they re-commence, 'Home I bring the bri-i-ide,' and again, with sorrowful faces, the chorus women sing, first one and then another of them raising their hands. But two chorus-girls speak to each other,— again a more vehement rapping with the stick. 'Have you come here to talk? Can't you gossip at home? You there in red breeches, come nearer. Look at me! Begin again!' Again 'Home I bring the bri-i-ide.' And so it goes on for one, two, three hours. The whole of such a rehearsal lasts six hours on end. Raps with the stick, repetitions, placings, corrections of the singers, of the orchestra, of the procession, of the dancers,—all seasoned with angry scolding. I heard the words, 'asses,' fools,' 'idiots,' 'swine,' addressed to the musicians and singers at least forty times in the course of one hour. And the unhappy individual to whom the abuse is addressed—flautist, horn-blower, or singer—physically and mentally demoralized, does not reply, and does what is demanded of him. Twenty times is repeated the one phrase, 'Home I bring the bri-i-ide,' and twenty times the striding about in yellow shoes with a halberd over the shoulder. The conductor knows that these people are so demoralized that they are no longer fit for anything but to blow trumpets and walk about with halberds and in yellow shoes, and that they are also so accustomed to dainty easy living that they will put up with anything rather than lose their luxurious life. He therefore gives free vent to his churlishness, especially as he has seen the same thing done in Paris and Vienna, and knows that this is the way the best conductors behave, and that it is a musical tradition of great artists to be so carried away by the great business of their art that they can-not pause to consider the feelings of other artists.

It would be difficult to find a more repulsive sight.

D

I have seen one workman abuse another for not supporting the weight piled upon him when goods were being unloaded, or at hay-stacking, the village Elder scold a peasant for not making the rick right, and the man submitted in silence. And however unpleasant it was to witness the scene, the unpleasantness was lessened by the consciousness that the business in hand was necessary and important and the fault for which the Elder scolded the labourer was one which might spoil a necessary undertaking.

But what was being done here? For what, and for whom? Very likely the conductor was tired out, like the workman I passed in the vaults; it was even evident that he was; but who made him tire himself? And why was he tiring himself? The opera he was rehearsing was one of the most ordinary of operas for people who are accustomed to them, but also one of the most gigantic absurdities that could possibly be devised. An Indian king wants to marry; they bring him a bride; he disguises himself as a minstrel; the bride falls in love with the minstrel and is in despair, but afterwards discovers that the minstrel is the king, and every one is highly delighted.

That there never were or could be such Indians, and that they were not only unlike Indians but that what they were doing was unlike anything on earth except other operas, was beyond all manner of doubt; that people do not converse in such a way as recitative, and do not place themselves at fixed distances, in a quartet, waving their arms to express their emotions; that nowhere except in theatres do people walk about in such a manner, in pairs, with tinfoil halberds and in slippers; that no one ever gets angry in such a way, or is affected in such a way, or laughs in such a way, or cries in such a way; and that no one on earth can be moved by such performances—all this is beyond the possibility of doubt.

Instinctively the question presents itself: For whom is this being done? Whom *can* it please? If there are occasionally good melodies in the opera, to which it is pleasant to listen, they could have been sung simply without these stupid costumes and all the processions and recitatives and hand-wavings.

The ballet, in which half-naked women make voluptuous movements, twisting themselves into various sensual wreathings, is simply a lewd performance.

So one is quite at a loss as to whom these things are done for. The man of culture is heartily sick of them, while to a real working man they are utterly incomprehensible. If any one can be pleased by these things (which is doubtful), it can only be some young footman or depraved artisan, who has contracted the spirit of the upper classes but is not yet satiated with their amusements, and wishes to show his breeding.

And all this nasty folly is prepared, not simply, nor with kindly merriment, but with anger and brutal cruelty.

It is said that it is all done for the sake of art and that art is a very important thing. But is it true that art is so important that such sacrifices should be made for its sake? This question is especially urgent because art, for the sake of which the labour of millions, the lives of men, and above all love between man and man, are all being sacrificed—this very art is becoming something more and more vague and uncertain to human perception.

Criticism, in which the lovers of art used to find support for their opinions, has latterly become so self-contradictory that if we exclude from the domain of art all to which the critics of various schools themselves deny the title, there is scarcely any art left.

The artists of various sects, like the theologians of various sects, mutually exclude and destroy one another. Listen to the artists of the schools of our times, and in all branches you will find each set of artists disowning others. In poetry the old romanticists deny the parnassians and the decadents; the parnassians disown the romanticists and the decadents; the decadents disown all their predecessors and the symbolists; the symbolists disown all their predecessors and *les mages*; and *les mages* disown all, all their predecessors. Among novelists we have naturalists, psychologists, and 'nature-ists,' all rejecting each other. And it is the same in dramatic art, in painting, and in music. So that art, which demands such tremendous labour-sacrifices from the people, which stunts human lives and transgresses against human love, is not only *not* a thing clearly and firmly defined, but is understood in such contradictory ways by its own devotees that it is difficult to say what is meant by art, and especially what is good, useful art,—art for the sake of which we might condone such sacrifices as are being offered at its shrine.

CHAPTER II

Does art compensate for so much evil? What is art? Confusion of opinions. Is it 'that which produces beauty'? The word 'beauty' in Russian. Chaos in æsthetics.

FOR the production of every ballet, circus, opera, operetta, exhibition, picture, concert, or printed book, the intense and unwilling labour of thousands and thousands of people is needed at what is often harmful and humiliating work. It were well if artists made all they require for themselves, but as it is, they all need the help of workmen, not only to produce art but also for their own usually luxurious maintenance. And one way or other they get it, either through payments from rich people, or through subsidies given by Government (in Russia, for instance, in grants of millions of rúbles to theatres, conservatoires, and academies). This money is collected from the people, some of whom have to sell their only cow to pay the tax, and who never get those æsthetic pleasures which art gives.

It was all very well for a Greek or Roman artist or even for a Russian artist of the first half of the nineteenth century (when there still were slaves and it was considered right that there should be) with a quiet mind to make people serve him and his art; but in our day, when in all men there is at least some dim perception of the equal rights of all, it is impossible to constrain people to labour unwillingly for art, without first deciding the question whether it is true that art is so good and so important an affair as to redeem this evil.

If not, we have the terrible probability to consider that while fearful sacrifices of the labour and lives of men and of morality itself are being made to art, that same art may be not only useless but even harmful.

And therefore it is necessary for a society in which works of art arise and are supported, to find out whether all that professes to be art is really art; whether (as is presupposed in our society) all that is art is good, and whether it is important and worth the sacrifices which it necessitates. It is still more necessary for every conscientious artist to know this, in order that he may be sure that all he does has a valid meaning—that it is not merely an infatuation of the small circle of people among whom he lives which excites in him the false assurance that he is doing a good work—and that what he takes from others for the support of his often very luxurious life will be compensated for by those productions at which he works. And that is why answers to the above questions are specially important in our time.

What is this art which is considered so important and necessary for humanity that for its sake these sacrifices of labour, of human life, and even of goodness, may be made?

'What is art? What a question! Art is architecture, sculpture, painting, music, and poetry in all its forms,' usually replies the ordinary man, the art amateur or even the artist himself, imagining the matter about which he is talking to be perfectly clear and uniformly understood by everybody. But in architecture, one inquires further, are there not simple buildings which are not objects of art, and buildings with artistic pretensions which are unsuccessful and ugly and therefore not to be considered works of art? Wherein lies the characteristic sign of a work of art?

It is the same in sculpture, in music, and in poetry. Art in all its forms is bounded on one side by the practically useful, and on the other by unsuccessful attempts at art. How is art to be marked off from each of these? The ordinary educated man of our circle, and even the artist who has not occupied himself specially with æsthetics, will not hesitate at this question either. He thinks the solution was found long ago and is well known to everyone.

'Art is activity that produces beauty,' says such a man.

If art consists in that,—then is a ballet or an operetta art? you inquire.

'Yes,' says the ordinary man, though with some hesitation, 'a good ballet or a graceful operetta is also art, in so far as it manifests beauty.'

But without even asking the ordinary man what differentiates the 'good' ballet and the 'graceful' operetta from their opposites (a question he would have much difficulty in answering), if you ask him whether the activity of costumers and hairdressers, who ornament the figures and faces of the women for the ballet and the operetta, is art; or the activity of Worth, the dressmaker; of scent-makers and mencooks, then he will in most cases deny that their activity belongs to the domain of art. But in this the ordinary man makes a mistake just because he is an ordinary man and not a specialist, and because he has not occupied himself with æsthetic questions. Had he looked into these matters he would have seen in the great Renan's book, *Marc-Aurèle*, a dissertation showing that the dressmaker's work is art, and that those who do not see in the adornment of woman an affair of the highest art are very small-minded and dull. '*C'est le grand art*,' says Renan. Moreover, he would have known that in many æsthetic systems—for instance, in the æsthetics of the learned Professor Kralik, *Weltschönheit, Versuch einer allgemeinen Æsthetik, von Richard Kralik*, and in *Les problèmes de l'esthétique contemporaine*, by Guyau—the arts of costume, of taste, and of touch, are included.

'*Es folgt nun ein Fünfblatt von Künsten, die der subjec-*

tiven Sinnlichkeit entkeimen' (There results then a penta-
foliate of arts, growing out of our subjective perceptions), says Kralik (p. 175). *'Sie sind die ästhetische
Behandlung der fünf Sinne.'* (They are the æsthetic treatment of the five senses.)

These five arts are the following:—

Die Kunst des Geschmacksinns—The art of the sense of
taste (p. 175).

Die Kunst des Geruchsinns—The art of the sense of
smell (p. 177).

Die Kunst des Tastsinns—The art of the sense of
touch (p. 180).

Die Kunst des Gehörsinns—The art of the sense of
hearing (p. 182).

Die Kunst des Gesichtsinns—The art of the sense of
sight (p. 184).

Of the first of these—*die Kunst des Geschmacksinns*—he
says: Man hält zwar gewöhnlich nur zwei oder höch-
stens drei Sinne für würdig den Stoff künstlerischer
Behandlung abzugeben, aber ich glaube nur mit be-
dingtem Recht. Ich will kein allzugrosses Gewicht dar-
auf legen, dass der gemeine Sprachgebrauch manch
andere Künste, wie zum Beispiel die Kochkunst
kennt.[1]

And further: Und es ist doch gewiss eine ästhetische
Leistung, wenn es der Kochkunst gelingt aus einem
thierischen Kadaver einen Gegenstand des Ge-
schmacks in jedem Sinne zu machen. Der Grundsatz
der Kunst des Geschmacksinns (die weiter ist als die
sogenannte Kochkunst) ist also dieser: Es soll alles
Geniessbare als Sinnbild einer Idee behandelt werden

---

[1] The art of the sense of taste. . . . Only two, or at most
three, senses are generally held worthy to supply matter
for artistic treatment, but I think this opinion is only
conditionally correct. I will not lay too much stress on the
fact that our common speech recognizes many other arts,
as, for instance, the art of cookery.

und in jedesmaligem Einklang zur auszudrückenden Idee.[1]

This author, like Renan, acknowledges a *Kostüm-kunst* (Art of Costume) (p. 200), etc.

Such is also the opinion of the French writer, Guyau, who is highly esteemed by some authors of our day. In his book, *Les Problèmes de l'esthétique contemporaine*, he speaks seriously of touch, taste, and smell, as giving or being capable of giving æsthetic impressions: 'Si la couleur manque au toucher, il nous fournit en revanche une notion que l'œil seul ne peut nous donner, et qui a une valeur esthétique considérable, celle du doux, du soyeux, du poli. Ce qui caractérise la beauté du velours c'est sa douceur au toucher non moins que son brillant. Dans l'idée que nous nous faisons de la beauté d'une femme le velouté de sa peau entre comme élément essentiel.

Chacun de nous probablement avec un peu d'attention se rappellera des jouissances du goût, qui ont été de véritables jouissances esthétiques.'[2] And he recounts how a glass of milk drunk by him in the mountains gave him æsthetic enjoyment.

---

[1] And yet it is certainly an æsthetic achievement when the art of cooking succeeds in making of an animal's corpse an object in all respects tasteful. The principle of the Art of Taste (which goes beyond the so-called Art of Cookery) is therefore this: All that is eatable should be treated as the symbol of some Idea, and always in harmony with the Idea to be expressed.

[2] If the sense of touch lacks colour, it gives us on the other hand a notion which the eye alone cannot afford, and one of considerable æsthetic value, namely, that of *softness, silkiness, polish*. The beauty of velvet is characterized not less by its softness to the touch than by its lustre. In our conception of a woman's beauty the softness of her skin enters as an essential element.

Each of us probably, with a little attention, can recall pleasures of taste which have been real æsthetic pleasures.

So it turns out that the conception of art as consisting in making beauty manifest is not at all so simple as it seemed, especially now when in this conception of beauty are included our sensations of touch and taste and smell, as they are by the latest æsthetic writers.

But the ordinary man either does not know or does not wish to know all this, and is firmly convinced that all questions of art may be simply and clearly solved by acknowledging beauty to be the content of art. To him it seems clear and comprehensible that art consists in manifesting beauty, and that a reference to beauty will serve to explain all questions about art.

But what is this beauty which forms the content of art? How is it defined? What is it?

As is always the case, the more cloudy and confused the conception conveyed by a word, with the greater *aplomb* and self-assurance do people use that word, pretending that what is understood by it is so simple and clear that it is not even worth while to discuss what it actually means.

This is how matters of orthodox religion are usually dealt with, and this is how people now deal with the conception of beauty. It is taken for granted that what is meant by the word beauty is known and understood by every one. And yet not only is this not known, but after whole mountains of books have been written on the subject by the most learned and profound thinkers during one hundred and fifty years (ever since Baumgarten founded æsthetics in the year 1750). the question, What is beauty? remains to this day quite unsolved, and in each new work on æsthetics it is answered in a new way. One of the last books I read on the subject was a not ill-written booklet by Julius Mithalter, called *Rätsel des Schönen* (*The Enigma of the Beautiful*). And that title precisely expresses the position of the question, What is beauty? After thousands of learned men have discussed it for one hundred and fifty years, the meaning of the word beauty remains an enigma still. The Germans answer the question in their manner, though in a hundred different ways; the physiological æstheticians, especially the Englishmen: Herbert Spencer, Grant Allen, and his school, answer it each in his own way; the French eclectics and the followers of Guyau and Taine, also each in his own way; and all these people know all the preceding solutions given by Baumgarten, and Kant, and Schelling, and Schiller, and Fichte, and Winckelmann, and Lessing, and Hegel, and Schopenhauer, and Hartmann, and Schasler, and Cousin, and Lévêque and others.

What is this strange conception of 'beauty,' which seems so simple to those who talk without thinking, but in defining which all the philosophers of various tendencies and different nationalities can in a century and a half come to no agreement? What is this conception of beauty on which the dominant doctrine of art rests?

In Russian, by the word *krasotá* (beauty) we mean only that which pleases the sight. And though latterly people have begun to speak of 'an ugly deed,' or of 'beautiful music,' it is not good Russian.

A Russian of the common folk, not knowing foreign languages, will not understand you if you tell him that a man who has given his last coat to another, or done anything similar, has acted 'beautifully,' that a man who has cheated another has done an 'ugly' action, or that a song is 'beautiful.'

In Russian a deed may be kind and good, or unkind and bad. Music may be pleasant and good, or unpleasant and bad; but there can be no such thing as 'beautiful' or 'ugly' music.

Beautiful may relate to a man, a horse, a house, a view, or a movement. Of actions, thoughts, character, or music, if they please us we may say that they are good, or if they do not please us that they are bad. But beautiful can be used only concerning that which pleases the sight. So that the word and conception 'good' includes the conception of 'beautiful,' but the reverse is not true, the conception 'beauty' does not include the conception 'good.' If we say 'good' of an article which we value for its appearance, we thereby say that the article is beautiful; but if we say it is 'beautiful,' it does not at all mean that the article is a good one.

Such is the meaning ascribed by the Russian language, and therefore by the sense of the people, to the words and conceptions 'good' and 'beautiful.'

In all the European languages, that is, in the languages of those nations among whom the doctrine has spread that beauty is the essential thing in art, the words '*beau*', '*schön*,' 'beautiful,' '*bello*,' etc., while keeping their meaning of beautiful in form, have come also to express 'goodness,' 'kindness,' that is to say, have come to act as substitutes for the word 'good.'

So that it has become quite natural in those languages to use such expressions as '*belle âme*,' '*schöne Gedanken*,' or 'beautiful deed.' Those languages no longer have a suitable word wherewith expressly to indicate beauty of form, and have to use a combination of words such as '*beau par la forme*,' '*beautiful to look at*,' and so forth, to convey that idea.

Observation of the divergent meanings which the words 'beauty' and 'beautiful' have in Russian on the one hand and in those European languages now permeated by this æsthetic theory on the other hand, shows us that the word 'beauty' has among the latter acquired a special meaning, namely, that of 'good.'

What is remarkable moreover is that since we Russians have begun more and more to adopt the European view of art, the same evolution has begun to show itself in our language also, and some people speak and write quite confidently, and without causing surprise, of beautiful music and ugly actions, and even of beautiful or ugly thoughts; whereas forty years ago, when I was young, the expressions 'beautiful music' and 'ugly actions' were not only unusual but incomprehensible. Evidently this new meaning given to beauty by European thought is beginning to be assimilated by Russian society.

And what really is this meaning? What is this 'beauty' as understood by the European peoples?

In order to answer this question I must here quote at least a small selection of those definitions of beauty most generally adopted in existing æsthetic systems. I particularly beg the reader not to be overcome by dulness but to read these extracts through, or still better to read some one of the erudite æsthetic authors. Not to mention the voluminous German æstheticians, a very good book for this purpose would be either the German book by Kralik, the English work by Knight, or the French one by Lévêque. It is necessary to read at least one of the learned æsthetic writers in order to form at first hand a conception of the variety of opinion and the frightful obscurity which reigns in this region of speculation, not in this important matter trusting to another's report.

This for instance is what the German æsthetician Schasler says in the preface to his famous, voluminous, and detailed work on æsthetics:—

'In hardly any sphere of philosophic science can we find such divergent methods of investigation and exposition, amounting even to self-contradiction, as in the sphere of æsthetics. On the one hand we have elegant phraseology without any substance, characterized in great part by most one-sided superficiality; and on the other hand, accompanying undeniable

profundity of investigation and richness of subject-
matter, we get a revolting awkwardness of philosophic
terminology clothing the simplest thoughts in an ap-
parel of abstract science, as though to render them
worthy to enter the consecrated palace of the system;
and finally, between these two methods of investigation and exposition, there is a third, forming as it were
the transition from one to the other, an eclectic
method,—now flaunting an elegant phraseology and
now a pedantic erudition. . . . A style of exposition
that falls into none of these three defects but is truly
concrete, and having important matter expresses it in
clear and popular philosophic language, can nowhere be found less often than in the domain of
esthetics.' [1]

One need only read Schasler's own book, for example, to convince oneself of the justice of this observation of his.

On the same subject the French writer, Véron, in
the preface to his very good work on æsthetics, says,
'Il n'y a pas de science qui ait été plus que l'esthétique
livrée aux rêveries des métaphysiciens. Depuis Platon
jusqu'aux doctrines officielles de nos jours, on a fait
de l'art je ne sais quel amalgame de fantaisies quintes-
senciées et de mystères transcendantaux qui trouvent
leur expression suprême dans la conception absolue
du Beau idéal, prototype immuable et divin des choses
réelles' (L'esthétique, 1878, p. 5). [2]

[1] M. Schasler, Kritische Geschichte der Aesthetik, 1872, vol.
I, p. 13.

[2] There is no science which has been handed over to the
dreams of the metaphysicians more entirely than æsthetics.
From Plato down to the received doctrines of our day,
people have made of art a strange amalgam of quintes-
sential fancies and transcendental mysteries, which find
their supreme expression in the conception of an absolute
ideal Beauty, immutable and divine prototype of actual
things.

If the reader will only be at the pains to peruse the following extracts defining beauty, taken from the chief writers on æsthetics, he may convince himself that this censure is thoroughly deserved.

I shall not quote the definitions of beauty attributed to the ancients,—Socrates, Plato, Aristotle, and others, down to Plotinus,—because, in reality, the ancients had not that conception of beauty separated from goodness which forms the basis and aim of æsthetics in our time. By referring the judgments of the ancients on beauty to our conception of it, as is usually done in æsthetics, we give the words of the ancients a meaning which is not theirs.[1]

---

[1] See on this matter Bernard's admirable book, *L'esthétique d'Aristote*, also Walter's *Geschichte der Aesthetik im Altertum.*

CHAPTER III

Summary of various æsthetic theories and definitions from Baumgarten to the present day.

This chapter shows that no satisfactory definition of art had been devised, but it is one that many readers will prefer to skip or to skim. It contains nothing of Tolstóy's own thought, except negatively in his comments.

I BEGIN with the founder of æsthetics, Baumgarten (1714–1762).

According to Baumgarten,[1] the object of logical knowledge is Truth, the object of æsthetic (*i.e.*, sensuous) knowledge is Beauty. Beauty is the Perfect (the Absolute), recognized through the senses; Truth is the Perfect perceived through reason; Goodness is the Perfect reached by moral will.

Beauty is defined by Baumgarten as a correspondence, that is, an order of parts in their mutual relations to each other and in their relation to the whole. The aim of beauty itself is to please and excite a desire, '*Wohlgefallen und Erregung eines Verlangens.*' (A position precisely the opposite to Kant's definition of the nature and sign of beauty.)

With reference to the manifestations of beauty Baumgarten considers that the highest embodiment of beauty is visible to us in nature, and he therefore thinks that the highest aim of art is to copy ·nature. (This position also is directly contradicted by the conclusions of the latest æstheticians.)

Passing over the unimportant followers of Baumgarten—Maier, Eschenburg, and Eberhard—who only slightly modified the doctrine of their teacher by dividing the pleasant from the beautiful, I will quote

[1] Schasler, p. 361.

the definitions given by writers who came immediately after Baumgarten and defined beauty in quite another way. These writers were Sulzer, Mendelssohn, and Moritz. They in contradiction to Baumgarten's main position recognize as the aim of art not beauty, but goodness. Thus Sulzer (1720–1777) says, only that can be considered beautiful which contains goodness. According to his theory, the aim of the whole life of humanity is welfare in social life. This is attained by the education of the moral feelings, to which end art should be subservient. Beauty is that which evokes and educates this feeling.

Beauty is understood almost in the same way by Mendelssohn (1729–1786). According to him art is the development of the beautiful, obscurely recognized by feeling, till it becomes the true and good. The aim of art is moral perfection.[1]

For the æstheticians of this school the ideal of beauty is a beautiful soul in a beautiful body; so that they completely wipe out Baumgarten's division of the Perfect (the Absolute) into the three forms of Truth, Goodness, and Beauty; and Beauty again merges into the Good and the True.

But this conception is not only not maintained by the later æstheticians, but the æsthetic doctrine of Winckelmann arises, again in complete opposition. This divides the mission of art from the aim of goodness in the sharpest and most positive manner, makes external beauty the aim of art and even limits it to visible beauty.

According to the celebrated work of Winckelmann (1717–1767) the law and aim of all art is beauty only —beauty quite separated from and independent of goodness. There are three kinds of beauty:—(1) beauty of form, (2) beauty of idea, expressing itself in the position of the figure (in plastic art), (3) beauty

[1] Schasler, p. 369.

of expression, attainable only when the two first conditions are present. This beauty of expression is the highest aim of art, and is attained in antique art; modern art should therefore aim at imitating ancient art.[1]

Art is similarly understood by Lessing, Herder, and afterwards by Goethe and by all the distinguished æstheticians of Germany till Kant, from whose day again a different conception of art arises.

Native æsthetic theories arose during this period in England, France, Italy, and Holland, and though not taken from the German, they were equally cloudy and contradictory. And all these writers, just like the German æstheticians, founded their theories on a conception of the Beautiful: understanding beauty in the sense of a something existing absolutely and more or less intermingled with Goodness, or having one and the same root. In England almost simultaneously with Baumgarten, even a little earlier, Shaftesbury, Hutcheson, Home, Burke, Hogarth, and others, wrote on art.

According to Shaftesbury (1670-1713), 'That which is beautiful is harmonious and proportionable, what is harmonious and proportionable is true, and what is at once both beautiful and true is of consequence agreeable and good.'[2] Beauty, he taught, is recognized by the mind only. God is fundamental beauty; beauty and goodness proceed from the same fount. So that although Shaftesbury regards beauty as being something separate from goodness, they again merge into something inseparable.

According to Hutcheson (1694-1747—*Inquiry into the Original of our Ideas of Beauty and Virtue*), the aim of art is beauty, the essence of which consists in evoking in us the perception of uniformity and variety. In the

[1] Schasler, pp. 388–390.
[2] Knight, *Philosophy of the Beautiful*, vol. i, pp. 165, 166.

recognition of what is art we are guided by 'an internal sense.' This internal sense may be in contradiction to the ethical one. So that according to Hutcheson beauty does not always correspond with goodness but separates from it and is sometimes contrary to it.[1]

According to Home, Lord Kames (1696–1782), beauty is that which is pleasant. Therefore beauty is defined by taste alone. The standard of true taste is that the maximum of richness, fulness, strength, and variety of impression, should be contained within the narrowest limits. That is the ideal of a perfect work of art.

According to Burke (1729–1797—*Philosophical Inquiry into the Origin of our Ideas of the Sublime and Beautiful*), the sublime and beautiful, which are the aim of art, have their origin in the promptings of self-preservation and of society. These feelings, examined at their source, are means for the maintenance of the race through the individual. The first (self-preservation) is attained by nourishment, defence, and war; the second (society) by intercourse and propagation. Therefore self-defence and war, which is bound up with it, are the source of the sublime; sociability and the sex-instinct, which is bound up with it, are the source of beauty.[2]

Such were the chief English definitions of art and beauty in the eighteenth century.

During the same period the writers on art in France were Père André and Batteux, with Diderot, D'Alembert, and to some extent Voltaire, following later.

According to Père André (*Essai sur le Beau*, 1741), there are three kinds of beauty—divine beauty, natural beauty, and artificial beauty.[3]

---

[1] Schasler, p. 289, Knight, pp. 168, 169.

[2] R. Kralik, *Weltschönheit, Versuch einer allgemeinen Aesthetik*, pp. 304–306.   [3] Knight, p. 101.

According to Batteux (1713–1780), art consists in imitating the beauty of nature, its aim being enjoyment.[1] Such also is Diderot's definition of art.

The French writers, like the English, hold that it is taste that decides what is beautiful; and the laws of taste are not only not laid down but it is admitted that they cannot be determined. The same view was held by D'Alembert and Voltaire.[2]

According to Pagano, the Italian æsthetician of that period, art consists in uniting the beauties dispersed in nature. The capacity to perceive these beauties is taste, the capacity to bring them into one whole is artistic genius. Beauty commingles with goodness, so that beauty is goodness made visible, and goodness is inner beauty.[3]

According to the opinion of other Italians: Muratori (1672–1750),—*Riflessioni sopra il buon gusto intorno le scienze e le arti,*—and especially Spaletti,[4]—*Saggio sopra la bellezza* (1765),—art amounts to an egotistical sensation founded (as with Burke) on the desire for self-preservation and society.

Among Dutch writers, Hemsterhuis (1720–1790), who had an influence on the German æstheticians and on Goethe, is remarkable. According to him, beauty is that which gives most pleasure, and that gives most pleasure which gives us the greatest number of perceptions in the shortest time. Enjoyment of the beautiful, because it gives the greatest quantity of perceptions in the shortest time, is the highest cognition to which man can attain.[5]

Such were the æsthetic theories outside Germany during the last century. In Germany after Winckelmann there again arose a completely new æsthetic theory, that of Kant (1724–1804), which more than

[1] Schasler, p. 316.   [2] Knight, pp. 102–104.
[3] R. Kralik, p. 124.   [4] Schasler, p. 328.
[5] Schasler, pp. 331–333.

all others clears up what this conception of beauty, and consequently of art, really amounts to.

The æsthetic teaching of Kant is founded as follows: —Man has a knowledge of nature outside him and of himself in nature. In nature outside himself he seeks for truth; in himself he seeks for goodness. The first is an affair of pure reason, the other of practical reason (free-will). Besides these two means of perception, there is also the judging capacity (*Urteilskraft*) which forms judgments without reasoning and produces pleasure without desire (*Urteil ohne Begriff und Vergnügen ohne Begehren*). This capacity is the basis of æsthetic feeling. Beauty, according to Kant, is, in its subjective meaning, that which in general and necessarily, without reasoning and without practical advantage, pleases; and in its objective meaning it is the form of an object suitable for its purpose in so far as that object is perceived without any conception of its utility.[1]

Beauty is defined in the same way by the followers of Kant, among whom was Schiller (1759-1805). According to Schiller, who wrote much on æsthetics, the aim of art is, as with Kant, beauty, the source of which is pleasure without practical advantage. So that art may be called a game, not in the sense of an unimportant occupation but in the sense of a manifestation of the beauties of life itself without other aim than that of beauty.[2]

Besides Schiller the most remarkable of Kant's followers in the sphere of æsthetics was Wilhelm Humboldt, who though he added nothing to the definition of beauty explained various forms of it,— the drama, music, humour, etc.[3]

After Kant, besides the second-rate philosophers, the writers on æsthetics were Fichte, Schelling, Hegel, and their followers.

[1] Schasler, pp. 525–528.   [2] Knight, pp. 61–63.
[3] Schasler, pp. 740–743.

Fichte (1762–1814) says that perception of the beautiful proceeds from this: the world—that is, nature—has two sides: it is the sum of our limitations and it is the sum of our free idealistic activity. In the first aspect the world is limited, in the second aspect it is free. In the first aspect every object is limited, distorted, compressed, confined—and we see deformity; in the second we perceive its inner completeness, vitality, regeneration—and we see beauty. So that the deformity or beauty of an object, according to Fichte, depends on the point of view of the observer. Beauty therefore exists not in the world but in the beautiful soul (*schöner Geist*). Art is the manifestation of this beautiful soul, and its aim is the education, not of the mind only—that is the business of the *savant*; not of the heart only—that is the affair of the moral preacher; but of the whole man. And so the characteristic of beauty lies not in anything external but in the presence of a beautiful soul in the artist.[1]

Following Fichte, and in the same direction, Friedrich Schlegel and Adam Müller also defined beauty. According to Schlegel (1772–1829), beauty in art is understood too incompletely, one-sidedly, and disconnectedly. Beauty exists not only in art but also in nature and in love; so that the truly beautiful is expressed by the union of art, nature, and love. Therefore Schlegel acknowledges moral and philosophic art as inseparably one with æsthetic art.[2]

According to Adam Müller (1779–1829), there are two kinds of beauty: the one, general beauty which attracts people as the sun attracts the planet—this is found chiefly in antique art—and the other, individual beauty which results from the observer himself becoming a sun attracting beauty,—this is the beauty of modern art. A world in which all contradictions are harmonized is the highest beauty. Every work of

[1] Schasler, pp. 769–771. [2] Schasler, pp. 786, 787.

art is a reproduction of this universal harmony.[1] The highest art is the art of life.[2]

Next after Fichte and his followers came a contemporary of his, the philosopher Schelling (1775-1845), who has had a great influence on the æsthetic conceptions of our times. According to Schelling's philosophy, art is the production or result of that conception of things by which the subject becomes its own object, or the object its own subject. Beauty is the perception of the infinite in the finite, and the chief characteristic of works of art is unconscious infinity. Art is the uniting of the subjective with the objective, of nature with reason, of the unconscious with the conscious, and therefore art is the highest means of knowledge. Beauty is the contemplation of things in themselves as they exist in the prototype (*in den Urbildern*). It is not the artist who by his knowledge or skill produces the beautiful, but the idea of beauty in him itself produces it.[3]

Of Schelling's followers the most noticeable was Solger (1780-1819—*Vorlesungen über Aesthetik*). According to him the idea of beauty is the fundamental idea of everything. In the world we see only distortions of the fundamental idea, but art, by imagination, may lift itself to the height of this idea. Art is therefore akin to creation.[4]

According to another follower of Schelling, Krause (1781-1832), true, positive beauty is the manifestation of the Idea in an individual form; art is the actualization of the beauty existing in the sphere of man's free spirit. The highest stage of art is the art of life, which directs its activity towards the adornment of life so that it may be a beautiful abode for beautiful man.[5]

[1] Kralik, p. 148.   [2] Kralik, p. 820.
[3] Schasler, pp. 828, 829, 834-841.   [4] Schasler, p. 891.
[5] Schasler, p. 917.

After Schelling and his followers came the new æsthetic doctrine of Hegel, which is held to this day consciously by many but by the majority unconsciously. This teaching is not only no clearer or better defined than the preceding ones but is if possible even more cloudy and mystical.

According to Hegel (1770–1831), God manifests himself in nature and in art in the form of beauty. God expresses himself in two ways: in the object and in the subject—in nature and in spirit. Beauty is the shining of the Idea through matter. Only the soul and what pertains to it is truly beautiful, and therefore the beauty of nature is only the reflection of the natural beauty of the spirit—the beautiful has only a spiritual content. But the spiritual must appear in sensuous form. The sensuous manifestation of spirit is only appearance (*Schein*), and this appearance is the only reality of the beautiful. Art is thus the production of this appearance of the Idea, and is a means, together with religion and philosophy, of bringing to consciousness, and expressing, the deepest problems of humanity and the highest truths of the spirit.

Truth and beauty according to Hegel are one and the same thing, the difference being only that truth is the Idea itself as it exists in itself and is thinkable. The Idea, manifested externally, becomes to the apprehension not only true but beautiful. The beautiful is the manifestation of the Idea.[1]

Following Hegel came his many adherents: Weisse, Arnold Ruge, Rosenkrantz, Theodor Vischer and others.

According to Weisse (1801–1867), art is the introduction (*Einbildung*) of the absolute spiritual reality of beauty into external, dead, indifferent matter, the perception of which latter apart from the beauty

[1] Schasler, pp. 946, 1085, 984, 985, 990.

brought into it presents the negation of all existence in itself (*Negation alles Fürsichseins*).

In the idea of truth, Weisse explains, lies a contradiction between the subjective and the objective sides of knowledge, in that an individual *ego* discerns the Universal. This contradiction can be removed by a conception that should unite into one the universal and the individual which fall asunder in our conceptions of truth. Such a conception would be reconciled (*aufgehoben*) truth. Beauty is such a reconciled truth.[1]

According to Ruge (1802–1880), a strict follower of Hegel, beauty is the Idea expressing itself. The spirit contemplating itself either finds itself expressed completely, and then that full expression of itself is beauty; or incompletely, and then it feels the need to alter this imperfect expression of itself and becomes creative art.[2]

According to Vischer (1807–1887), beauty is the Idea in the form of a finite phenomenon. The Idea itself is not indivisible but forms a system of ideas which may be represented by ascending and descending lines. The higher the idea the more beauty it contains; but even the lowest contains beauty because it forms an essential link of the system. The highest form of the Idea is personality, and therefore the highest art is that which has for its subject-matter the highest personality.[3]

Such were the theories of the German æstheticians in the Hegelian direction, but they did not monopolize æsthetic dissertations. In Germany, side by side and simultaneously with the Hegelian theories, there appeared theories of beauty not only independent of Hegel's position (that beauty is the manifestation of the Idea), but directly contrary to this view, denying and ridiculing it. Such was the line taken by Herbart and more particularly by Schopenhauer.

[1] Schasler, pp. 966, 655, 956.   [2] Schasler, p. 1017.
[3] Schasler, pp. 1065, 1066.

According to Herbart (1776–1841), there is not and cannot be any such thing as beauty existing in itself. What does exist is only our opinion, and it is necessary to find the basis of this opinion (*Ästhetisches Elementarurtheil*). Such bases are connected with our impressions. There are certain relations which we term beautiful; and art consists in finding these relations, which are simultaneous in painting, the plastic art, and architecture; successive and simultaneous in music; and purely successive in poetry. In contradiction to the former æstheticians, Herbart holds that objects are often beautiful which express nothing at all, as, for instance, the rainbow, which is beautiful for its lines and colours and not for its mythological connexion with Iris or Noah's rainbow.[1]

Another opponent of Hegel was Schopenhauer, who denied Hegel's whole system, his æsthetics included.

According to Schopenhauer (1788–1860), Will objectivizes itself in the world on various planes, and although the higher the plane on which it is objectivized the more beautiful it is, yet each plane has its own beauty. Renunciation of one's individuality and contemplation of one of these planes of manifestation of Will gives us a perception of beauty. All men, says Schopenhauer, possess the capacity to objectivize the Idea on different planes. The genius of the artist has this capacity in a higher degree and therefore makes a higher beauty manifest.[2]

After these more eminent writers there followed in Germany less original and less influential ones such as Hartmann, Kirchmann, Schnaase, and, to some extent, Helmholtz (as an æsthetician), Bergmann, Jungmann, and an innumerable host of others.

According to Hartmann (1842), beauty lies not in the external world nor in 'the thing in itself,' neither does it reside in the soul of man, but it lies in the

[1] Schasler, pp. 1097–1100.   [2] Schasler, pp. 1124, 1107.

'seeming' (*Schein*) produced by the artist. The thing in itself is not beautiful, but it is transformed into beauty by the artist.[1]

According to Schnaase (1798–1875), there is no perfect beauty in the world. In nature there is only an approach towards it. Art gives what nature cannot give. In the energy of the free *ego*, conscious of harmony not found in nature, beauty is disclosed.[2]

Kirchmann (1802–1884) wrote on experimental æsthetics. All aspects of history in his system are joined by pure chance. Thus according to him there are six realms of history:—the realm of Knowledge, of Wealth, of Morality, of Faith, of Politics, and of Beauty, and activity in the last-named realm is art.[3]

According to Helmholtz (1821–1894), who wrote on beauty as it relates to music, beauty in musical productions is attained only by following unalterable laws. These laws are not known to the artist, so that beauty is manifested by the artist unconsciously and cannot be subjected to analysis.[4]

According to Bergmann (b. 1840) (*Ueber das Schöne*, 1887), to define beauty objectively is impossible. Beauty is only perceived subjectively, and therefore the problem of æsthetics is to define what pleases whom.[5]

According to Jungmann (d. 1885), firstly, beauty is a suprasensible quality of things; secondly, beauty produces in us pleasure by merely being contemplated; and thirdly, beauty is the foundation of love.[6]

The æsthetic theories of the chief representatives of France, England, and other nations, in recent times have been the following:—

In France during this period the prominent writers

[1] Knight, pp. 81, 82.   [2] Knight, p. 83.
[3] Schasler, p. 1121.   [4] Knight, pp. 85, 86.
[5] Knight, p. 88.   [6] Knight, p. 112.

on æsthetics were Cousin, Jouffroy, Pictet, Ravaisson, Lévêque.

Cousin (1792–1867) was an eclectic and a follower of the German idealists. According to his theory, beauty always has a moral foundation. He disputes the doctrine that art is imitation and that the beautiful is what pleases. He affirms that beauty may be defined objectively and that it essentially consists in variety in unity.[1]

After Cousin came Jouffroy (1796–1842), who was a pupil of Cousin's and also a follower of the German æstheticians. According to his definition, beauty is the expression of the invisible by those natural signs which manifest it. The visible world is the garment by means of which we see beauty.[2]

The Swiss writer Pictet repeated Hegel and Plato, supposing beauty to exist in the direct and free manifestation of the divine Idea revealing itself in sense forms.[3]

Lévêque was a follower of Schelling and Hegel. He holds that beauty is something invisible behind nature—a force or spirit revealing itself in ordered energy.[4]

Similar vague opinions about the nature of beauty were expressed by the French metaphysician Ravaisson, who considered beauty to be the ultimate aim and purpose of the world. 'La beauté la plus divine et principalement la plus parfaite contient le secret du monde.'[5] And again:—'Le monde entier est l'œuvre d'une beauté absolue, qui n'est la cause des choses que par l'amour qu'elle met en elles.'[6]

---

[1] Knight, p. 88.   [2] Knight, p. 116.
[3] Knight, pp. 118, 119.   [4] Knight, pp. 123, 124.
[5] 'The most divine and especially the most perfect beauty contains the secret of the world,' La philosophie en France, p. 232.
[6] 'The whole world is the work of an absolute beauty,

I purposely quote these metaphysical expressions in the original, because, however cloudy the Germans may be, the French, once they absorb the theories of the Germans and take to imitating them, far surpass them in uniting heterogeneous conceptions into one expression and putting forward one meaning or another indiscriminately. For instance, the French philosopher Lachelier, when discussing beauty, says:
—Ne craignons pas de dire, qu'une vérité, qui ne serait pas belle, ne serait qu'un jeu logique de notre esprit et que la seule vérité solide et digne de ce nom c'est la beauté.[1]

Besides the æsthetic idealists who wrote and still write under the influence of German philosophy, the following recent writers have also influenced the comprehension of art and beauty in France: Taine, Guyau, Cherbuliez, Coster, and Véron.

According to Taine (1828–1893), beauty is the manifestation of the essential characteristic of any important idea more completely than it is expressed in reality.[2]

Guyau (1854–1888) taught that beauty is not something exterior to the object itself,—is not as it were a parasitic growth on it,—but is itself the actual blossoming forth of that on which it appears. Art is the expression of reasonable and conscious life evoking in us both the deepest consciousness of existence and the highest feelings and loftiest thoughts. Art lifts man from his personal life into the universal life, not only by participation in the same ideas and beliefs but also by similarity in feeling.[3]

which is only the cause of things by the love it puts into them.'

[1] 'Let us not fear to say that a truth which is not beautiful is but a logical play of our intelligence, and that the only truth that is solid and worthy of the name is beauty.' *Du fondement de l'induction.*

[2] *Philosophie de l'art*, vol. i, 1893, p. 47.

[3] Knight, p. 139–141.

According to Cherbuliez, art is an activity, (1) satisfying our innate love of forms (*apparences*), (2) endowing these forms with ideas, (3) affording pleasure alike to our senses, heart, and reason. Beauty is not inherent in objects, but is an act of our souls. Beauty is an illusion; there is no absolute beauty. But what we consider characteristic and harmonious appears beautiful to us.

Coster held that the ideas of the beautiful, the good, and the true, are innate. These ideas illumine our minds and are identical with God, who is Goodness, Truth, and Beauty. The idea of Beauty includes unity of essence, variety of constitutive elements, and order, which brings unity into the various manifestations of life.[1]

For the sake of completeness I will further cite some of the very latest writings upon art.

La Psychologie du beau et de l'art, par Mario Pilo (1895), says that beauty is a product of our physical feelings. The aim of art is pleasure, but this pleasure (for some reason) he considers to be necessarily highly moral.

The *Essai sur l'art contemporain, par Fierens Gevaert* (1897), says that art rests on its connexion with the past and on the religious ideal of the present which the artist holds when giving to his work the form of his individuality.

Then again Sar Peladan's *L'art idéaliste et mystique* (1894) says that beauty is one of the manifestations of God. 'Il n'y a pas d'autre Réalité que Dieu, il n'y a pas d'autre Vérité que Dieu, il n'y a pas d'autre Beauté que Dieu' (p. 33).[2] This book is very fantastic and very illiterate, but is characteristic in the positions it takes up, and noticeable on account of a certain

---

[1] Knight, pp. 134.

[2] There is no other Reality than God, there is no other Truth than God, there is no other Beauty than God.

success it is having with the younger generation in France.

All the æsthetics diffused in France up to the present time are similar in kind, but among them Véron's *L'esthétique* (1878) forms an exception, being reasonable and clear. This work, though it does not give an exact definition of art, at least rids æsthetics of the cloudy conception of an absolute beauty.

According to Véron (1825–1889), art is the manifestation of emotion, transmitted externally by a combination of lines, forms, colours, or by a succession of movements, sounds, or words subjected to certain rhythms.[1]

In England during this period, writers on æsthetics define beauty more and more frequently not by its own qualities but by taste, and the discussion of beauty is superseded by a discussion of taste.

After Reid (1704–1796), who acknowledged beauty as being entirely dependent on the spectator, Alison in his *Essay on the Nature and Principles of Taste* (1790) proved the same thing. From another side this was also asserted by Erasmus Darwin (1731–1802), grandfather of the celebrated Charles Darwin.

He says that we consider beautiful that which is connected in our conception with what we love. Richard Knight's work, *An Analytical Inquiry into the Principles of Taste*, also tends in the same direction.

Most of the English theories of æsthetics are on the same lines. The prominent writers on æsthetics in England during the nineteenth century were Charles Darwin (to some extent), Herbert Spencer, Grant Allen, Ker, and Knight.

According to Charles Darwin (1809–1882—*Descent of Man*, 1871), beauty is a feeling natural not only to man but also to animals and consequently to the ancestors of man. Birds adorn their nests and esteem

[1] *L'esthétique*, p. 106.

beauty in their mates. Beauty has an influence on marriages. Beauty includes a variety of diverse conceptions. The origin of the art of music is the call of the males to the females.[1]

According to Herbert Spencer (b. 1820), the origin of art is play, a thought previously expressed by Schiller. In the lower animals all the energy of life is expended in life-maintenance and race-maintenance; in man however there remains after these needs are satisfied some superfluous strength. This excess is used in play which passes over into art. Play is an imitation of real activity, so is art. The sources of æsthetic pleasure are threefold:—(1) That 'which exercises the faculties affected in the most complete way, with the fewest drawbacks from excess of exercise,' (2) 'the difference of a stimulus in large amount, which awakens a glow of agreeable feeling,' (3) the partial revival of the same with special combinations.[2]

In Todhunter's *Theory of the Beautiful* (1872), beauty is infinite loveliness which we apprehend both by reason and by the enthusiasm of love. The recognition of beauty as being such, depends on taste; there can be no criterion for it. The only approach to a definition is found in culture. (What culture is, is not defined.) Intrinsically, art—that which affects us through lines, colours, sounds, or words—is not the product of blind forces but of reasonable ones working with mutual helpfulness towards a reasonable aim. Beauty is the reconciliation of contradictions.[3]

Grant Allen is a follower of Spencer, and in his *Physiological Æsthetics* (1877) he says that beauty has a physical origin. Æsthetic pleasures come from the contemplation of the beautiful, but the conception of beauty is obtained by a physiological process. The origin of art is play: when there is a superfluity of

[1] Knight, p. 238.   [2] Knight, pp. 239, 240.
[3] Knight, pp. 240–243.

physical strength man gives himself to play; when there is a superfluity of receptive power man gives himself to art. The beautiful is that which affords the maximum of stimulation with the minimum of waste. Differences in the estimation of beauty proceed from taste. Taste can be educated. We must have faith in the judgments 'of the finest-nurtured and most discriminative' men. These people form the taste of the next generation.[1]

According to Ker's *Essay on the Philosophy of Art* (1883), beauty enables us to make part of the objective world intelligible to ourselves without being troubled by reference to other parts of it as is inevitable in science. So that art destroys the opposition between the one and the many, between the law and its manifestation, between the subject and its object, by uniting them. Art is the revelation and vindication of freedom because it is free from the darkness and incomprehensibility of finite things.[2]

According to Knight's *Philosophy of the Beautiful*, Part II (1893), beauty is (as with Schelling) the union of object and subject, the drawing forth from nature of that which is cognate to man, and the recognition in oneself of what is common to all nature.

The opinions on beauty and on art here mentioned are far from exhausting what has been written on the subject. And every day fresh writers on æsthetics arise in whose disquisitions appear the same enchanted confusion and contradictoriness in defining beauty. Some through inertia continue the mystical æsthetics of Baumgarten and Hegel with sundry variations; others transfer the question to the region of subjectivity and seek for the foundation of the beautiful in questions of taste; others—the æstheticians of the very latest school—seek the origin of beauty in the laws of physiology; and finally, others again investigate the ques-

[1] Knight, pp. 250–252. [2] Knight, pp. 258, 259.

E

tion quite independently of the conception of beauty. Thus Sully in his *Sensation and Intuition: Studies in Psychology and Æsthetics* (1874) dismisses the conception of beauty altogether; art, by his definition, being the production of some permanent object or passing action fitted to supply active enjoyment to the producer and a pleasurable impression to a number of spectators or listeners quite apart from any personal advantage derived from it.[1]

[1] Knight, p. 243.

CHAPTER IV

Definitions of art founded on beauty. Taste not definable. A clear definition needed to enable us to recognize works of art.

TO what do these definitions of beauty amount? Not reckoning the thoroughly inaccurate definitions of beauty which fail to cover the conception of art, and suppose beauty to consist either in utility, or in adjustment to a purpose, or in symmetry, or in order, or in proportion, or in smoothness, or in harmony of the parts, or in unity amid variety, or in various combinations of these,—not reckoning these unsatisfactory attempts at objective definition, all the æsthetic definitions of beauty lead to two fundamental conceptions. The first is that beauty is something having an independent existence (existing in itself), that it is one of the manifestations of the absolutely Perfect, of the Idea, of the Spirit, of Will, or of God; the other is that beauty is a kind of pleasure received by us not having personal advantage for its object.

The first of these definitions was accepted by Fichte, Schelling, Hegel, Schopenhauer, and the philosophizing Frenchmen: Cousin, Jouffroy, Ravaisson, and others, not to enumerate the second-rate æsthetic philosophers. And this same objective-mystical definition of beauty is held by a majority of educated people of our day. It is a conception very widely spread especially among the elder generation.

The second view, that beauty is a certain kind of pleasure received by us not having personal advantage for its aim, finds favour chiefly among the English æsthetic writers and is shared by the other part of our society, principally by the younger generation.

So there are (and it could not be otherwise) only two definitions of beauty: the one objective, mystical, merging this conception into that of the highest perfection, God—a fantastic definition, founded on nothing; the other on the contrary a very simple, and intelligible, subjective one, which considers beauty to be that which pleases (I do not add to the word 'pleases' the words 'without the aim of advantage,' because 'pleases' naturally presupposes the absence of the idea of profit).

On the one hand beauty is viewed as something mystical and very elevated, but unfortunately at the same time very indefinite, and consequently embracing philosophy, religion, and life itself (as in the theories of Schelling and Hegel and their German and French followers); or on the other hand (as necessarily follows from the definition of Kant and his adherents), beauty is simply a certain kind of disinterested pleasure received by us. And this conception of beauty, although it seems very clear, is unfortunately again inexact; for it widens out on the other side, that is, it includes the pleasure derived from drink, from food, from touching a delicate skin, and so forth, as is acknowledged by Guyau, Kralik, and others.

It is true that, following the development of the æsthetic doctrines of beauty, we may notice that though at first (in the times when the foundations of the science of æsthetics were being laid) the metaphysical definition of beauty prevailed, yet the nearer we get to our own times the more does an experimental definition (recently assuming a physiological form) come to the front, so that at last we even meet with æstheticians such as Véron and Sully, who try to escape entirely from the conception of beauty. But such æstheticians have very little success, and with the majority of the public as well as of artists and the learned, a conception of beauty is firmly held which agrees with the definitions contained in most of the æsthetic treatises, that is, which regards beauty either as something mystical or metaphysical, or as a special kind of enjoyment.

What then is this conception of beauty, so stubbornly held to by people of our circle and day as furnishing a definition of art?

In its subjective aspect, we call beauty that which supplies us with a particular kind of pleasure.

In its objective aspect, we call beauty something absolutely perfect, and we acknowledge it to be so only because we receive from the manifestation of this absolute perfection a certain kind of pleasure: so that this objective definition is nothing but the subjective conception differently expressed. In reality both conceptions of beauty amount to one and the same thing, namely, the reception by us of a certain kind of pleasure; that is to say, we call 'beauty' that which pleases us without evoking in us desire.

Such being the position of affairs it would seem only natural that the science of art should decline to content itself with a definition of art based on beauty (that is, on that which pleases), and should seek a general definition applicable to all artistic productions, by reference to which we might decide whether a certain article belonged to the realm of art or not. But no such definition is supplied, as the reader may see from those summaries of æsthetic theories which I have given, and as he may discover even more clearly from the original æsthetic works if he will be at the pains to read them. All attempts to define absolute beauty in itself—whether as an imitation of nature, or as suitability to its object, or as a correspondence of parts, or as symmetry, or as harmony, or as unity in variety, and so forth—either define nothing at all, or define only some traits of some artistic pro-

anything's not of a ci

ductions and are far from including all that everybody has always held and still holds to be art.

There is no objective definition of beauty. The existing definitions (both the metaphysical and the experimental) amount only to one and the same subjective definition, which is (strange as it seems to say so), that art is that which makes beauty manifest, and beauty is that which pleases (without exciting desire). Many æstheticians have felt the insufficiency and instability of such a definition, and in order to give it a firm basis have asked themselves why a thing pleases. And they have converted the discussion on beauty into a question of taste, as did Hutcheson, Voltaire, Diderot, and others. But all attempts to define what taste is must lead to nothing, as the reader may see both from the history of æsthetics and experimentally. There is and can be no explanation of why one thing pleases one man and displeases another, or *vice versa*; so that the whole existing science of æsthetics fails to do what we might expect from it as a mental activity calling itself a science, namely, it does not define the qualities and laws of art, or of the beautiful (if that be the content of art), or the nature of taste (if taste decides the question of art and its merit), and then on the basis of such definitions acknowledge as art those productions which correspond to these laws and reject those which do not come under them. But this science of æsthetics consists in first acknowledging a certain set of productions to be art (because they please us), and then framing such a theory of art as all these productions which please a certain circle of people can be fitted into. There exists an art-canon according to which certain productions favoured by our circle are acknowledged as being art,—the works of Phidias, Sophocles, Homer, Titian, Raphael, Bach, Beethoven, Dante, Shakespeare, Goethe, and others, —and the æsthetic laws must be such as to embrace all *such is properly called criticism, not aesthetics.*

these productions. In æsthetic literature you will constantly meet with opinions on the merit and importance of art, founded not on any certain laws by which this or that is held to be good or bad, but merely on consideration as to whether this art tallies with the art-canon we have drawn up.

The other day I was reading a far from ill-written book by Folgeldt. Discussing the demand for morality in works of art, the author plainly says that we must not demand morality in art. And in proof of this he advances the fact that, if we admit such a demand, Shakespeare's *Romeo and Juliet* and Goethe's *Wilhelm Meister* would not come within the definition of good art; but since both these books are included in our canon of art, he concludes that the demand is unjust. And therefore it is necessary to find a definition of art which shall fit the works; and instead of a demand for morality Folgeldt postulates as the basis of art a demand for the important (*Bedeutungsvolles*). *"meaningful"*

All the existing æsthetic standards are built on this plan. Instead of giving a definition of true art and then deciding what is and what is not good art by judging whether a work conforms or does not conform to this definition, a certain class of works which for some reason pleases a certain circle of people is accepted as being art, and a definition of art is then devised to cover all these productions. I recently came upon a remarkable instance of this method in a very good German work, *The History of Art in the Nineteenth Century*, by Muther. Describing the pre-Raphaelites, the Decadents, and the Symbolists (who are already included in the canon of art), he not only does not venture to blame their tendency, but earnestly endeavours to widen his standard so that it may include them all, since they appear to him to represent a legitimate reaction from the excesses of realism. No matter what insanities appear in art, when once they find acceptance among the upper classes of our society a theory is quickly invented to explain and sanction them; just as if there had never been periods in history when certain special circles of people recognized and approved false, deformed, and insensate, art which subsequently left no trace and has been utterly forgotten. And to what lengths the insanity and deformity of art may go, especially when as in our days it knows that it is considered infallible, may be seen by what is being done in the art of our circle to-day.

So that the theory of art founded on beauty, expounded by æsthetics and in dim outline professed by the public, is nothing but the setting up as good of that which has pleased and pleases us, that is, pleases a certain class of people.

In order to define any human activity, it is necessary to understand its sense and importance; and in order to do this it is primarily necessary to examine that activity in itself, in its dependence on its causes and in connexion with its effects, and not merely in relation to the pleasure we can get from it.

If we say that the aim of any activity is merely our pleasure and define it solely by that pleasure, our definition will evidently be a false one. But this is precisely what has occurred in the efforts to define art. Now if we consider the food question it will not occur to any one to affirm that the importance of food consists in the pleasure we receive when eating it. Everybody understands that the satisfaction of our taste cannot serve as a basis for our definition of the merits of food, and that we have therefore no right to presuppose that dinners with cayenne pepper, Limburg cheese, alcohol, and so on, to which we are accustomed and which please us, form the very best human food.

In the same way beauty, or that which pleases us,

can in no sense serve as a basis for the definition of art; nor can a series of objects which afford us pleasure serve as the model of what art should be.

To see the aim and purpose of art in the pleasure we get from it, is like assuming (as is done by people of the lowest moral development, for instance by savages) that the purpose and aim of food is the pleasure derived when consuming it.

Just as people who conceive the aim and purpose of food to be pleasure cannot recognize the real meaning of eating, so people who consider the aim of art to be pleasure cannot realize its true meaning and purpose, because they attribute to an activity the meaning of which lies in its connexion with the other phenomena of life, the false and exceptional aim of pleasure. People come to understand that the meaning of eating lies in the nourishment of the body, only when they cease to consider that the object of that activity is pleasure. And it is the same with regard to art. People will come to understand the meaning of art only when they cease to consider that the aim of that activity is beauty, that is to say, pleasure. The acknowledgment of beauty (that is, of a certain kind of pleasure received from art) as being the aim of art, not only fails to assist us in finding a definition of what art is, but on the contrary by transferring the question into a region quite foreign to art (into metaphysical, psychological, physiological, and even historical, discussions as to why such a production pleases one person and such another displeases or pleases some one else), it renders such definition impossible. And since discussions as to why one man likes pears and another prefers meat do not help towards finding a definition of what is essential in nourishment, so the solution of questions of taste in art (to which the discussions on art involuntarily come) not only does not help to make clear in what this particular human activity which we call art really consists, but renders such elucidation quite impossible until we rid ourselves of a conception which justifies every kind of art at the cost of confusing the whole matter.

To the question, What is this art to which is offered up the labour of millions, the very lives of men, and even morality itself? we have extracted replies from the existing æsthetics which all amount to this: that the aim of art is beauty, that beauty is recognized by the enjoyment it gives, and that artistic enjoyment is a good and important thing, because it *is* enjoyment. In a word, that enjoyment is good because it is enjoyment. Thus what is considered the definition of art is no definition at all, but only a shuffle to justify existing art. Therefore, however strange it may seem to say so, in spite of the mountains of books written about art, no exact definition of art has been constructed. And the reason of this is that the conception of art has been based on the conception of beauty.

CHAPTER V

Definitions of art not founded on beauty. Tolstóy's definition. The extent and necessity of art. How people in the past distinguished good from bad in art.

WHAT is art if we put aside the conception of beauty, which confuses the whole matter? The latest and most comprehensible definitions of art, apart from the conception of beauty, are the following:—(1) *a*, Art is an activity arising even in the animal kingdom, and springing from sexual desire and the propensity to play (Schiller, Darwin, Spencer), and *b*, accompanied by a pleasurable excitement of the nervous system (Grant Allen). This is the physiological-evolutionary definition. (2) Art is the external manifestation, by means of lines, colours, movements, sounds, or words, of emotions felt by man (Véron). This is the experimental definition. According to the very latest definition (Sully), (3) Art is 'the production of some permanent object or passing action which is fitted not only to supply an active enjoyment to the producer, but to convey a pleasurable impression to a number of spectators or listeners, quite apart from any personal advantage to be derived from it.'

Notwithstanding the superiority of these definitions to the metaphysical definitions which depended on the conception of beauty, they are yet far from exact. The first, the physiological-evolutionary definition (1) *a*, is inexact, because instead of speaking about the artistic activity itself, which is the real matter in hand, it treats of the derivation of art. The modification of it, *b*, based on the physiological effects on the human organism, is inexact because within the limits of such definition many other human activities can be included, as has occurred in the neo-æsthetic theories which reckon as art the preparation of handsome clothes, pleasant scents, and even of victuals.

The experimental definition, (2), which makes art consist in the expression of emotions, is inexact because a man may express his emotions by means of lines, colours, sounds, or words and yet may not act on others by such expression—and then the manifestation of his emotions is not art.

The third definition (that of Sully) is inexact because in the production of objects or actions affording pleasure to the producer and a pleasant emotion to the spectators or hearers apart from personal advantage, may be included the showing of conjuring tricks or gymnastic exercises, and other activities which are not art. And further, many things the production of which does not afford pleasure to the producer and the sensation received from which is unpleasant, such as gloomy, heart-rending scenes in a poetic description or a play, may nevertheless be undoubted works of art.

The inaccuracy of all these definitions arises from the fact that in them all (as also in the metaphysical definitions) the object considered is the pleasure art may give, and not the purpose it may serve in the life of man and of humanity.

In order to define art correctly it is necessary first of all to cease to consider it as a means to pleasure, and to consider it as one of the conditions of human life. Viewing it in this way we cannot fail to observe that art is one of the means of intercourse between man and man.

Every work of art causes the receiver to enter into a certain kind of relationship both with him who produced or is producing the art, and with all those who, simultaneously, previously, or subsequently, receive the same artistic impression.

*this is not as
unmoved as T.
wants it to
appear*

Speech transmitting the thoughts and experiences of men serves as a means of union among them, and art serves a similar purpose. The peculiarity of this latter means of intercourse, distinguishing it from intercourse by means of words, consists in this, that whereas by words a man transmits his thoughts to another, by art he transmits his feelings.

The activity of art is based on the fact that a man receiving through his sense of hearing or sight another man's expression of feeling, is capable of experiencing the emotion which moved the man who expressed it. To take the simplest example: one man laughs, and another who hears becomes merry, or a man weeps, and another who hears feels sorrow. A man is excited or irritated, and another man seeing him is brought to a similar state of mind. By his movements or by the sounds of his voice a man expresses courage and determination or sadness and calmness, and this state of mind passes on to others. A man suffers, manifesting his sufferings by groans and spasms, and this suffering transmits itself to other people; a man expresses his feelings of admiration, devotion, fear, respect, or love, to certain objects, persons, or phenomena, and others are infected by the same feelings of admiration, devotion, fear, respect, or love, to the same objects, persons, or phenomena.

And it is on this capacity of man to receive another man's expression of feeling and to experience those feelings himself, that the activity of art is based.

If a man infects another or others directly, immediately, by his appearance or by the sounds he gives vent to at the very time he experiences the feeling; if he causes another man to yawn when he himself cannot help yawning, or to laugh or cry when he himself is obliged to laugh or cry, or to suffer when he himself is suffering—that does not amount to art.

Art begins when one person with the object of join-

ing another or others to himself in one and the same
feeling, expresses that feeling by certain external indications. To take the simplest example: a boy having
experienced, let us say, fear on encountering a wolf,
relates that encounter, and in order to evoke in others
the feeling he has experienced, describes himself, his
condition before the encounter, the surroundings, the
wood, his own lightheartedness, and then the wolf's
appearance, its movements, the distance between
himself and the wolf, and so forth. All this, if only the
boy when telling the story again experiences the feelings he had lived through, and infects the hearers and
compels them to feel what he had experienced—is art.
Even if the boy had not seen a wolf but had frequently
been afraid of one, and if wishing to evoke in others
the fear he had felt, he invented an encounter with a
wolf and recounted it so as to make his hearers share
the feelings he experienced when he feared the wolf,
that also would be art. And just in the same way it is
art if a man, having experienced either the fear of
suffering or the attraction of enjoyment (whether in
reality or in imagination), expresses these feelings on
canvas or in marble so that others are infected by
them. And it is also art if a man feels, or imagines to
himself, feelings of delight, gladness, sorrow, despair,
courage, or despondency, and the transition from one
to another of these feelings, and expresses them by
sounds so that the hearers are infected by them and
experience them as they were experienced by the
composer.

The feelings with which the artist infects others may
be most various—very strong or very weak, very important or very insignificant, very bad or very good:
feelings of love of one's country, self-devotion and
submission to fate or to God expressed in a drama,
raptures of lovers described in a novel, feelings of
voluptuousness expressed in a picture, courage ex-

pressed in a triumphal march, merriment evoked by a dance, humour evoked by a funny story, the feeling of quietness transmitted by an evening landscape or by a lullaby, or the feeling of admiration evoked by a beautiful arabesque—it is all art.

If only the spectators or auditors are infected by the feelings which the author has felt, it is art.

To evoke in oneself a feeling one has once experienced and having evoked it in oneself then by means of movements, lines, colours, sounds, or forms expressed in words, so to transmit that feeling that others experience the same feeling—this is the activity of art.

Art is a human activity consising in this, that one man consciously by means of certain external signs, hands on to others feelings he has lived through, and that others are infected by these feelings and also experience them.

Art is not, as the metaphysicians say, the manifestation of some mysterious Idea of beauty or God; it is not, as the æsthetic physiologists say, a game in which man lets off his excess of stored-up energy; it is not the expression of man's emotions by external signs; it is not the production of pleasing objects; and, above all, it is not pleasure; but it is a means of union among men joining them together in the same feelings, and indispensable for the life and progress towards well-being of individuals and of humanity.

As every man, thanks to man's capacity to express thoughts by words, may know all that has been done for him in the realms of thought by all humanity before his day, and can in the present, thanks to this capacity to understand the thoughts of others, become a sharer in their activity and also himself hand on to his contemporaries and descendants the thoughts he has assimilated from others as well as those that have arisen in himself; so, thanks to man's capacity to be infected with the feelings of others by means of art, all that is being lived through by his contemporaries is accessible to him, as well as the feelings experienced by men thousands of years ago, and he has also the possibility of transmitting his own feelings to others.

If people lacked the capacity to receive the thoughts conceived by men who preceded them and to pass on to others their own thoughts, men would be like wild beasts, or like Kasper Hauser.[1]

And if men lacked this other capacity of being infected by art, people might be almost more savage still, and above all more separated from, and more hostile to, one another.

And therefore the activity of art is a most important one, as important as the activity of speech itself and as generally diffused.

As speech does not act on us only in sermons, orations, or books, but in all those remarks by which we interchange thoughts and experiences with one another, so also art in the wide sense of the word permeates our whole life, but it is only to some of its manifestations that we apply the term in the limited sense of the word.

We are accustomed to understand art to be only what we hear and see in theatres, concerts, and exhibitions; together with buildings, statues, poems, and novels. . . . But all this is but the smallest part of the art by which we communicate with one another in life. All human life is filled with works of art of every kind—from cradle-song, jest, mimicry, the ornamentation of houses, dress, and utensils, to church services,

---

[1] 'The foundling of Nuremberg,' found in the market-place of that town on 23rd May 1828, apparently some sixteen years old. He spoke little and was almost totally ignorant even of common objects. He subsequently explained that he had been brought up in confinement underground and visited by only one man, whom he saw but seldom.

buildings, monuments, and triumphal processions. It is all artistic activity. So that by art, in the limited sense of the word, we do not mean all human activity transmitting feelings but only that part which we for some reason select from it and to which we attach special importance.

This special importance has always been given by men to that part of this activity which transmits feelings flowing from their religious perception, and this small part they have specifically called art, attaching to it the full meaning of the word.

That was how men of old—Socrates, Plato, and Aristotle—looked on art. Thus did the Hebrew prophets and the ancient Christians regard art. Thus it was, and still is, understood by the Mohammedans, and thus it still is understood by religious folk among our own peasantry.

Some teachers of mankind—such as Plato in his *Republic*, and people like the primitive Christians, the strict Mohammedans, and the Buddhists—have gone so far as to repudiate all art.

People viewing art in this way (in contradiction to the prevalent view of to-day which regards any art as good if only it affords pleasure) held and hold that art (as contrasted with speech, which need not be listened to) is so highly dangerous in its power to infect people against their wills, that mankind will lose far less by banishing all art than by tolerating each and every art.

Evidently such people were wrong in repudiating all art, for they denied what cannot be denied—one of the indispensable means of communication without which mankind could not exist. But not less wrong are the people of civilized European society of our class and day in favouring any art if it but serves beauty, that is, gives people pleasure.

Formerly people feared lest among works of art

there might chance to be some causing corruption, and they prohibited art altogether. Now they only fear lest they should be deprived of any enjoyment art can afford, and they patronize any art. And I think the last error is much grosser than the first and that its consequences are far more harmful.

CHAPTER VI

How art for pleasure's sake has come into esteem. Religions indicate what is good and bad. Church Christianity. The Renaissance. Scepticism of the upper classes. They confuse beauty with goodness.

BUT how could it happen that that very art which in ancient times was merely tolerated (if tolerated at all), should have come in our times to be invariably considered a good thing if only it affords pleasure?

It has resulted from the following causes. The estimation of the value of art (or rather, of the feelings it transmits) depends on men's perception of the meaning of life; depends on what they hold to be the good and the evil of life. And what is good and what is evil is defined by what are termed religions.

Humanity unceasingly moves forward from a lower, more partial and obscure, understanding of life to one more general and more lucid. And in this as in every movement there are leaders—those who have understood the meaning of life more clearly than others—and of these advanced men there is always one who has in his words and by his life expressed this meaning more clearly, lucidly, and strongly, than others. This man's expression of the meaning of life, together with those superstitions, traditions, and ceremonies, which usually form round the memory of such a man, is what is called a religion. Religions are the exponents of the highest comprehension of life accessible to the best and foremost men at a given time in a given society—a comprehension towards which all the rest of that society must inevitably and irresistibly advance. And therefore religions alone have always served, and still serve, as bases for the valuation of human sentiments. If feelings bring men nearer the ideal their religion indicates, if they are in harmony with it and do not contradict it, they are good; if they estrange men from it and oppose it they are bad.

If the religion places the meaning of life in worshipping one God and fulfilling what is regarded as His will, as was the case among the Jews, then the feelings flowing from love of that God and of His law, when successfully transmitted through the art of poetry, by the prophets, by the psalms, or by the epic of the book of Genesis, are good, high art. All opposing that, as for instance the transmission of feelings of devotion to strange gods, or of feelings incompatible with the law of God, would be considered bad art. Or if, as was the case among the Greeks, the religion places the meaning of life in earthly happiness, in beauty and in strength, then art successfully transmitting the joy and energy of life would be considered good art, but art transmitting feelings of effeminacy or despondency would be bad art. If the meaning of life is seen in the well-being of one's nation, or in honouring one's ancestors and continuing the mode of life led by them, as was the case among the Romans and the Chinese respectively, then art transmitting feelings of joy at the sacrifice of one's personal well-being for the common weal, or at the exaltation of one's ancestors and the maintenance of their traditions, would be considered good art; but art expressing feelings contrary to these would be regarded as bad. If the meaning of life is seen in freeing oneself from the yoke of animalism, as is the case among the Buddhists, then art successfully transmitting feelings that elevate the soul and humble the flesh will be good art, and all that transmits feelings strengthening the bodily passions will be bad art.

In every age and in every human society there

exists a religious sense of what is good and what is bad common to that whole society, and it is this religious conception that decides the value of the feelings transmitted by art. Therefore among all nations art which transmitted feelings considered to be good by the general religious sense was recognized as being good and was encouraged, but art which transmitted feelings considered bad by this general religious sense was recognized as being bad and was rejected. All the rest of the immense field of art by means of which people communicate one with another was not esteemed at all and was only noticed when it ran counter to the religious conception of its age, and then merely to be repudiated. Thus it was among all nations—Greeks, Jews, Indians, Egyptians, and Chinese—and so it was when Christianity appeared.

The Christianity of the first centuries recognized as productions of good art only legends, lives of saints, sermons, prayers, and hymn-singing, evoking love of Christ, emotion at his life, desire to follow his example, renunciation of worldly life, humility, and the love of others; all productions transmitting feelings of personal enjoyment they considered to be bad, and therefore rejected; for instance, tolerating plastic representations only when they were symbolical, they rejected all the pagan sculptures.

This was so among the Christians of the first centuries, who accepted Christ's teaching if not quite in its true form at least not in the perverted, paganized form in which it was subsequently held.

But besides this Christianity, from the time of the wholesale conversion of nations by order of the authorities, as in the days of Constantine, Charlemagne, and Vladímir, there appeared another, a Church-Christianity, which was nearer to paganism than to Christ's teaching. And in accord with its own teaching, this Church-Christianity estimated quite otherwise the feelings of people and the productions of art which transmitted those feelings.

This Church-Christianity not only did not acknowledge the fundamental and essential positions of true Christianity,—the immediate relationship of each man to the Father, the consequent brotherhood and equality of all men, and the substitution of humility and love in place of any kind of violence,—but on the contrary, having set up a heavenly hierarchy similar to the pagan mythology, and having introduced the worship of Christ, of the Virgin, of angels, of apostles, of saints, and of martyrs, and not only of these divinities themselves but also of their images, it made blind faith in the Church and in its ordinances the essential point of its teaching.

However foreign this teaching may have been to true Christianity, however degraded, not only in comparison with true Christianity but even with the conception of life of Romans such as Julian and others, for all that it was to the barbarians who accepted it, a higher doctrine than their former adoration of gods, heroes, and good and bad spirits. And therefore this teaching was a religion to them, and on the basis of this religion the art of that time was assessed. And art transmitting pious adoration of the Virgin, Jesus, the saints, and the angels, a blind faith in and submission to the Church, fear of torments, and hope of blessedness in a life beyond the grave, was considered good, while all art opposed to this was held to be bad.

The teaching on the basis of which this art arose was a perversion of Christ's teaching, but the art which sprang up on this perverted teaching was for all that a true art, since it corresponded to the religious view of life held by the people among whom it arose.

The artists of the Middle Ages, vitalized by the same source of feeling—religion—as the mass of the people, and transmitting in architecture, sculpture, painting, music, poetry, or drama, the feelings and states of mind they experienced, were true artists; and their activity, founded on the highest conceptions accessible to their age and common to the entire people—though for our times a mean art—was nevertheless a true one, shared by the whole community.

And this was the state of things until in the upper, rich, more educated, classes of European society doubt arose as to the truth of the understanding of life which was expressed by Church-Christianity. When after the Crusades and the maximum development of papal power and its abuses, people of the rich classes became acquainted with the wisdom of the classics, and saw on the one hand the reasonable lucidity of the teaching of the ancient sages, and on the other hand the incompatibility of the Church doctrine with the teaching of Christ, it became impossible for them to continue to believe the Church teaching.

If in externals they still kept to the forms of Church teaching, they could no longer believe in it, and held to it only by inertia and to influence the masses, who continued to believe blindly in Church doctrine and whom the upper classes for their own advantage considered it necessary to encourage in those beliefs.

So that a time came when Church-Christianity ceased to be the general religious doctrine of all Christian people: some—the masses—continued blindly to believe in it, but the upper classes—those in whose hands lay the power and wealth, and therefore the leisure to produce art and the means to stimulate it—ceased to believe that teaching.

In regard to religion the upper circles of the Middle Ages found themselves in the position educated Romans were in before Christianity arose, that is, they no longer believed in the religion of the masses but had no beliefs to put in place of the worn-out

Church doctrine which for them had lost its meaning.

There was only this difference, that whereas for the Romans who lost faith in their emperor-gods and household-gods it was impossible to extract anything further from all the complex mythology they had borrowed from conquered nations, and it was consequently necessary to find a completely new conception of life, the people of the Middle Ages when they doubted the truth of the Church teaching had no need to seek a fresh one. That Christian teaching which they professed in a perverted form as Church doctrine, had mapped out the path of human progress so far ahead that they needed only to rid themselves of those perversions which hid the teaching announced by Christ and to adopt its real meaning— if not completely, at least in a greater degree than the Church had done. And this was partially accomplished not only in the reformations of Wyclif, Huss, Luther, and Calvin, but by the whole current of non-Church Christianity represented in earlier times by the Paulicians and the Bogomilites,[1] and afterwards by the Waldenses and other non-Church Christians, who were called heretics. But this could be, and was, done chiefly by poor people—who did not rule. A few of the rich and strong, such as Francis of Assisi and others, accepted the Christian teaching in its full significance even though it undermined their privileged positions. But most people of the upper classes (though in the depth of their souls they had lost faith in the Church teaching) could not or would not act thus, because the essence of that Christian view of life which stood ready to be adopted when once they rejected the Church faith, was a teaching of the

[1] Eastern sects well known in early Church history, who rejected the Church's rendering of Christ's teaching and were cruelly persecuted.—A. M.

brotherhood (and therefore the equality) of man, and this condemned the privileges by which they lived, in which they had grown up and been educated, and to which they were accustomed. Not in the depth of their hearts believing in the Church teaching—which had outlived its age and had no longer any true meaning for them—and not being strong enough to accept true Christianity, men of these rich, governing classes —popes, kings, dukes, and all the great ones of the earth—were left without any religion, with but the external forms of one, which they supported as being profitable and even necessary for themselves since these forms maintained a teaching which justified the privileges they made use of. In reality these people believed in nothing, just as the Romans of the first centuries of our era believed in nothing. But at the same time they were the people who had the power and the wealth, and they were the people who rewarded art and directed it.

And it should be remarked that it was just among these people that there grew up an art esteemed not according to its success in expressing men's religious feelings, but in proportion to its beauty—in other words, according to the enjoyment it gave.

No longer able to believe in the Church religion whose falsehood they had detected, and incapable of accepting true Christian teaching which denounced their whole manner of life, these rich and powerful people, stranded with no religious conception of life, involuntarily returned to the pagan view of things which places life's meaning in personal enjoyment. And then took place among the upper classes what is called the Renaissance of science and art, which was really not only a denial of every religion, but also an assertion that religion is unnecessary.

The Church doctrine is so coherent a system that it cannot be altered or corrected without destroying it altogether. As soon as doubt arose with regard to the infallibility of the Pope (and this doubt was then in the minds of all educated people), doubt inevitably followed as to the truth of tradition. But doubt as to the truth of tradition is fatal not only to popery and Catholicism but also to the whole Church creed with all its dogmas: the divinity of Christ, the resurrection, and the Trinity; and it destroys the authority of the Scriptures, since they were considered to be inspired only because the tradition of the Church so decided.

So that the majority of the highest classes of that age, even the popes and the ecclesiastics, really believed in nothing at all. In the Church doctrine these people did not believe, for they saw its insolvency; but neither could they follow Francis of Assisi, Peter of Chelczic,[1] and most of the heretics, in acknowledging the moral, social, teaching of Christ, for that teaching undermined their social position. So these people remained without any religious view of life; and having none, they could have no standard whereby to estimate what was good and what was bad art, except that of personal enjoyment. And having acknowledged their criterion of what was good to be pleasure, that is beauty, these people of the upper classes of European society went back in their comprehension of art to the gross conception of the primitive Greeks, which Plato had already condemned. And conformably to this understanding of life a theory of art was formulated.

[1] Peter of Chelczic, a Bohemian, was one of the successors of John Huss. In 1457 he was leader of the nonresistants called the United Brethren. He was the author of a remarkable book, *The Net of Faith*, directed against Church and State. It is mentioned in Tolstóy's *The Kingdom of God is Within You.*—A. M.

CHAPTER VII

An æsthetic theory framed to suit the view of life of the ruling classes.

FROM the time that people of the upper classes lost faith in Church-Christianity, beauty (that is to say, the pleasure received from art) became their standard of good and bad art. And in accordance with that view an æsthetic theory naturally sprang up among those upper classes, justifying such a conception—a theory according to which the aim of art is to exhibit beauty. The partisans of this æsthetic theory, in confirmation of its truth, affirmed that it was no invention of their own, but existed in the nature of things and was recognized even by the ancient Greeks. But this assertion was quite arbitrary and had no foundation other than the fact that among the ancient Greeks, in consequence of the low level of their moral ideal as compared with the Christian, the conception of what is good, τὸ ἀγαθόν, was not yet sharply divided from their conception of the beautiful, τὸ καλόν.

The highest perfection of goodness (not only not identical with beauty but for the most part contrasting with it) discerned by the Jews even in the times of Isaiah, and fully expressed by Christianity, was quite unknown to the Greeks. They supposed that the beautiful must necessarily also be the good. It is true that their foremost thinkers—Socrates, Plato, Aristotle—felt that goodness may happen not to coincide with beauty. Socrates expressly subordinated beauty to goodness; Plato to unite the two conceptions spoke of spiritual beauty; while Aristotle demanded from art that it should have a moral influence on people (κάθαρσις).

But notwithstanding all this, they could not quite dismiss the notion that beauty and goodness coincide.

Consequently in the language of the period, a compound word (καλοκἀγαθία, beauty-goodness) came into use to express that notion.

Evidently the Greek sages began to draw near to the perception of goodness expressed in Buddhism and in Christianity, but got entangled in defining the relation between goodness and beauty. Plato's reasoning about beauty and goodness is full of contradictions. And it was just this confusion of ideas that the Europeans of a later age, who had lost all faith, tried to elevate into a law. They tried to prove that this union of beauty and goodness is inherent in the very essence of things; that beauty and goodness must coincide; and that the word and conception καλοκἀγαθία (which had a meaning for Greeks but has none at all for Christians) represents humanity's highest ideal. On this misunderstanding the new science of æsthetics was built up; and to justify its existence the teachings of the ancients on art were twisted so that it should appear that this invented science of æsthetics had existed among the Greeks.

In reality the reasoning of the ancients on art was quite unlike ours. As Benard, in his book on the æsthetics of Aristotle, quite justly remarks: 'Pour qui veut y regarder de près, la théorie du beau et celle de l'art sont tout à fait séparées dans Aristote, comme elles le sont dans Platon et chez tous leurs successeurs' (*L'esthétique d'Aristote et de ses successeurs*, Paris, 1889, p. 28).[1] And indeed the reasoning of the ancients on art not only does not confirm our science of æsthetics, but rather contradicts its doctrine of beauty. But nevertheless all the æsthetic guides, from

[1] Any one examining closely may see that the theory of beauty and that of art are quite separated in Aristotle as they are in Plato and in all their successors.

Schasler to Knight, declare that the science of the beautiful—æsthetic science—was begun by the ancients, by Socrates, Plato, Aristotle, and was continued, they say, to some extent by the Epicureans and Stoics, by Seneca and Plutarch, down to Plotinus. But it is supposed that this science, by some unfortunate accident, suddenly vanished in the fourth century and stayed away for about 1,500 years, and only after these 1,500 years had passed revived in Germany, A.D. 1750, in Baumgarten's doctrine.

After Plotinus, says Schasler, fifteen centuries passed away during which there was not the slightest scientific interest shown for the world of beauty and art. These one and a half thousand years, says he, have been lost to æsthetics and have contributed nothing towards the erection of the learned edifice of this science.[1]

[1] 'Die Lücke von fünf Jahrhunderten welche zwischen den Kunst-philosophischen Betrachtungen des Plato und Aristoteles und die des Plotins fällt, kann zwar auffällig erscheinen; dennoch kann man eigentlich nicht sagen, dass in dieser Zwischenziet überhaupt von ästhetischen Dingen nicht die Rede gewesen; oder dass gar ein völliger Mangel an Zusammenhang zwischen den Kunst-anschauungen des letztgenamten Philosophen und denen die ersteren existire. Freilich wurde die von Aristotle begründete Wissenschaft in Nichts dadurch gefördert! immerhin aber zeigt sich in jener Zwischenzeit noch ein gewisses Interesse für ästhetische Fragen. Nach Plotin aber, die wenigen, ihm in der Ziet nahestehenden Philosophen, wie Longin, Augustin, u. s. f. kommen, wie wir gesehen, kaum in Betracht und schliessen sich übrigens in ihrer Anschauungsweise an ihn an,—vergehen nicht fünf, sondern *fünfzehen Jahrhunderte*, in denen von irgend einer wissenschaftlichen Interesse für die Welt des Schönen und der Kunst nichts zu spüren ist.

Diese anderthalbtausend Jahre, innerhalb deren der Weltgeist durch die mannigfachsten Kämpfe hindurch zu einer völlig neuen Gestaltung des Lebens sich durch-

In reality nothing of the kind happened. The science of æsthetics, the science of the beautiful, neither did nor could vanish, because it never existed. The Greeks (just like everybody else, always and everywhere) simply considered art (like everything else) good only when it served goodness (as they understood goodness), and bad when it was in opposition to that goodness. And the Greeks themselves were so little developed morally that goodness and beauty seemed to them to coincide. On that obsolete Greek view of life was erected the science of æsthetics, invented by men of the eighteenth century, and especially shaped and mounted in Baumgarten's theory. The Greeks (as any one may see who will read Benard's

arbeitete, sind für die Aesthetik, hinsichtlich des weiteren Ausbaus dieser Wissenschaft verloren.'—*Kritische Geschichte der Aesthetik*, von Max Schasler. Berlin, 1872, p. 253, § 25.

The gap of five hundred years which occurred between the artistic-philosophic observations of Plato and Aristotle and those of Plotinus, may indeed appear striking, but one cannot exactly say that in this interval of time there was absolutely no mention of æsthetic matters; or even that a complete lack of correspondence exists between the art-views of the last-named philosopher and that of the former. It is true that the science founded by Aristotle was not in any way advanced thereby; but, for all that, during this interval a certain interest in æsthetic questions still appears. But after Plotinus (the few philosophers near him in time, such as Longinus, Augustinus and so forth, hardly come into question as we have seen, and moreover they adhere to him in their views) there passed not five, but *fifteen centuries* in which there is no indication of any sort of scientific interest for the world of the beautiful and of art.

These one-and-a-half-thousand years, during which the world-spirit worked out a completely new foundation of life, are lost for æsthetics as regards any further construction of this science.

admirable book on Aristotle and his successors, and Walter's work on Plato) never had a science of æsthetics.

Æsthetic theories arose about one hundred and fifty years ago among the wealthy classes of the Christian European world and arose simultaneously among different nations,—German, Italian, Dutch, French, and English. The founder and organizer of it, who gave it a scientific and theoretic form, was Baumgarten.

With a characteristically German external exactitude, pedantry, and symmetry, he devised and expounded this extraordinary theory. And notwithstanding its obvious lack of substance, no one else's theory so pleased the cultured crowd or was accepted so readily and with such an absence of criticism. It so suited the people of the upper classes that to this day, notwithstanding its entirely fantastic character and the arbitrary nature of its assertions, it is repeated by learned and unlearned as though it were something indubitable and self-evident.

Pro captu lectoris habent sua fata libelli,[1] and so, or even more so, theories *habent sua fata* according to the condition of error in which the society lives among whom, and for whom, the theories are invented. If a theory justifies the false position in which a certain part of a society is living, then however unfounded or even obviously false the theory may be, it is accepted and becomes an article of faith to that section of society. Such, for instance, was the celebrated and unfounded theory expounded by Malthus, of the tendency of the population of the world to increase in geometrical progression but of the means of subsistence to increase only in arithmetical progression, and of the consequent over-population of the world; such also was the theory (an outgrowth of the Malthusian) of selection and struggle for existence as the basis of

[1] The fate of books depends on the head of the reader.

human progress. Such again is Marx's theory, which regards that gradual destruction of small private production by large capitalistic production now going on around us, as an inevitable decree of fate. However unfounded such theories are, however contrary to all that is known and confessed by humanity, and however obviously immoral they may be, they are credulously accepted, pass uncriticized, and are preached, perhaps for centuries, until the conditions are destroyed which they served to justify, or until their absurdity has become too evident. To this class belongs the astonishing theory of the Baumgartenian Trinity: Goodness, Beauty, and Truth, according to which it appears that the very best that can be done by the art of nations after 1900 years of Christian teaching is to choose as the ideal of their life the ideal that was held by a small, semi-savage, slave-holding people who lived 2000 years ago, imitated the nude human body extremely well, and erected buildings pleasant to look at. All these incompatibilities pass completely unnoticed. Learned people write long, cloudy treatises on beauty as a member of the æsthetic trinity of Beauty, Truth, and Goodness; *das Schöne, das Wahre, das Gute; le Beau, le Vrai, le Bon*, are repeated with capital letters by philosophers, æstheticians, and artists, by private individuals, by novelists, and by *feuilletonistes*; and they all think when pronouncing these sacrosanct words that they speak of something quite definite and solid—something on which they can base their opinions. In reality these words not only have no definite meaning, but hinder us in attaching any definite meaning to existing art; they are wanted only for the purpose of justifying the false importance we attribute to an art that transmits every kind of feeling if only those feelings afford us pleasure.[1]

[1] *What is Art?* was translated by me from Tolstóy's MSS., which he sent me chapter by chapter as he wrote

it. He revised his work to such an extent that some chapters were re-written three times over after he first sent them to me for translation. The following passages belonging to an early version of this chapter, not retained in his final revision, seem worth preserving. I therefore give them here in a foot-note.

'We only need escape for a moment from the habit of considering this trinity of Goodness, Beauty, and Truth presented to us by Baumgarten, to be as true as the Trinity of religion, and need only ask ourselves what we all have always understood by the words which form this triad, to be convinced of the utterly fantastic nature of the union into one, of three absolutely different words and conceptions, which are not even commensurable in meaning.

'Goodness, Beauty, and Truth are put on one level, and all three conceptions are treated as though they were fundamental and metaphysical: whereas in reality such is not at all the case.

'Goodness is the eternal, the highest, aim of our life. However we may understand goodness our life is nothing but a striving towards the good, that is, towards God.

'Goodness is really the fundamental metaphysical perception which forms the essence of our consciousness: a perception not defined by reason.

'Goodness is that which cannot be defined by anything else but which defines everything else.

'But Beauty—if we do not want mere words, but speak of what we understand—beauty is nothing but what pleases us. The notion of beauty not only does not coincide with goodness, but rather is contrary to it; for the good most often coincides with victory over the passions while beauty is at the root of our passions.

'The more utterly we surrender ourselves to beauty the farther we depart from goodness. I know that to this people always reply that there is a moral and spiritual beauty, but this is merely playing with words, for by spiritual and moral beauty nothing else is understood but goodness. For the most part, beauty of soul, or goodness, not only does not coincide with what is ordinarily understood as beauty but is opposed to it.

'As to truth—still less can we attribute to this member of

F

the trinity identity with goodness, or even any independent existence at all.

'By truth we merely mean the correspondence of an expression or of the definition of an object, with reality, or with an understanding of the object common to every one, and therefore it is a means of arriving at the good. But what is there in common between the conceptions of beauty and truth on the one hand, and of goodness on the other? Truth spoken expressly to cause annoyance certainly does not harmonize with goodness.

'Not only are beauty and truth not conceptions equivalent to goodness, and not only do they not form one entity with goodness, but they do not even coincide with it. For instance, Socrates and Pascal as well as many others, considered that learning the truth about unnecessary things does not accord with goodness. With beauty, truth has not even anything in common, but for the most part is in contradiction with it, for truth generally exposes the deception and destroys the illusion which is a chief condition of beauty.

'And lo and behold! the arbitrary conjunction into one, of these three conceptions which are not commensurable but foreign to one another, has served as the basis for that amazing theory according to which the difference between good art transmitting good feeling, and bad art transmitting bad feeling, is completely obliterated, and one of the lowest manifestations of art, art merely for enjoyment—that art against which all the teachers of humanity have warned mankind—has come to be considered the highest art.'

Why Tolstóy deleted these passages is uncertain. They clearly express his perception of the fact that beauty, truth, and goodness, are not one but three different conceptions. Perhaps he noticed that the remarks about beauty, if detached from the context, could be used to support the delusion that his avoidance of the word 'beauty' in framing his definition of art, arose not from the fact that beauty is a word that itself needs definition, but because he 'hated beauty,' as some critics have foolishly alleged.—A. M.

CHAPTER VIII

Who have adopted this æsthetic theory? Real art needful for all men. Our art too expensive, too unintelligible, and too harmful, for the masses. The theory of 'the elect' in art.

BUT if art is a human activity having for its purpose the transmission to others of the highest and best feelings to which men have risen, how could it be that humanity for a certain rather considerable period of its existence (from the time people ceased to believe in Church doctrine down to the present day) should exist without this important activity, and instead of it should put up with an insignificant artistic activity only affording pleasure?

To answer this question it is necessary first of all to correct the current error people make in attributing to our art the significance of true, universal art. We are so accustomed not only naïvely to consider the Circassian family the best stock of people, but also the Anglo-Saxon race the best race if we are Englishmen or Americans, or the Teutonic if we are Germans, or the Gallo-Latin if we are French, or the Slavonic if we are Russians, that when speaking of our own art we feel fully convinced not only that our art is true art but even that it is the best and only true art. But in reality our art is not only not the only art (as the Bible was once held to be the only Book)—it is not even the art of the whole of Christendom, only of a small section of our part of humanity. It was correct to speak of a national Jewish, Greek, or Egyptian art, and one may speak of a now-existing Chinese, Japanese, or Indian art, shared by a whole people. Such art common to a whole nation existed in Russia till Peter I's time, and existed in the rest of Europe until the thirteenth or fourteenth century, but since the upper classes of European society, having lost faith in the Church teaching, did not accept real Christianity but remained without any faith, one can no longer speak of an art of the Christian nations in the sense of the whole of art. Since the upper classes of the Christian nations lost faith in Church-Christianity the art of those upper classes has separated itself from the art of the rest of the people and there have been two arts —the art of the people, and genteel art. Therefore the answer to the question how it could happen that humanity lived for a certain period without real art, replacing it by art which served enjoyment only, is that not the whole of humanity, nor even any considerable portion of it, lived without real art, but only the highest classes of European Christian society, and even they only for a comparatively short time—from the commencement of the Renaissance down to our own day.

The consequence of this absence of true art showed itself inevitably in the corruption of this class which nourished itself on false art. All the confused unintelligible theories of art, all the false and contradictory judgments on art—and particularly the self-confident stagnation of our art in its false channels—arise from the assertion, which has come into common use and is accepted as an unquestioned truth but is yet amazingly and palpably false, the assertion namely that the art of our upper classes [1] is the whole of art: the true, the only, the universal art. And although this assertion (which is precisely similar to the assertion made by religious people of the various Churches who consider that theirs is the only true religion) is quite arbitrary and obviously unjust, yet

[1] The contrast made is between the classes and the masses: between those who do not and those who do earn their bread by productive manual labour, the middle classes being taken as an offshoot of the upper classes.—A. M.

it is calmly repeated by all the people of our circle with full faith in its infallibility.

The art we have is the whole of art, the real, the only art, and yet two-thirds of the human race (all the peoples of Asia and Africa) live and die knowing nothing of this sole and supreme art. And even in our Christian society hardly one per cent of the people make use of this art, which we speak of as being the *whole* of art; the remaining ninety-nine per cent live and die, generation after generation, crushed by toil and never tasting this art, which moreover is of such a nature that if they could get it they would not understand anything of it. According to the current æsthetic theory, we acknowledge art either as one of the highest manifestations of the Idea, God, Beauty, or as the highest spiritual enjoyment; furthermore we hold that all people have equal rights, if not to material at any rate to spiritual well-being, and yet ninety-nine per cent of our European population live and die, generation after generation, crushed by toil, much of which toil is necessary for the production of our art which they never use, and we in face of this, calmly assert that the art which we produce is the real, true, only art—all of art!

To the remark that if our art is the true art every-one should have the benefit of it, the usual reply is that if everybody at present does not make use of existing art, the fault lies not in the art but in the false organi-zation of society; that one can imagine to oneself in the future a state of things in which physical labour will be partly superseded by machinery, partly light-ened by its just distribution, and that labour for the production of art will be taken in turns: that there is no need for some people always to sit below the stage moving the decorations, winding up the machinery, working at the piano or French horn, and setting type and printing books, but that the people who do all this work might be so engaged only a few hours per day, and in their leisure time might enjoy all the blessings of art.

That is what the defenders of our exclusive art say; but I think they do not themselves believe it. They cannot help knowing that fine art can arise only on the slavery of the masses of the people, and can continue only as long as that slavery lasts; and they cannot help knowing that only under conditions of intense hardship for the workers can specialists—writers, musicians, dancers, and actors—arrive at that fine degree of perfection to which they do attain, or produce their refined works of art, and that only under the same conditions can there be a fine public to appreciate such productions. Free the slaves of capital, and it will be impossible to produce such refined art.

But even were we to admit the inadmissible, and say that means may be found by which art (that art which is considered to be art among us) may be made accessible to the whole people, another consideration presents itself showing that fashionable art cannot be the whole of art, namely the fact that it is completely unintelligible to the people. Formerly men wrote poems in Latin, but now their artistic productions are as unintelligible to the common folk as if they were written in Sanskrit. The usual reply to this is, that if the people do not now understand this art of ours it only proves that they are undeveloped, and that this has been so at each fresh step forward made by art. It has never been understood at first, but afterwards people have become accustomed to it.

It will be the same with our present art; it will be understood when everybody is as well educated as are we—the people of the upper classes—who produce it, say the defenders of our art. But this assertion is evidently even more untrue than the former, for we know that the majority of the productions of the art of the upper classes, such as various odes, poems, dramas, cantatas, pastorals, pictures, and so forth, which delighted people of the upper classes when they were produced, never were afterwards either understood or valued by the great masses of mankind, but have remained, what they were at first, a mere pastime for the rich people of their time, for whom alone they ever were of any importance. It is also often urged in proof of the assertion that the people will some day understand our art, that some productions of so-called classical poetry, music, or painting, which formerly did not please the masses, do—now that they have been offered to them from all sides—begin to please these same masses; but this only shows that the crowd, especially the half-spoilt town crowd, can easily (its taste having been perverted) be accustomed to any sort of art. Moreover this art is not produced by these masses, nor even chosen by them, but is energetically thrust upon them in those public places in which art is accessible to the people. For the great majority of working people our art, besides being inaccessible on account of its costliness, is strange in its very nature, transmitting as it does the feelings of people far removed from those conditions of laborious life which are natural to the great body of humanity. That which is enjoyment to a man of the rich classes is incomprehensible as a pleasure to a working man, and evokes in him either no feeling at all or a feeling quite contrary to that which it evokes in an idle and satiated man. Such feelings as form the chief subjects of present-day art—say, for instance, honour,[1] patriotism, and amorousness—evoke in a working man only bewilderment and contempt, or indignation. So that even if a possibility were given to the labouring classes

[1] Duelling was still customary among the higher circles in Russia, as in other Continental countries, when this was written.—A. M.

to see, to read, and to hear, in their leisure time, all that forms the flower of contemporary art (as is done to some extent in towns, by means of picture-galleries, popular concerts, and libraries), the working man (to the extent to which he is a labourer, and has not begun to pass into the ranks of those perverted by idleness) would be able to make nothing of our fine art, and if he did understand it, what he understood would not elevate his soul but would certainly in most cases pervert it. To thoughtful and sincere people there can therefore be no doubt that the art of our upper classes never can be the art of the whole people. But if art is an important matter, a spiritual blessing essential for all men (like religion, as the devotees of art are fond of saying), then it should be accessible to every one. And if, as in our day, it is not accessible to all men, then either art is not the vital matter it is represented to be, or that art which we call art is not the real thing.

The dilemma is inevitable, and therefore clever and immoral people avoid it by denying one side of it, namely, denying that the common people have a right to art. These people simply and boldly speak out and say (what goes to the heart of the matter) that the participators in and utilizers of what in their esteem is highly beautiful art, that is, art furnishing the greatest enjoyment, can only be *schöne Geister*, the elect, as the romanticists called them, the *Uebermenschen*, as they are called by the followers of Nietzsche; the vulgar herd which remains, incapable of experiencing these pleasures, must serve the exalted pleasures of this superior breed of people. The people who express these views at least do not pretend, and do not try to combine the incompatible, but frankly admit what is the case, that our art is an art of the upper classes only. So in reality art has been, and is, understood by every one engaged on it in our society.

CHAPTER IX

The perversion of our art. It has lost its natural subject-matter. Has no flow of fresh feeling. Transmits chiefly three base emotions.

THE unbelief of the upper classes of the European world had this effect, that instead of an artistic activity aiming at transmitting the highest feelings to which humanity has attained—those flowing from religious perception—we have an activity which aims at affording the greatest enjoyment to a certain class of society. And from all the immense domain of art, that part has been fenced off and is alone called art which affords enjoyment to the people of this particular circle.

Apart from the moral effects on European society of such a selection out of the whole sphere of art of what did not deserve such a valuation, and the acknowledgment of it as important, this perversion of art has weakened art itself and well-nigh destroyed it. The first great result was that art was deprived of the infinite, varied, and profound, religious subject-matter proper to it. The second result was that, having only a small circle of people in view, it lost its beauty of form and became affected and obscure; and the third and chief result was that it ceased to be natural or even sincere and became thoroughly artificial and brain-spun.

The first result—the impoverishment of subject-matter—followed because only that is a true work of art which transmits fresh feelings not previously experienced by man. As thought-product is only then real thought-product when it transmits new conceptions and thoughts and does not merely repeat what was

known before, so also an art-product is only then a
genuine art-product when it brings a new feeling
(however insignificant) into the current of human
life. This explains why children and youths are so
strongly impressed by those works of art which first
transmit to them feelings they had not experienced
before.

The same powerful impression is made on people by
feelings which are quite new and have never before
been expressed by man. And it is the source from
which such feelings flow, that the art of the upper
classes has deprived itself of by estimating feelings not
in conformity with a religious perception but according
to the degree of enjoyment they afford. There is
nothing older and more hackneyed than enjoyment,
and there is nothing fresher than the feelings springing
from the religious consciousness of each age. It could
not be otherwise: man's enjoyment has limits established by his nature, but the movement forward of
humanity which expresses itself in religious consciousness has no limits. At every forward step taken by
humanity—and such steps are taken in consequence
of a greater and greater elucidation of religious
perception—men experience new and fresh feelings.
And therefore only on the basis of religious perception
(which shows the highest level of life-comprehension
reached by the people of a certain period) can fresh
emotion, never before felt by man, arise. From the
religious perception of the ancient Greeks flowed the
really new, important, and endlessly varied feelings
expressed by Homer and the tragic writers. It was
the same among the Jews, who attained the religious
conception of a single God; from that perception
flowed all those new and important emotions expressed by the prophets. It was the same for the poets
of the Middle Ages, who if they believed in a heavenly
hierarchy believed also in the Catholic commune;

and it is the same for a man of to-day who has grasped the religious conception of true Christianity—the brotherhood of man.

The variety of fresh feelings flowing from religious perception is endless, and they are all new, for religious perception is nothing else than the first indication of that which is coming into existence, namely, a new relation of man to the world around him. But the feelings flowing from the desire for enjoyment are, on the contrary, not only limited but were long ago experienced and expressed. And therefore the lack of belief of the upper classes of Europe has left them with an art fed on the poorest subject-matter.

The impoverishment of the subject-matter of upper-class art was further increased by the fact that ceasing to be religious it ceased also to be popular, and this again diminished the range of feelings it transmitted, for the range of feelings experienced by the powerful and the rich who have no experience of labour for the support of life, is far poorer, more limited, and more insignificant, than the range of feelings natural to working people.

People of our circle, æstheticians, usually think and say just the contrary of this. I remember how Goncharév the author, a very clever and educated man but a thorough townsman and an æsthetician, said to me that after Turgénev's *Sportsman's Notebook* there was nothing left to write about in peasant life. It was all used up. The life of working people seemed to him so simple that Turgénev's peasant stories had used up all there was to describe. The life of our wealthy people, with their love affairs and dissatisfaction with themselves, seemed to him full of inexhaustible subject-matter. One hero kissed his lady on the palm of her hand, another on her elbow, and a third somewhere else. One man is discontented through idleness, and another because people don't love him. And

Goncharév thought that in this sphere there is no end of variety. And this opinion—that the life of working people is poor in subject-matter but that our life, the life of the idle, is full of interest—is shared by very many people in our society. The life of a labouring man, with its endlessly varied forms of labour and the dangers connected with labour on sea and underground: his migrations, his intercourse with his employers, overseers, and companions, and with men of other religions and other nationalities: his struggles with nature and with wild beasts, his association with domestic animals, his work in the forest, on the steppe, in the field, the garden, the orchard: his intercourse with wife and children, not only as with people near and dear to him but as with co-workers and helpers in labour, replacing him in time of need: his concern in all economic questions, not as matters of display or discussion but as problems of life for himself and family: his pride in self-suppression and the service of others, his pleasures of refreshment; and the permeation of all these interests by a religious reaction towards the facts: all this to us who have not these interests, and possess no religious perception, seems monotonous in comparison with the small enjoyments and insignificant cares of our life—a life not of labour or production but of consumption and destruction of what others have produced for us. We think the feelings experienced by people of our day and our class are very important and varied; but in reality almost all the feelings of people of our class amount to but three very insignificant and simple feelings—the feeling of pride, the feeling of sexual desire, and the feeling of weariness of life. These three feelings, with their off-shoots, form almost the sole subject-matter of the art of the rich classes.

At first, at the very beginning of the separation of the exclusive art of the upper classes from universal art, its chief subject-matter was the feeling of pride. It was so at the time of the Renaissance and after it, when the chief subject of works of art was the laudation of the strong—popes, kings, and dukes. Odes and madrigals were written in their honour, they were extolled in cantatas and hymns, and their portraits were painted, and their statues carved, in various adulatory ways.

Next, the element of sexual desire began more and more to enter into art, and—with very few exceptions, and in novels and dramas almost without exception—it has now become an essential feature of every art product of the wealthy classes.

The third feeling transmitted by the art of the rich —that of discontent with life—appeared yet later in modern art. This feeling, which at the commencement of the present [XIXth] century was expressed only by exceptional men: by Byron, by Leopardi, and afterwards by Heine, has latterly become fashionable and is expressed by the most ordinary and empty people. Most justly does the French critic Doumic characterize the works of the new writers: . . . c'est la lassitude de vivre, le mépris de l'époque présente, le regret d'un autre temps aperçu à travers l'illusion de l'art, le goût du paradoxe, le besoin de se singulariser, une aspiration de raffinés vers la simplicité, l'adoration enfantine du merveilleux, la séduction maladive de la rêverie, l'ébranlement des nerfs,— surtout l'appel exaspéré de la sensualité (Les Jeunes, René Doumic).[1] And, as a matter of fact, of these three

---

[1] . . . it is weariness of life, contempt for the present epoch, regret for another age seen through the illusion of art, a taste for paradox, a desire to be singular, a sentimental aspiration towards simplicity, an infantile adoration of the marvellous, a sickly tendency towards reverie, a shattered condition of nerves,—and, above all, the exasperated demand of sensuality.

feelings it is sensuality, the lowest (accessible not only to all men but even to all animals), which forms the chief subject-matter of the works of art of recent times.

From Boccaccio to Marcel Prévost, novels, poems, and verses, invariably transmit the feeling of sexual love in its different forms. Adultery is not only the favourite, but almost the only theme of all the novels. A performance is not a performance unless under some pretext women appear with naked busts and limbs. Songs and romances—all are expressions of lust idealized in various degrees.

A majority of the pictures by French artists represent female nakedness in various forms. In recent French literature there is hardly a page or a poem in which nakedness is not described, and in which, relevantly or irrelevantly, their favourite thought and word *nu* is not repeated a couple of times. There is a certain writer, Rémy de Gourment, who gets printed and is considered talented. To obtain an idea of the new writers I read his novel, *Les Chevaux de Diomède*. It is a consecutive and detailed account of the sexual connexions some gentleman had with various women. Every page contains lust-kindling descriptions. It is the same in Pierre Louÿs' book, *Aphrodite*, which met with success; it is the same in a book I lately chanced upon, Huysmans' *Certains*, and with but few exceptions it is the same in all French novels. They are all the productions of people suffering from erotic mania. And these people are evidently convinced that as their whole life, in consequence of their diseased condition, is concentrated on amplifying various sexual abominations, therefore the life of all the world is similarly concentrated. And these people, suffering from erotic mania, are imitated throughout the whole artistic world of Europe and America.

Thus, in consequence of the lack of belief and the exceptional manner of life of the wealthy classes, the art of these classes became impoverished in subject-matter and has sunk to the transmission of the feelings of pride, discontent with life, and above all of sexual desire.

CHAPTER X

Loss of comprehensibility. Decadent art. Recent French art. Have we a right to say it is bad? The highest art has always been comprehensible to normal people. What fails to infect normal people is not art.

IN consequence of their unbelief the art of the upper classes became poor in subject-matter. But besides that, becoming continually more and more exclusive, it became at the same time continually more and more involved, affected, and obscure.

When a universal artist (such as were some of the Greek artists or the Jewish prophets) composed his work he naturally strove to say what he had to say so that it should be intelligible to all men. But when an artist composed for a small circle of people placed in exceptional conditions, or even for a single individual and his courtiers—for popes, cardinals, kings, dukes, queens, or for a king's mistress—he naturally aimed only at influencing these people, who were well known to him and lived in exceptional conditions familiar to him. And this was an easier task, and the artist was involuntarily drawn to express himself by allusions comprehensible only to the initiated, and obscure to every one else. In the first place more could be said in that way; and secondly, there is (for the initiated) even a certain charm in the cloudiness of such a manner of expression. This method, which showed itself both in euphuism and in mythological and historical allusions, came more and more into use until apparently it reached its utmost limits in the so-called art of the Decadents. It has come finally to this: that not only are haziness, mysteriousness, obscurity, and exclusiveness (shutting out the masses) elevated to the rank of a merit and a condition of poetic art, but even inaccuracy, indefiniteness, and lack of eloquence, are held in esteem.

Théophile Gautier in his preface to the celebrated *Fleurs du Mal* says that Baudelaire as far as possible banished from poetry eloquence, passion, and truth too strictly copied ('*l'éloquence, la passion, et la vérité calquée trop exactement*').

And Baudelaire not only did this, but maintained this thesis in his verses, and yet more strikingly in the prose of his *Petits Poèmes en Prose*, the meanings of which have to be guessed like a rebus and remain for the most part undiscovered.

The poet Verlaine (who followed next after Baudelaire and was also esteemed great) even wrote an *Art poétique*, in which he advises this style of compositon:—

> De la musique avant toute chose,
> Et pour cela préfère l'Impair
> Plus vague et plus soluble dans l'air,
> Sans rien en lui qui pèse ou qui pose.
>
> Il faut aussi que tu n'ailles point
> Choisir tes mots sans quelque méprise:
> Rien de plus cher que la chanson grise
> Où l'Indécis au Précis se joint.

. . . .

And again:—

> De la musique encore et toujours!
> Que ton vers soit la chose envolée
> Qu'on sent qui fuit d'une âme en allée
> Vers d'autres cieux à d'autres amours.
>
> Que ton vers soit la bonne aventure
> Éparse au vent crispé de matin,
> Qui va fleurant la menthe et le thym . . .
> Et tout le reste est littérature.[1]

---

[1] Music, music before all things!
The eccentric still prefer,
Vague in air, and nothing weighty,
Soluble. Yet do not err,

After these two comes Mallarmé, considered the most important of the young poets, and he plainly says that the charm of poetry lies in our having to guess its meaning—that in poetry there should always be a puzzle:—

'Je pense qu'il faut qu'il n'y ait qu'allusion', says he. 'La contemplation des objets, l'image s'envolant des rêveries suscitées par eux, sont le chant: les Parnassiens, eux, prennent la chose entièrement et la montrent; par là ils manquent de mystère; ils retirent aux esprits cette joie délicieuse de croire qu'ils créent.' *Nommer un objet, c'est supprimer les trois quarts de la jouissance du poème, qui est faite du bonheur de deviner peu à peu: le suggérer, voilà le rêve.* C'est le parfait usage de ce mystère qui constitue le symbole: évoquer petit à petit un objet pour montrer un état d'âme, ou, inversement, choisir un objet et en dégager un état d'âme, par une série de déchiffrements.

'. . . Si un être d'une intelligence moyenne, et d'une préparation littéraire insuffisante, ouvre par hasard un livre ainsi fait et prétend en jouir, il y a un malentendu, il faut remettre les choses à leur place. *Il doit y avoir toujours énigme en poésie*, et c'est le but de la littéra-

---

Choosing words; still do it lightly,
Do it with contemptuous mind:
Dearest are grey songs where mingle
The Defined and Undefined!

. . . .

Music always, now and ever!
Be thy verse the thing that flies
From a soul that's gone, escaping,
Gone to other loves and skies.

Gone to other loves and regions,
Following fortunes that allure,
Mint and thyme and morning crispness . .
All the rest's mere literature.

ture, il n'y en a pas d'autre,—d'évoquer les objets.'
Enquête sur l'évolution littéraire, Jules Huret, pp. 60,
61).[1]

Thus is obscurity elevated into a dogma among the
new poets. As the French critic Doumic (who has not
yet accepted the dogma) quite correctly says:—

'Il serait temps aussi d'en finir avec cette fameuse
"théorie de l'obscurité" que la nouvelle école a élevée,
en effet à la hauteur d'un dogme.' (*Les Jeunes, études
et portraits*, René Doumic).[2]

But it is not only French writers who think thus. The
poets of all other countries think and act in the same
way: German, and Scandinavian, and Italian, and
Russian, and English. So also do the artists of the
new period in all branches of art: in painting, in
sculpture, and in music. Relying on Nietzsche and
Wagner, the artists of the new age conclude that it is
unnecessary for them to be intelligible to the vulgar

---

[1] I think there should be nothing but allusions. The
contemplation of objects, the flying image of reveries
evoked by them, make the song. The Parnassians state the
thing completely, and show it, and thereby lack mystery;
they deprive the mind of that delicious joy of imagining
that it creates. To *name an object is to take away three-fourths
of the enjoyment of the poem, which consists in the happiness of
guessing little by little: to suggest it, that is the dream*. It is the perfect use of this mystery that constitutes the symbol: little by
little to evoke an object in order to show a state of the soul;
or inversely, to choose an object and from it to disengage
a state of the soul by a series of decipherings.
... If a being of mediocre intelligence and insufficient
literary preparation chances to open a book made in this
way and pretends to enjoy it, there is a misunderstanding—
things must be put back into their places. *There should
always be an enigma in poetry*, and the aim of literature—it
has no other—is to evoke objects.

[2] It were time also to have done with this famous 'theory
of obscurity', which the new school has practically raised
to the height of a dogma.

crowd; it is enough for them to evoke poetic emotion in 'the finest nurtured,' to borrow a phrase from an English æsthetician.

In order that what I am saying may not seem to be mere assertion, I will quote at least a few examples from the French poets who have led this movement. The name of these poets is legion. I have taken French writers because they, more decidedly than any others, indicate the new direction of art and are imitated by most European writers.

Besides those whose names are already considered famous, such as Baudelaire and Verlaine, here are the names of a few of them: Jean Moréas, Charles Morice, Henri de Régnier, Charles Vignier, Adrien Remacle, René Ghil, Maurice Maeterlinck, G. Albert Aurier, Rémy de Gourment, Saint-Pol-Roux-le-Magnifique, Georges Rodenbach, le comte Robert de Montesquiou-Fezensac. These are Symbolists and Decadents. Next we have the 'Magi': Joséphin Péladan, Paul Adam, Jules Bois, M. Papus, and others.

Besides these there are yet a hundred and forty-one others whom Doumic mentions in the book referred to above.

Here are some examples from the work of those of them who are considered to be the best, beginning with that most celebrated man, acknowledged to be a great artist worthy of a monument—Baudelaire. This is a poem from his celebrated *Fleurs du mal*:—

No. XXIV

Je t'adore à l'égal de la voûte nocturne,
O vase de tristesse, ô grande taciturne,
Et t'aime d'autant plus, belle, que tu me fuis,
Et que tu me parais, ornement de mes nuits,
Plus ironiquement accumuler les lieues
Qui séparent mes bras des immensités bleues.
Je m'avance à l'attaque, et je grimpe aux assauts,
Comme après un cadavre un chœur de vermisseaux,

Et je chéris, ô bête implacable et cruelle,
Jusqu'à cette froideur par où tu m'es plus belle![1]

And this is another by the same writer:—

No. XXXVI
DUELLUM

Deux guerriers ont couru l'un sur l'autre; leurs armes
Ont éclaboussé l'air de lueurs et de sang.
Ces jeux, ces cliquetis du fer sont les vacarmes
D'une jeunesse en proie à l'amour vagissant.

Les glaives sont brisés! comme notre jeunesse,
Ma chère! Mais les dents, les ongles acérés,
Vengent bientôt l'épée et la dague traîtresse.
O fureur des cœurs mûrs par l'amour ulcérés!

Dans le ravin hanté des chats-pards et des onces
Nos héros, s'étreignant méchamment, ont roulé,
Et leur peau fleurira l'aridité des ronces.
Ce gouffre, c'est l'enfer, de nos amis peuplé!
Roulons-y sans remords, amazone inhumaine,
Afin d'éterniser l'ardeur de notre haine![1]

To be exact, I should mention that the collection
contains verses less comprehensible than these, but
not one poem which is plain and can be understood
without a certain effort—an effort seldom rewarded,
for the feelings the poet transmits are evil and very
base ones. And these feelings are always, and purposely, expressed by him with eccentricity and lack
of clearness. This premeditated obscurity is especially noticeable in his prose, where the author could
speak plainly if he wanted to.

Take, for instance, the first piece from his *Petits
poèmes en prose*:—

L'ÉTRANGER

Qui aimes-tu le mieux, homme énigmatique, dis? ton
père, ta mère, ta sœur, ou ton frère?
Je n'ai ni père, ni mère, ni sœur, ni frère.

---

[1] For translation, see Appendix I.   [2] *ibid.*

Tes amis?

Vous vous servez là d'une parole dont le sens m'est resté jusqu'à ce jour inconnu.

Ta patrie?

J'ignore sous quelle latitude elle est située.

La beauté?

Je l'aimerais volontiers, déesse et immortelle.

L'or?

Je le hais, comme vous haïssez Dieu.

Et qu'aimes-tu donc, extraordinaire étranger?

J'aime les nuages . . . les nuages qui passent . . . là-bas, . . . les merveilleux nuages![1]

The piece called *La Soupe et les nuages* is probably intended to express the unintelligibility of the poet even to her whom he loves. This is the piece in question:—

'Ma petite folle bien-aimée me donnait à dîner, et par la fenêtre ouverte de la salle à manger je contemplais les mouvantes architectures que Dieu fait avec les vapeurs, les merveilleuses constructions de l'impalpable. Et je me disais, à travers ma contemplation: "Toutes ces fantasmagories sont presque aussi belles que les yeux de ma belle bien-aimée, la petite folle monstrueuse aux yeux verts."

'Et tout-à-coup je reçus un violent coup de poing dans le dos, et j'entendis une voix rauque et charmante, une voix hystérique et comme enrouée par l'eau-de-vie, la voix de ma chère petite bien-aimée, qui me disait, "Allez-vous bientôt manger votre soupe, s . . . . b . . . . de marchand de nuages?"'[2]

However artificial these two pieces may be, it is still possible with some effort to guess at what the author meant them to express, but some of the pieces are absolutely incomprehensible—at least to me. *Le Galant Tireur* is a piece I was quite unable to understand.

---

[1] For translation, see Appendix I.   [2] *ibid.*

LE GALANT TIREUR

'Comme la voiture traversait le bois, il la fit arrêter dans le voisinage d'un tir, disant qu'il lui serait agréable de tirer quelques balles pour *tuer* le Temps. Tuer ce monstre-là, n'est-ce pas l'occupation la plus ordinaire et la plus légitime de chacun?—Et il offrit galamment la main à sa chère, délicieuse et exécrable femme, à cette mystérieuse femme à laquelle il doit tant de plaisirs, tant de douleurs, et peut-être aussi une grande partie de son génie.

'Plusieurs balles frappèrent loin du but proposé; l'une d'elles s'enfonça même dans le plafond; et comme la charmante créature riait follement, se moquant de la maladresse de son époux, celui-ci se tourna brusquement vers elle, et lui dit: "Observez cette poupée, là-bas, à droite, qui porte le nez en l'air et qui a la mine si hautaine. Eh bien! cher ange, *je me figure que c'est vous.*" Et il ferma les yeux et il lâcha la détente. La poupée fut nettement décapitée.

Alors s'inclinant vers sa chère, sa délicieuse, son exécrable femme, son inévitable et impitoyable Muse, et lui baisant respectueusement la main, il ajouta: "Ah! mon cher ange, combien je vous remercie de mon adresse!" ' [1]

The productions of another celebrity, Verlaine, are not less affected and unintelligible. This, for instance is the first poem in the section called *Ariettes oubliées*:

'Le vent dans la plaine
Suspend son haleine.'—FAVART.

C'est l'extase langoureuse,
C'est la fatigue amoureuse,
C'est tous les frissons des bois
Parmi l'étreinte des brises,
C'est, vers les ramures grises,
Le chœur des petites voix.

---

[1] For translation, see Appendix I.

> O le frêle et frais murmure!
> Cela gazouille et susurre,
> Cela ressemble au cri doux
> Que l'herbe agitée expire . . .
> Tu dirais, sous l'eau qui vire,
> Le roulis sourd des cailloux.
>
> Cette âme qui se lamente
> En cette plainte dormante,
> C'est la nôtre, n'est-ce pas?
> La mienne, dis, et la tienne,
> Dont s'exhale l'humble antienne
> Par ce tiède soir, tout bas?[1]

What '*chœur des petites voix*,' and what '*cri doux que l'herbe agitée expire*,' and what it all means, remains altogether unintelligible to me.

And here is another Ariette:—

VIII

> Dans l'interminable
> Ennui de la plaine,
> La neige incertaine
> Luit comme du sable.
>
> Le ciel est de cuivre,
> Sans lueur aucune.
> On croirait voir vivre
> Et mourir la lune.
>
> Comme des nuées
> Flottent gris les chênes
> Des forêts prochaines
> Parmi les buées.
>
> Le ciel est de cuivre,
> Sans lueur aucune.
> On croirait voir vivre
> Et mourir la lune.
>
> Corneille poussive
> Et vous, les loups maigres,
> Par ces bises aigres,
> Quoi donc vous arrive?

---

[1] For translation, see Appendix I.

Dans l'interminable
Ennui de la plaine,
La neige incertaine
Luit comme du sable.[1]

How does the moon seem to live and die in a copper heaven? And how can snow shine like sand? The whole thing is not merely unintelligible, but under pretence of conveying an impression it passes off a string of incorrect comparisons and words.

Besides these artificial and obscure poems there are others which are intelligible, but make up for it by being altogether bad both in form and in content. Such are all the poems under the heading *La Sagesse*. The chief place in these verses is occupied by a very poor expression of the most commonplace Roman Catholic and patriotic sentiments. For instance, one meets with verses such as this:—

Je ne veux plus penser qu'a ma mère Marie,
Siège de la sagesse et source de pardons,
Mère de France aussi DE QUI NOUS ATTENDONS
INÉBRANLABLEMENT L'HONNEUR DE LA PATRIE.[2]

Before citing examples from other poets I must pause to note the amazing celebrity of these two versifiers, Baudelaire and Verlaine, who are now accepted as being great poets. How the French, who had Chénier, Musset, Lamartine, and above all Hugo,— and among whom quite recently flourished the so-called Parnassians: Leconte de Lisle, Sully-Prud-homme, etc.—could attribute such importance to these two versifiers who were far from skilful in form and most contemptible and commonplace in

[1] For translation, see Appendix I.
[2] I do not wish to think any more, except about my
    mother Mary,
Seat of wisdom and source of pardon,
Also Mother of France, *from whom we*
Steadfastly expect the honour of our country;

subject-matter, is to me incomprehensible. The philosophy of life of one of them, Baudelaire, consisted in elevating gross egotism into a theory and replacing morality by a cloudy conception of beauty —especially artificial beauty. Baudelaire had a preference, which he expressed, for a woman's face painted rather than in its natural colour, and for metal trees and a theatrical imitation of water rather than real trees and real water.

The conception of life of the other, Verlaine, consisted in weak profligacy, in confession of moral impotence, and as an antidote to that impotence, in the grossest Roman Catholic idolatry. Both moreover were quite lacking in naïveté, sincerity, and simplicity, and both overflowed with artificiality, forced originality, and self-assurance. So that in their least bad productions one sees more of M. Baudelaire or M. Verlaine than of what they are describing. But these two indifferent versifiers form a school, and lead hundreds of followers after them.

There is only one explanation of this fact: it is that the art of the society in which these versifiers lived is not a serious, important matter of life, but a mere amusement; and all amusements grow wearisome by repetition. And in order to make wearisome amusement again tolerable it is necessary to find some means to freshen it up. When, at cards, ombre grows stale, whist is introduced; when whist grows stale, écarté is substituted; when écarté grows stale, some other novelty is invented, and so on. The substance of the matter remains the same, only its form is changed. It is the same with this kind of art. The subject-matter of the art of the upper classes growing continually more and more limited, it has come at last to this, that to the artists of these exclusive classes it seems as if everything has already been said, and that to find anything new to say is impossible. And therefore to freshen up this art they look out for fresh forms.

Baudelaire and Verlaine invent such a new form, furbish it up moreover with hitherto unused pornographic details, and—the critics and the public of the upper classes hail them as great writers.

This is the only explanation of the success not of Baudelaire and Verlaine only, but of all the Decadents.

For instance, there are poems by Mallarmé and Maeterlinck which have no meaning, and yet, for all that, or perhaps on that very account, are printed by tens of thousands, not only in various publications but even in collections of the best works of the younger poets.

This, for example, is a sonnet by Mallarmé:—

> A la nue accablante tu
> Basse de basalte et de laves
> A même les échos esclaves
> Par une trompe sans vertu.
> Quel sépulcral naufrage (tu
> Le soir, écume, mais y baves)
> Suprême une entre les épaves
> Abolit le mât dévêtu.
>
> Ou cela que furibond faute
> De quelque perdition haute
> Tout l'abîme vain éployé
> Dans le si blanc cheveu qui traîne
> Avarement aura noyé
> Le flanc enfant d'une sirène.[1]

('Pan,' 1895, No. 1.)

This poem is not exceptional in its incomprehensibility. I have read several other poems by Mallarmé and they also had no meaning whatever. I give a sample of his prose in Appendix II. There is a whole

[1] This sonnet seems too unintelligible for translation.—Trans.

volume of this prose, called *Divagations*. It is impossible to understand any of it. And that is evidently what the author intended.

And here is a song by Maeterlinck, another celebrated author of to-day:—

Quand il est sorti,
(J'entendis la porte)
Quand il est sorti
Elle avait souri . . .

Mais quand il rentra,
(J'entendis la lampe)
Mais quand il rentra
Une autre était là . . .

Et j'ai vu la mort,
(J'entendis son âme)
Et j'ai vu la mort
Qui l'attend encore . . .

On est venu dire,
(Mon enfant, j'ai peur)
On est venu dire
Qu'il allait partir . . .

Ma lampe allumée,
(Mon enfant, j'ai peur)
Ma lampe allumée
Me suis approchée . . .

A la première porte,
(Mon enfant, j'ai peur)
A la première porte
La flamme a tremblé . . .

A la seconde porte,
(Mon enfant, j'ai peur)
A la seconde porte
La flamme a parlé . . .

A la troisième porte,
(Mon enfant, j'ai peur)
A la troisième porte
La lumière est morte . . .

Et s'il revenait un jour,
Que faut-il lui dire?
Dites-lui qu'on l'attendit
Jusqu'à s'en mourir . . .

Et s'il m'interroge encore
Sans me reconnaître?
Parlez-lui comme une sœur.
Il souffre peut-être . . .

Et s'il demande où vous êtes
Que faut-il répondre?
Donnez-lui mon anneau d'or
Sans rien lui répondre . . .

Et s'il veut savoir pourquoi
La salle est déserte?
Montrez-lui la lampe éteinte
Et la porte ouverte . . .

Et s'il m'interroge alors
Sur la dernière heure?
Dites-lui que j'ai souri
De peur qu'il ne pleure . . .[1]

('Pan,' 1895, No. 2.)

Who went out? Who came in? Who is speaking? Who died?

I beg the reader to take the trouble to read through the samples I cite in Appendix III of the celebrated and esteemed young poets: Régnier, Griffin, Verhaeren, Moréas, and Montesquiou. It is important to do so in order to form a clear conception of the present position of art, and not to suppose as many do, that Decadentism is an accidental and transient phenomenon. To avoid the reproach of having selected the worst verses, I have copied out of each volume whatever poem happened to stand on page 28.

All the other productions of these poets are equally unintelligible, or can only be understood with great difficulty and then not fully. All the productions of

[1] For translation, see Appendix I.

those hundreds of poets of whom I have named a few, are the same in kind. And among the Germans, Swedes, Norwegians, Italians, and us Russians, similar verses are printed. And such productions are printed and made up into book-form if not by the million then by the hundred-thousand (some of these separate works sell in tens of thousands). For type-setting, paging, printing, and binding, these books, millions and millions of working days are spent—not less, I think, than went to build the Great Pyramid. Nor is this all. The same is going on in all the other arts: millions and millions of working days are being spent on the production of equally incomprehensible works in painting, in music, and in drama.

Painting not only does not lag behind poetry in this matter, but rather outstrips it. Here is an extract from the diary of an amateur of art,[1] written when visiting the Paris exhibitions in 1894:—

'I was to-day at three exhibitions: the Symbolists', the Impressionists', and the Neo-Impressionists'. I looked at the pictures conscientiously and carefully, but again felt the same stupefaction and ultimate indignation. The first exhibition, that of Camille Pissarro, was comparatively the most comprehensible, though the pictures were out of drawing, had no content, and the colourings were most improbable. The drawing was so indefinite that you were some-times unable to make out which way an arm or a head was turned. The subject was generally, "*effets*"—*Effet de brouillard, Effet du soir, Soleil couchant*. There were some pictures with figures but without subjects.

'In the colouring, bright blue and bright green predominated. And each picture had its special colour with which the whole picture was, as it were, splashed. For instance in "A Girl guarding Geese"

[1] Tolstóy's eldest daughter, Tatiána, Mme. Sukhotín; who was herself a gifted art-student.—A. M.

the special colour is *vert de gris*, and dots of it were splashed about everywhere: on the face, the hair, the hands, and the clothes. In the same gallery—that of Durand-Ruel—were other pictures: by Puvis de Chavannes, Manet, Monet, Renoir, Sisley, who are all Impressionists. One of them, whose name I could not make out—it was something like Redon—had painted a blue face in profile. On the whole face there is only this blue tone, with white-of-lead. Pissarro has a water-colour all done in dots. In the foreground is a cow entirely painted with various-coloured dots. The general colour cannot be distinguished, however much one stands back from, or draws near to, the picture. From there I went to see the Symbolists. I looked at them long without asking any one for an explanation, trying to guess the meaning; but it is beyond human comprehension. One of the first things to catch my eye was a wooden *haut-relief*, wretchedly executed, representing a woman (naked) who with both hands is squeezing from her two breasts streams of blood. The blood flows down, becoming lilac in colour. Her hair first descends and then rises again and turns into trees. The figure is all coloured yellow and the hair is brown.

'Next—a picture: a yellow sea on which something swims which is neither a ship nor a heart; on the horizon is a profile with a halo and yellow hair, which changes into the sea, in which it is lost. Some of the painters lay on their colours so thick that the effect is something between painting and sculpture. A third exhibit was even less comprehensible: a man's profile; before him a flame and black stripes—leeches, as I was afterwards told. At last I asked a gentleman who was there what it meant, and he explained to me that the *haut-relief* was a symbol, and represented "*La Terre*." The heart swimming in a yellow sea was "*Illusion perdue*," and the gentleman with the leeches was "*Le Mal.*" There were also some Impressionist pictures: elementary profiles, holding some sort of flowers in their hands; in monotone, out of drawing, and either quite blurred or else marked out with wide black outlines.'

This was in 1894; the same tendency is now even more strongly defined, and we have Böcklin, Stuck, Klinger, Sasha Schneider, and others.

The same thing is taking place in the drama. The play-writers give us an architect who for some reason has not fulfilled his former high intentions, and consequently climbs on to the roof of a house he has erected and tumbles down head foremost;[1] or an incomprehensible old woman (who exterminates rats), and who for an unintelligible reason takes a poetic child to the sea and there drowns him;[2] or some blind men, who, sitting on the sea-shore, for some reason always repeat one and the same thing;[3] or a bell of some kind, which flies into a lake and there rings.[4]

And the same is happening in music—in that art which more than any other one would have thought should be intelligible to everybody.

An acquaintance of yours, a musician of repute, sits down to the piano and plays you what he says is a new composition of his own, or of one of the new composers. You hear the strange, loud sounds, and admire the gymnastic exercises performed by his fingers, and you see that the performer wishes to convey to you that the sounds he is producing express various poetic strivings of the soul. You see his intention, but no feeling whatever, except weariness, is transmitted to you. The execution lasts long, at least it seems very long to you because you do not receive

---

[1] Ibsen's *The Master-Builder.*—A. M.
[2] Ibsen's *Little Eyolf.*—A. M.
[3] Maeterlinck's *Les Aveugles.*—A. M.
[4] G. Hauptmann's *Die versunkene Glocke.*—A. M.

any clear impression, and involuntarily you remember the words of Alphonse Karr, '*Plus ça va vite, plus ça dure longtemps.*'[1] And it occurs to you that perhaps it is all a mystification; perhaps the performer is trying you—just throwing his hands and fingers wildly about the key-board in the hope that you will fall into the trap and praise him, and then he will laugh and confess that he only wanted to see if he could hoax you, but when at last the piece does finish and the perspiring and agitated musician rises from the piano obviously anticipating praise, you see that it was all done in earnest.

The same thing takes place at all the concerts with pieces by Liszt, Wagner, Berlioz, Brahms, and (newest of all) Richard Strauss, and the numberless other composers of the new school who unceasingly produce opera after opera, symphony after symphony, piece after piece.

The same is occurring in a domain in which it seemed hard to be unintelligible—in the sphere of novels and short stories.

Read *Là-Bas* by Huysmans, or some of Kipling's short stories, or *L'Annonciateur* by Villiers de L'Isle-Adam in his *Contes cruels*, etc., and you will find them not only '*abscons*' (to use a word adopted by the new writers) but absolutely unintelligible both in form and in substance. Such again is the work by E. Morel, *Terre Promise*, now appearing in the *Revue Blanche*, and such are most of the new novels. The style is very high-flown, the feelings seem to be most elevated, but you can't make out what is happening, to whom it is happening, and where it is happening. And such is the bulk of the young art of our time.

People who grew up in the first half of this century admiring Goethe, Schiller, Musset, Hugo, Dickens, Beethoven, Chopin, Raphael, da Vinci, Michael-

[1] 'The quicker it goes the longer it lasts.'

G

angelo, and Delaroche, being unable to make head or tail of this new art simply attribute its productions to tasteless insanity and wish to ignore them. But such an attitude towards this new art is quite unjustifiable because, in the first place, this art is spreading more and more and has already conquered for itself a firm position in society similar to that occupied by the Romanticists in the third decade of this [the XIXth] century; and secondly and chiefly because, if it is permissible to judge in this way of the productions of the latest form of art, called by us Decadent art, merely because we do not understand it, then remember, there are an enormous number of people—all the labourers and many of the non-labouring folk—who, in just the same way, do not comprehend those productions of art which we consider admirable: the verses of our favourite artists—Goethe, Schiller, and Hugo; the novels of Dickens, the music of Beethoven and Chopin, the pictures of Raphael, Michaelangelo, da Vinci, and so forth.

If I have a right to think that great masses of people, because they are not sufficiently developed, fail to understand and do not like what I consider undoubtedly good, then I have no right to deny that perhaps the reason why I cannot understand and cannot like the new productions of art is merely that I am still insufficiently developed to understand them. If I have a right to say that I, and the majority of people who are in sympathy with me, do not understand the productions of the new art simply because there is nothing in it to understand, and because it is bad art, then with just the same right the still larger majority, the whole labouring mass, who do not understand what I consider admirable art, can say that what I reckon as good art is bad art and there is nothing in it to understand.

I once saw the injustice of such condemnation of the

new art with especial clearness, when in my presence a certain poet who writes incomprehensible verses ridiculed incomprehensible music with gay self-assurance; and shortly afterwards a certain musician who composes incomprehensible symphonies laughed at incomprehensible poetry with equal self-confidence. I have no right and no authority to condemn the new art on the ground that I (a man educated in the first half of the nineteenth century) do not understand it; I can only say that it is incomprehensible to me. The only advantage the art I acknowledge has over the Decadent art lies in the fact that the art I recognize is comprehensible to a somewhat larger number of people than present-day art.

The fact that I am accustomed to a certain exclusive art and can understand it, but am unable to understand another still more exclusive art, does not give me a right to conclude that my art is the real, true art, and that the other one, which I do not understand, is an unreal, a bad, art. I can only conclude that art, becoming ever more and more exclusive, has become more and more incomprehensible to an ever-increasing number of people, and that in this, its progress towards greater and greater incomprehensibility (on one level of which I am standing with the art familiar to me), it has reached a point where it is understood by a very small number of the elect, and the number of these chosen people is becoming ever smaller and smaller.

As soon as ever the art of the upper classes separated itself from universal art a conviction arose that art may be art and yet be incomprehensible to the masses. And as soon as this position was admitted it had inevitably to be admitted also that art may be intelligible only to the very smallest number of the elect and eventually to two, or to one, of our nearest friends, or to oneself alone—which is practically what is being said by modern artists:—'I create and understand myself, and if any one does not understand me so much the worse for him.'

The assertion that art may be good art and at the same time incomprehensible to a great number of people, is extremely unjust, and its consequences are ruinous to art itself; but at the same time it is so common and has so eaten into our conceptions, that it is impossible to make sufficiently clear its whole absurdity.

Nothing is more common than to hear it said of reputed works of art that they are very good but very difficult to understand. We are quite used to such assertions, and yet to say that a work of art is good but incomprehensible to the majority of men, is the same as saying of some kind of food that it is very good but most people can't eat it. The majority of men may not like rotten cheese or putrefying grouse, dishes esteemed by people with perverted tastes; but bread and fruit are only good when they are such as please the majority of men. And it is the same with art. Perverted art may not please the majority of men, but good art always pleases every one.

It is said that the very best works of art are such that they cannot be understood by the masses, but are accessible only to the elect who are prepared to understand these great works. But if the majority of men do not understand, the knowledge necessary to enable them to understand should be taught and explained to them. But it turns out that there is no such knowledge, that the works cannot be explained, and that those who say the majority do not understand good works of art, still do not explain those works, but only tell us that in order to understand them one must read, and see, and hear, these same works over and over again. But this is not to explain, it is only to habituate! And people may habituate themselves to anything, even to the very worst things. As people may habituate themselves to bad food, to spirits, tobacco, and opium, just in the same way they may habituate themselves to bad art—and that is exactly what is being done.

Moreover it cannot be said that the majority of people lack the taste to esteem the highest works of art. The majority always have understood and still understand what we also recognize as being the very best art: the epic of Genesis, the Gospel parables, folk-legends, fairy-tales, and folk-songs, are understood by all. How can it be that the majority has suddenly lost its capacity to understand what is high in our art?

Of a speech it may be said that it is admirable but incomprehensible to those who do not know the language in which it is delivered. A speech delivered in Chinese may be excellent, and yet remain incomprehensible to me if I do not know Chinese; but what distinguishes a work of art from all other mental activity is just the fact that its language is understood by all, and that it infects all without distinction. The tears and laughter of a Chinaman infect me just as the laughter and tears of a Russian; and it is the same with painting and music, and also poetry when it is translated into a language I understand. The songs of a Kirghiz or of a Japanese touch me, though in a lesser degree than they touch a Kirghiz or a Japanese. I am also touched by Japanese painting, Indian architecture, and Arabian stories. If I am but little touched by a Japanese song and a Chinese novel, it is not that I do not understand these productions, but that I know and am accustomed to higher works of art. It is not because their art is above me. Great works of art are only great because they are accessible and comprehensible to every one. The story of Joseph translated into the Chinese language touches a Chinese. The story of Sakya Muni (Buddha) touches us.

And there are, and must be, buildings, pictures, statues, and music, of similar power. So that if art fails to move men, it cannot be said that this is due to the spectators' or hearers' lack of understanding, but the conclusion to be drawn may be, and should be, that such art is either bad or is not art at all.

Art is differentiated from activity of the understanding, which demands preparation and a certain sequence of knowledge (so that one cannot learn trigonometry before knowing geometry), by the fact that it acts on people independently of their state of development and education, that the charm of a picture, of sounds, or of forms, infects any man whatever his plane of development.

The business of art lies just in this: to make that understood and felt which in the form of an argument might be incomprehensible and inaccessible. Usually it seems to the recipient of a truly artistic impression that he knew the thing before, but had been unable to express it.

And such has always been the nature of good, supreme art; the *Iliad*, the *Odyssey*; the stories of Isaac, Jacob, and Joseph; the Hebrew prophets, the psalms, the Gospel parables; the story of Sakya Muni and the hymns of the Vedas, all transmit very exalted feelings and are nevertheless quite comprehensible now to us, educated or uneducated, just as they were comprehensible to the men of those times, long ago, who were even less educated than our labourers. People talk about incomprehensibility; but if art is the transmission of feelings flowing from man's religious perception, how can a feeling be incomprehensible which is founded on religion, that is, on man's relation to God? Such art should be, and has actually always been, comprehensible to everybody, because every man's relation to God is one and the same. This is why the churches and the images in them were always comprehensible to every one. The hindrance to an understanding of the best and highest feelings (as is said in the Gospel) lies not at all in deficiency of development or learning, but on the contrary in false development and false learning. A good and lofty work of art may be incomprehensible, but not to simple, unperverted, peasant labourers (what is highest is understood by them)—it may be and often is unintelligible to erudite, perverted people destitute of religion. And this continually occurs in our society in which the highest feelings are simply not understood. For instance, I know people who consider themselves most refined, and who say that they do not understand the poetry of love of one's neighbour, of self-sacrifice, or of chastity.

So that good, great, universal, religious art may be incomprehensible to a small circle of spoilt people, but certainly not to any large number of plain men.

Art cannot be incomprehensible to the great masses only because it is very good—as artists of our day are fond of telling us. Rather we are bound to conclude that this art is unintelligible to the great masses only because it is very bad art, or even is not art at all. So that the favourite argument (naïvely accepted by the cultured crowd), that in order to feel art one has first to understand it (which really only means habituate oneself to it), is the truest indication that what we are asked to understand by such a method is either very bad, exclusive art, or is not art at all.

People say that works of art do not please the people because they are incapable of understanding them. But if the aim of works of art is to infect people with the emotion the artist has experienced, how can one talk about not understanding?

A man of the people reads a book, sees a picture, hears a play or a symphony, and is touched by no feeling. He is told that this is because he cannot

understand. People promise to let a man see a certain
show; he enters and sees nothing. He is told that this
is because his sight is not prepared for this show. But
the man knows for certain that he sees quite well, and
if he does not see what people promised to show him
he only concludes (as is quite just) that those who
undertook to show him the spectacle have not fulfilled
their engagement. And it is perfectly just for a man
who does feel the influence of some works of art, to
come to this conclusion concerning artists who do not
by their works evoke feeling in him. To say that the
reason a man is not touched by my art is because he
is still too stupid, besides being very self-conceited and
also rude, is to reverse the rôles, and for the sick to
send the hale to bed.

Voltaire said that '*Tous les genres sont bons, hors le
genre ennuyeux*';[1] but with even more right one may
say of art that *Tous les genres sont bons, hors celui qu'on ne
comprend pas*, or *qui ne produit pas son effet*,[2] for of what
value is an article which fails to accomplish that for
which it was intended?

Mark this above all: if only it be admitted that art
may be unintelligible to any one of sound mind and
yet be art, there is no reason why any circle of perverted people should not compose works tickling their
own perverted feelings and comprehensible to no one
but themselves, and call it 'art,' as is actually being
done by the so-called Decadents.

The direction art has taken may be compared to
placing on a large circle other circles, smaller and
smaller, until a cone is formed, the apex of which is no
longer a circle at all. That is what has happened to
the art of our times.

[1] All styles are good except the wearisome style.
[2] All styles are good except that which is not understood, *or* which fails to produce its effect.

CHAPTER XI

Counterfeits of art produced by: Borrowing; Imitation; being Striking; Interesting. Qualifications needful for the production of real works of art, and those sufficient for the production of counterfeits.

BECOMING ever poorer and poorer in subject-matter and more and more unintelligible in form, the art of the upper classes in its latest productions has even lost all the characteristics of art and has been replaced by imitations of art. Not only has upper-class art in consequence of its separation from universal art become poor in subject-matter and bad in form, that is, ever more and more unintelligible—it has in course of time ceased even to be art at all, and has been replaced by counterfeits.

This has resulted from the following causes: Universal art arises only when some one of the people, having experienced a strong emotion, feels the necessity of transmitting it to others. The art of the rich classes, on the other hand, arises not from the artist's inner impulse but chiefly because people of the upper classes demand amusement and pay well for it. They demand from art the transmission of feelings that please them, and this demand artists try to meet. But it is a very difficult task, for people of the wealthy classes, spending their lives in idleness and luxury, desire to be continually diverted by art; and art, even the lowest, cannot be produced at will, but has to generate spontaneously in the artist's inner self. And therefore to satisfy the demands of people of the upper classes artists have had to devise methods of producing imitations of art. And such methods have been devised.

These methods are those of (1) borrowing, (2)

imitation, (3) striking (producing effects), and (4) interesting.

The first method consists in borrowing whole subjects, or merely separate features, from former works recognized by every one as being poetic, and in so reshaping them with sundry additions that they should have an appearance of novelty.

Such works, evoking in people of a certain class memories of artistic feelings formerly experienced, produce an impression similar to art, and provided only that they conform to other needful conditions they pass for art among those who seek for pleasure from art. Subjects borrowed from previous works of art are usually called poetic subjects. Objects and people thus borrowed are called poetic objects and people. Thus, in our circle, all sorts of legends, sagas, and ancient traditions are considered poetic subjects. Among poetic people and objects we reckon maidens, warriors, shepherds, hermits, angels, devils of all sorts, moonlight, thunder, mountains, the sea, precipices, flowers, long hair, lions, lambs, doves, and nightingales. In general all those objects are considered poetic which have most frequently been used by former artists in their productions.

Some forty years ago a stupid but highly cultured—*ayant beaucoup d'acquis*—lady (since deceased) asked me to listen to a novel she had written. It began with a heroine who, in a poetic white dress and with poetically flowing hair, was reading poetry near some water in a poetic wood. The scene was in Russia, but suddenly from behind the bushes the hero appears, wearing a hat with a feather *à la Guillaume Tell* (the book specially mentioned this) and accompanied by two poetical white dogs. The authoress deemed all this highly poetic, and it might have passed muster if only it had not been necessary for the hero to speak. But as soon as the gentleman in the hat *à la Guillaume*

Tell began to converse with the maiden in the white dress it became obvious that the authoress had nothing to say, but had merely been moved by poetic memories of other works and imagined that by ringing the changes on those memories she could produce an artistic impression. But an artistic impression, that is to say, infection, is only received when an author has in the manner peculiar to himself experienced the feeling which he transmits, and not when he passes on another man's feeling previously transmitted to him. Such poetry from poetry cannot infect people, it can only simulate a work of art, and even that only to people of perverted æsthetic taste. The lady in question being very stupid and devoid of talent, it was at once apparent how the case stood; but when such borrowing is resorted to by people who are erudite and talented and have cultivated the technique of their art, we get those borrowings from the Greek, the antique, the Christian or mythological world, which have become so numerous, and which, particularly in our day, continue to increase and multiply and are accepted by the public as works of art if only the borrowings are well mounted by means of the technique of the particular art to which they belong.

As a characteristic example of such counterfeits of art in the realm of poetry, take Rostand's *Princesse Lointaine*, in which there is not a spark of art, but which seems very poetic to many people, and probably also to its author.

The second method of imparting a semblance of art is that which I have called imitation. The essence of this method consists in supplying details accompanying the thing described or depicted. In literary art this method consists in describing in minutest detail the external appearance, the faces, the clothes, the gestures, the tones, and the habitations, of the characters represented, with all the occurrences met with in life. For instance in novels and stories, when one of the characters speaks we are told in what voice he spoke and what he was doing at the time. And the things said are not given so that they should have as much sense as possible, but as they are in life, disconnectedly and with interruptions and omissions. In dramatic art, besides such imitation of real speech, this method consists in having all the accessories and all the people just like those in real life. In painting, this method assimilates painting to photography and destroys the difference between them. And strange to say, this method is used also in music: music tries to imitate, not only by its rhythm but also by its very sounds, the sounds which in real life accompany the thing it wishes to represent.

The third method is by action, often purely physical, on the outer senses. Work of this kind is said to be 'striking' and 'effective'. In all arts these effects consist chiefly in contrasts: in bringing together the terrible and the tender, the beautiful and the hideous, the loud and the soft, darkness and light, the most ordinary and the most extraordinary. In verbal art, besides effects of contrast there are also effects consisting in the description of things that have never before been described. These are usually pornographic details evoking sexual desire, or details of suffering and death evoking feelings of horror, such, for instance, as when describing a murder, to give a detailed medical account of the lacerated tissues, of the swellings, of the smell, quantity, and appearance, of the blood. It is the same in painting: besides all kinds of other contrasts one is coming into vogue which consists in giving careful finish to one object and being careless about all the rest. The chief and usual effects in painting are effects of light and the presentation of the horrible. In the drama the most common effects, besides contrasts, are tempests, thunder, moonlight, scenes at sea or by the sea-shore, changes of costume, exposure of the female body, madness, murder, and death generally: the dying person exhibiting in detail all the phases of agony. In music the most usual effects are a *crescendo* passing from the softest and simplest sounds to the loudest and most complex crash of the full orchestra; a repetition of the same sounds *arpeggio* in all the octaves and on various instruments; or for the harmony, tone, and rhythm, to be not at all those naturally flowing from the course of the musical thought, but such as strike one by their unexpectedness. Besides these, the commonest effects in music are produced in a purely physical manner by strength of sound, especially in an orchestra.

Such are some of the most usual effects in the various arts, but there yet remains one common to them all, namely, to convey by means of one art what it would be natural to convey by another: for instance, to make music describe (as is done by the programme music of Wagner and his followers), or to make painting, the drama, or poetry, induce a frame of mind (as is aimed at by all the Decadent art).

The fourth method is that of interesting (that is, occupying the mind) in connexion with works of art. The interest may lie in an intricate plot—a method till quite recently much employed in English novels and French plays—but now going out of fashion and being replaced by realism, that is, by detailed description of some historic period or some branch of contemporary life. For example in a novel, the interest may consist in a description of Egyptian or Roman life, the life of miners, or that of the clerks in a big shop. The reader becomes interested, and mistakes this interest for an artistic impression. The interest may also depend on the very method of expression—a kind of interest that has now come much into use. Both verse and prose, as well as pictures, plays, and music, are constructed so that they must be guessed like riddles, and this process of guessing, again, affords pleasure and gives a semblance of the feeling received from art.

It is often said that a work of art is very good because it is poetic, or realistic, or striking, or interesting; whereas not only can neither the first, nor the second, nor the third, nor the fourth, of these attributes supply a standard of excellence in art, but they have not even anything in common with art.

Poetic—means borrowed. All borrowing merely recalls to the reader, spectator, or listener, some dim recollection of artistic impressions received from previous works of art and does not infect with feeling experienced by the artist himself. A work founded on something borrowed, like Goethe's *Faust* for instance, may be very well executed and be full of mind and every beauty, but because it lacks the chief characteristic of a work of art—completeness, oneness, the inseparable unity of form and content expressing the feeling the artist has experienced—it cannot produce a really artistic impression. In availing himself of this method the artist only transmits the feeling received by him from a previous work of art; therefore every borrowing, whether it be of whole subjects or of various scenes, situations, or descriptions, is but a reflection of art, a simulation of it, but is not art itself. And therefore, to say that a certain production is good because it is poetic—that is, resembles a work of art —is like saying of a coin that it is good because it resembles real money.

Equally little can imitation, realism, serve, as many people suppose, as a measure of the quality of art. Imitation cannot be such a measure, for the chief characteristic of art is the infection of others with the feelings the artist has experienced, and infection with a feeling is not only not identical with description of the accessories of what is transmitted, but is usually hindered by superfluous details. The attention of the receiver of the artistic impression is diverted by all these well-observed details, and they hinder the transmission of feeling even when the feeling exists.

To value a work of art by the degree of its realism, by the accuracy of the details reproduced, is as strange as to judge of the nutritive quality of food by its external appearance. When we appraise a work according to its realism we only show that we are talking not of a work of art but of its counterfeit.

Neither does the third method of imitating art—by the use of what is striking or effective—coincide with real art any better than the two former methods, for in effectiveness (the effects of novelty, of the unexpected, of contrasts, of the horrible) there is no transmission of feeling but only an action on the nerves. If an artist were to paint a bloody wound admirably, the sight of the wound would strike me, but it would not be art. One prolonged note on a powerful organ will produce a striking impression, will often even cause tears, but there is no music in it, because no feeling is transmitted. Yet such physiological effects are constantly mistaken for art by people of our circle, and this not only in music but also in poetry, painting, and the drama. It is said that art has become refined. On the contrary, thanks to the pursuit of effects, it has become very coarse. A new piece is brought out and accepted all over Europe, such, for instance, as *Hanneles Himmelfahrt*,[1] in which play the author wishes to transmit to the spectators pity for a persecuted girl. To evoke this feeling in the audience by means of art, the author should either make one of the characters express this pity in such a way as to infect every one, or should describe the girl's feelings correctly. But he cannot or will not do this, and chooses another way,

[1] By G. Hauptmann.

more complicated in stage management but easier for the author. He makes the girl die on the stage; and still further to increase the physiological effect on the spectators, he extinguishes the lights in the theatre, leaving the audience in the dark, and to the sound of dismal music shows how the girl is pursued and beaten by her drunken father. The girl shrinks—screams—groans—and falls. Angels appear and carry her away. And the audience, experiencing some excitement while this is going on, are fully convinced that this is true æsthetic feeling. But there is nothing æsthetic in such excitement, for there is no infection of man by man, but only a mingled feeling of pity for another and of self-congratulation that it is not I who am suffering: it is like what we feel at the sight of an execution, or what the Romans felt in their circuses.

The substitution of effect for æsthetic feeling is particularly noticeable in musical art—that art which by its nature has an immediate physiological action on the nerves. Instead of transmitting by means of a melody the feelings he has experienced, a composer of the new school accumulates and complicates sounds, and by now strengthening, now weakening them, he produces on the audience a physiological effect of a kind that can be measured by an apparatus invented for that purpose.[1] And the public mistake this physiological effect for the effect of art.

As to the fourth method—that of interesting—it also is frequently confounded with art. One often hears it said, not only of a poem, a novel, or a picture, but even of a musical work, that it is interesting. What does this mean? To speak of an interesting work of art means either that we receive from a work of art

---

[1] An apparatus exists by means of which a very sensitive arrow, in dependence on the tension of a muscle of the arm, will indicate the physiological action of music on the nerves and muscles.—L. T.

information new to us, or that the work is not fully intelligible and that little by little, and with effort, we arrive at its meaning and experience a certain pleasure in the process of guessing it. In neither case has the interest anything in common with artistic impression. Art aims at infecting people with feeling experienced by the artist. But the mental effort necessary to enable the spectator, listener, or reader, to assimilate the new information contained in the work, or to guess the puzzles propounded, hinders this infection by distracting him. And therefore the interest of a work not only has nothing to do with its excellence as a work of art, but rather hinders than assists artistic impression.

We may in a work of art meet with what is poetic, and realistic, and striking, and interesting, but these things cannot replace the essential of art—feeling experienced by the artist. Latterly in upper-class art most of the objects given out as being works of art are of the kind which only resemble art and are devoid of its essential quality—feeling experienced by the artist. And for the diversion of the rich such objects are continually being produced in enormous quantities by the artisans of art.

Many conditions must be fulfilled to enable a man to produce a real work of art. It is necessary that he should stand on the level of the highest life-conception of his time, that he should experience feeling, and have desire and capacity to transmit it, and that he should moreover have a talent for some one of the forms of art. It is very seldom that all these conditions necessary for the production of true art are combined. But in order to produce unceasingly—aided by the customary methods of borrowing, imitating, introducing effects, and interesting—counterfeits of art which pass for art in our society and are well paid for, it is only necessary to have a talent for some branch of art, and this is very often to be met with. By talent I mean ability: in literary art the ability to express one's thoughts and impressions easily and to notice and remember characteristic details; in graphic arts to distinguish and remember lines, forms, and colours; in music to distinguish the intervals and to remember and transmit the sequence of sounds. And a man in our time, if only he possesses such a talent and selects some speciality, may, after learning the methods of counterfeiting used in his branch of art—if he has patience and if his æsthetic feeling (which would render such productions revolting to him) be atrophied—turn out unceasingly to the end of his life works which will pass for art in our society.

To produce such counterfeits, definite rules or recipes exist in each branch of art. So the talented man having assimilated them, may produce such works à froid, cold-drawn, without feeling.

In order to write poems a man of literary talent needs only these qualifications: to acquire the knack, conformably with the requirements of rhyme and rhythm, of using instead of the one really suitable word ten others meaning approximately the same; to learn how to take any phrase which to be clear has but one natural order of words, and despite all possible dislocations still to retain some sense in it; and lastly, to be able to devise, guided by the words required for the rhymes, some semblance of thoughts, feelings, or descriptions, to suit these words. Having acquired these qualifications he may unceasingly produce poems—short or long, religious, amatory, or patriotic, according to the demand.

If a man of literary talent wishes to write a story or novel he need only form his style—that is, learn how to describe all that he sees—and accustom himself to remember or note down details. When he has accustomed himself to this he can, according to his inclination or the demand, unceasingly produce novels or stories—historical, naturalistic, social, erotic, psychological, or even religious, for which latter kind a demand and fashion begins to show itself. He can take subjects from books or from the events of life, and can copy the characters of the people in his book from his acquaintances.

And such novels and stories, if only they are decked out with well-observed and carefully noted details, preferably erotic ones, will be considered works of art even though they may not contain a spark of feeling experienced.

To produce art in dramatic form a talented man, in addition to all that is required for novels and stories, must also learn to furnish his characters with as many smart and witty sentences as possible, must know how to utilize theatrical effects, and how to entwine the action of his characters so that there shall be no long conversations, but as much bustle and movement on the stage as possible. If the writer is able to do this, he may produce dramatic works one after another without stopping, selecting his subjects from the reports of the law courts, or from the latest society topic, such as hypnotism, heredity, etc., or from deep antiquity, or even from the realms of fancy.

In the sphere of painting and sculpture it is still easier for the talented man to produce imitations of art. He need only learn to draw, paint, and model—especially naked bodies. Thus equipped he can continue to paint pictures, or model statues, one after another, choosing subjects according to his bent: mythological, or religious, or fantastic, or symbolic; or he may depict what is written about in the papers: a coronation, a strike, the Turko-Grecian war, famine scenes; or commonest of all he may just copy anything he thinks beautiful—from naked women to copper basins.

For the production of musical art the talented man needs still less of what constitutes the essence of art, that is, feeling wherewith to infect others, but on the other hand he requires more physical, gymnastic labour than for any other art, unless it be dancing. To produce works of musical art he must first learn to move his fingers on some instrument as rapidly as those who have reached the highest perfection; next he must know how in former times polyphonic music was written, must study what are called counterpoint and fugue; and, furthermore, he must learn orchestration, that is, how to utilize the effects of the instruments. But once he has learned all this, the composer may unceasingly produce one work after another: whether programme-music, opera, or song (devising sounds more or less corresponding to the words), or chamber music, that is, he may take another man's themes and work them up into definite forms by means of counterpoint and fugue; or, what is commonest of all, he may compose fantastic music, that is, he may take a conjunction of sounds which happens to come to hand and pile every sort of complication and ornamentation on to this chance combination.

Thus in all realms of art counterfeits of art are manufactured to a ready-made, pre-arranged recipe, and these counterfeits the public of our upper classes accepts for real art.

And this substitution of counterfeits for real works of art was the third and most important consequence of the separation of the art of the upper classes from universal art.

CHAPTER XII

Causes of production of counterfeits. Professionalism. Criticism. Schools of art. Perfection of form necessary to produce the infection which characterizes a true work of art.

IN our society three conditions co-öperate to cause the production of objects of counterfeit art. They are (1) the considerable remuneration of artists for their productions and the professionalism which this has produced among artists, (2) art criticism, and (3) schools of art.

While art was as yet undivided, and only religious art was valued and rewarded while indiscriminate art was left unrewarded, there were no counterfeits of art or, if any existed, being exposed to the criticism of the whole people they quickly disappeared. But as soon as that division occurred and the upper classes acclaimed every kind of art as good if only it afforded them pleasure, and began to reward such art more highly than any other social activity, a large number of people immediately devoted themselves to this activity, and art assumed quite a different character and became a profession.

And as soon as this occurred the chief and most precious quality of art—its sincerity—was at once greatly weakened and eventually quite destroyed.

The professional artist lives by his art and has continually to invent subjects for his works, and does invent them. And it is obvious how great a difference must exist between works of art produced on the one hand by men such as the Jewish prophets, the authors of the Psalms, Francis of Assisi, the authors of the *Iliad* and *Odyssey*, of folk-stories, legends, and folk-songs, many of whom not only received no remuneration for their work but did not even attach their names to it, and on the other hand works produced by court poets, dramatists, and musicians receiving honours and remuneration, and later on by professional artists who lived by the trade, receiving remuneration from newspaper editors, publishers, impresarios, and in general from the agents who come between the artists and the consumers of art.

Professionalism is the first condition of the diffusion of false, counterfeit art.

The second condition is the growth in recent times of art-criticism, that is, the valuation of art not by everybody, and above all not by plain men, but by erudite, that is, by perverted and at the same time self-confident, individuals.

A friend of mine, speaking of the relation of critics to artists, half-jokingly defined it thus: 'Critics are the stupid who discuss the wise.' However partial, inexact, and rude, this definition may be, it is yet partly true, and incomparably more just than the definition which considers critics to be men who can explain works of art.

'Critics explain!' What do they explain?

The artist, if a real artist, has by his work transmitted to others the feeling he experienced. What is there, then, to explain?

If a work is a good work of art, then the feeling expressed by the artist—be it moral or immoral—transmits itself to other people. If it is transmitted to others, then they feel it, and all interpretations are superfluous. If the work does not infect people, no explanation can make it contagious. An artist's work cannot be interpreted. Had it been possible to *explain* in words what he wished to convey, the artist would have expressed himself in words. He expressed it by his art, only because the feeling he experienced could not be otherwise transmitted. The interpretation of works of art by words only indicates that the interpreter is himself incapable of feeling the infection of art. And this is actually the case, for, however strange it may seem to say so, critics have always been people less susceptible than other men to the contagion of art. For the most part they are able writers, educated and clever, but with their capacity for being infected by art quite perverted or atrophied. And therefore their writings have always largely contributed, and still contribute, to the perversion of the taste of that public which reads them and trusts them.

Art criticism did not exist—could not and cannot exist—in societies where art is undivided, and where consequently it is appraised by the religious conception of life common to the whole people. Art criticism grew, and could grow, only on the art of the upper classes who did not acknowledge the religious perception of their time.

Universal art has a definite and indubitable internal criterion—religious perception; upper-class art lacks this, and therefore the appreciators of that art are obliged to cling to some external criterion. And they find it in 'the judgments of the finest-nurtured,' as an English æsthetician has phrased it, that is, in the authority of the people who are considered educated; nor in this alone, but also in a tradition of such authorities. This tradition is extremely misleading, both because the opinions of 'the finest-nurtured' are often mistaken, and also because judgments which were valid once cease to be so with the lapse of time. But the critics, having no basis for their judgments, never cease to repeat their traditions. The classical tragedians were once considered good, and therefore criticism considers them to be so still. Dante was esteemed a great poet, Raphael a great painter, Bach a great musician—and the critics, lacking a standard by which to separate good art from bad, not only

consider these artists great, but regard all their productions as admirable and worthy of imitation.
Nothing has contributed, and still contributes, so
much to the perversion of art as these authorities set
up by criticism. A man produces a work of art expressing in his own peculiar manner, like every true
artist, a feeling he has experienced. Most people are
infected by the artist's feeling and his work becomes
known. Then criticism, discussing the artist, says that
the work is not bad, but all the same the artist is not
a Dante, nor a Shakespeare, nor a Goethe, nor a
Raphael, nor what Beethoven was in his last period.
And the young artist sets to work to copy those held
up for his imitation, and he produces not only feeble
works but false works, counterfeits of art.

Thus, for instance, our Púshkin writes his short
poems, *Evgéni Onégin*, *The Gipsies*, and his stories—
works varying in quality, but all true art. But then,
under the influence of false criticism extolling Shakespeare, he writes *Borís Godunóv*, a cold, brain-spun
work, and this production is lauded by the critics, set
up as a model, and imitations of it appear: *Mínin* by
Ostróvski, and *Tsar Borís* by Alexéy Tolstóy, and such
imitations of imitations as crowd all literatures with
insignificant productions. The chief harm done by
the critics is this, that themselves lacking the capacity
to be infected by art (and that is the characteristic of
all critics, for did they not lack this they could not
attempt the impossible—the interpretation of works
of art), they pay most attention to, and eulogize, brain-
spun, invented works, and set these up as models
worthy of imitation. That is the reason they so confidently extol, in literature, the Greek tragedians,
Dante, Tasso, Milton, Shakespeare, Goethe (almost
all he wrote), and among recent writers Zola and
Ibsen; in music, Beethoven's last period, and Wagner.
To justify their praise of these brain-spun, invented

works, they devise entire theories (of which the famous theory of beauty is one); and not only dull but also talented people compose works in strict deference to these theories, and often even real artists, doing violence to their genius, submit to them.

Every false work extolled by the critics serves as a door through which the hypocrites of art at once crowd in.

It is solely due to the critics who in our times still praise rude, savage, and, for us, often meaningless works of the ancient Greeks: Sophocles, Euripides, Æschylus, and especially Aristophanes; or, of modern writers, Dante, Tasso, Milton, Shakespeare; in painting, all of Raphael, all of Michaelangelo including his absurd 'Last Judgment'; in music, the whole of Bach, and the whole of Beethoven, including his last period,—thanks only to them, have the Ibsens, Maeterlincks, Verlaines, Mallarmés, Puvis de Chavannes, Klingers, Böcklins, Stucks, Schneiders; in music, the Wagners, Liszts, Berliozes, Brahmses, and Richard Strausses, etc., and all that immense mass of good-for-nothing imitators of these imitators, become possible in our day.

As a good illustration of the harmful influence of criticism, take its relation to Beethoven. Among his innumerable hasty productions written to order, there are, notwithstanding their artificiality of form, works of true art. But he grows deaf, cannot hear, and begins to write invented, unfinished works which are consequently often meaningless and musically unintelligible. I know that musicians can imagine sounds vividly enough and can almost hear what they read, but imaginary sounds can never be the same as real ones and every composer must hear his production in order to perfect it. Beethoven however could not hear, could not perfect his work, and consequently published productions which are artistic ravings. But criticism, having once acknowledged him to be a great composer, seizes on just these abnormal works with special gusto and searches for extraordinary beauties in them. And to justify its praises (perverting the very meaning of musical art) it attributed to music the property of describing what it cannot describe. And imitators appear—an innumerable host of imitators of these abnormal attempts at artistic productions which Beethoven wrote when he was deaf.

Then Wagner appears, who at first in critical articles praises just Beethoven's last period, connecting this music with Schopenhauer's mystical theory that music is the expression of Will—not of separate manifestations of will objectivised on various planes, but of its very essence—which is in itself as absurd as this music of Beethoven. And afterwards he composes music of his own on this theory, in conjunction with another still more erroneous system of the union of all the arts. After Wagner yet new imitators appear, diverging yet farther from art: Brahms, Richard Strauss, and others.

Such are the results of criticism. But the third condition of the perversion of art, namely, art schools, is almost more harmful still.

As soon as art became not art for the whole people but for a rich class, it became a profession; as soon as it became a profession, methods were devised to teach it; people who chose this profession of art began to learn these methods, and thus professional schools sprang up: classes of rhetoric or literature in the public schools, academies for painting, conservatoires for music, schools for dramatic art.

In these schools art is taught! But art is the transmission to others of a special feeling experienced by the artist. How can this be taught in schools?

No school can evoke feeling in a man, and still less can it teach him how to manifest it in the one particular manner natural to him alone. But the essence of art lies in these things.

The one thing these schools can teach is how to transmit feelings experienced by other artists in the way those other artists transmitted them. And this is just what the professional schools do teach; and such instruction not only does not assist the spread of true art but on the contrary by diffusing counterfeits of art does more than anything else to deprive people of the capacity to understand true art.

In literary art people are taught how to write a many-paged composition, without having anything they wish to say, on a theme about which they have never thought, and moreover to write it so that it should resemble the work of an author admitted to be celebrated. This is taught in schools.

In painting the chief training consists in learning to draw and paint from copies and models, principally the naked body (the very thing that is never seen and which a man occupied with real art hardly ever has to depict), and to draw and paint as former masters drew and painted. The composition of pictures is taught by giving out themes similar to those which have been treated by former acknowledged celebrities.

So also in dramatic schools—the pupils are taught to recite monologues just as tragedians considered celebrated declaimed them.

It is the same in music. The whole theory of music is nothing but a disconnected repetition of those methods which the acknowledged masters of composition made use of.

I have elsewhere quoted the profound remark of the Russian artist Bryulóv on art, but I cannot here refrain from repeating it, because nothing better illustrates what can, and what can not, be taught in the schools. Once when correcting a pupil's study, Bryulóv just touched it in a few places and the poor dead study immediately became animated. 'Why, you only touched it a *wee bit*, and it is quite another thing!' said one of the pupils. 'Art begins where the *wee bit* begins,' replied Bryulóv, indicating by these words just what is most characteristic of art. The remark is true of all the arts, but its justice is particularly noticeable in the performance of music. That musical execution should be artistic, should be art, that is, should carry infection, three chief conditions must be observed. There are many others needed for musical perfection: the transition from one sound to another must be interrupted or continuous; the sound must increase or diminish steadily; it must be blended with one and not with another sound; the sound must have this or that timbre, and much besides,—but take the three chief conditions: the pitch, the time, and the strength of the sound. Musical execution is only then art, only then infects, when the sound is neither higher nor lower than it should be, that is, when exactly the infinitely small centre of the required note is taken; when that note is continued exactly as long as is needed; and when the strength of the sound is neither more nor less than is required. The slightest deviation of pitch in either direction, the slightest increase or decrease in time, or the slightest strengthening or weakening of the sound beyond what is needed, destroys the perfection and consequently the infectiousness of the work. So that the feeling of infection by the art of music, which seems so simple and so easily obtained, is a thing we receive only when the performer finds those infinitely minute degrees which are necessary to perfection in music. It is the same in all arts: a wee bit lighter, a wee bit darker, a wee bit higher, lower, to the right or the left—in painting; a wee bit weaker or stronger in intonation, a wee bit sooner or later—in dramatic art; a wee bit omitted, over-emphasised, or exaggerated—in poetry, and there is no contagion. Infection is only obtained when an artist finds those infinitely minute degrees of which a work of art consists, and only to the extent to which he finds them. And it is quite impossible to teach people by external means to find these minute degrees: they can only be found when a man yields to his feeling. No instruction can make a dancer catch just the time of the music, or a singer or a fiddler take exactly the infinitely minute centre of his note, or a sketcher draw of all possible lines the only right one, or a poet find the only right arrangement of the only suitable words. All this is found only by feeling. And therefore schools may teach what is necessary in order to produce something resembling art, but not art itself.

The teaching of the schools stops where the *wee bit* begins—consequently where art begins.

Accustoming people to something resembling art disaccustoms them to the comprehension of real art. And that is how it comes about that none are more dull to art than those who have passed through the professional schools and been most successful in them. Professional schools produce an hypocrisy of art precisely akin to that hypocrisy of religion which is produced by theological colleges for training priests, pastors, and religious teachers generally. As it is impossible in a school to train a man so as to make a religious teacher of him, so it is impossible to teach a man how to become an artist.

Art schools are thus doubly destructive of art: first, in that they destroy the capacity to produce real art in those who have the misfortune to enter them and go through a seven or eight years' course; and secondly, in that they generate enormous quantities of that counterfeit art which perverts the taste of the masses and overflows our world. In order that born artists may know the methods of the various arts elaborated by former artists, there should exist in all elementary schools such classes for drawing and music (singing) that, after passing through them, every talented scholar may, by using existing models accessible to all, be able to perfect himself in his art independently.

These three conditions—the professionalization of artists, art criticism, and art schools—have had this effect: that most people in our times are quite unable even to understand what is art, and accept as art the grossest counterfeits of it.

CHAPTER XIII

Wagner's 'Nibelungen Ring' a type of counterfeit art. Its success and the reasons thereof.

TO what an extent people of our circle and time have lost the capacity to receive real art and have become accustomed to accept as art things that have nothing in common with it, is best seen from the works of Richard Wagner, which have latterly come to be more and more esteemed not only by the Germans, but also by the French and the English, as the very highest art revealing new horizons to us.

The peculiarity of Wagner's music, as is known, consists in this, that he considered that music should serve poetry, expressing all the shades of a poetical work.

The union of the drama with music, devised in the fifteenth century in Italy for the revival of what they imagined to have been the ancient Greek music-drama, is an artificial form which had, and has, success only among the upper classes, and among them only when gifted composers such as Mozart, Weber, Rossini, and others, drawing inspiration from a dramatic subject, yielded freely to the inspiration and subordinated the text to the music, so that in their operas the important thing to the audience is merely the music on a certain text, and not the text at all, which latter even when it was utterly absurd, as for instance in the *Magic Flute*, still does not prevent the music from producing an artistic impression.

Wagner wishes to correct the opera by letting music submit to the demands of poetry and unite with it. But each art has its own definite realm which is not identical with the realm of other arts, but merely comes in contact with them; and therefore if the manifestations, I will not say of several but even of two arts —the dramatic and the musical—be united in one complete production, then the demands of the one art will make it impossible to fulfil the demands of the other, as has always occurred in the ordinary operas, where the dramatic art has submitted to, or rather yielded place to, the musical. Wagner wishes musical art to submit to dramatic art, and that both should appear in full strength. But this is impossible, for every work of art, if it be a true one, is an expression of the intimate feelings of the artist, which are quite peculiar to him and not like anything else. Such is a musical production, and such is a dramatic work, if they be true art. And therefore in order that a production in the one branch of art should coincide with a production in the other branch, it is necessary that the impossible should happen: that two works from different realms of art should be absolutely exceptional, unlike anything that existed before, and yet should coincide and be exactly alike.

And this cannot be, just as there cannot be two men, or even two leaves on a tree, exactly alike. Still less can two works from different realms of art, the musical and the literary, be absolutely alike. If they coincide, then either one is a work of art and the other a counterfeit, or both are counterfeits. Two live leaves cannot be exactly alike, but two artificial leaves may be. And so it is with works of art. They can only coincide completely when neither the one nor the other is art but both are only cunningly devised semblances of it.

If poetry and music may be joined, as occurs in hymns, songs, and *romances*—(though even in these the music does not follow the changes of each verse of the text as Wagner wishes, but the song and the music merely produce a coincident effect on the mind)—

this occurs only because lyrical poetry and music have to some extent one and the same aim: to produce a mental condition, and the conditions produced by lyrical poetry and by music can, more or less, coincide. But even in these conjunctions the centre of gravity always lies in one of the two productions, so that it is one of them that produces the artistic impression, while the other remains unregarded. And still less is it possible for such union to exist between epic or dramatic poetry and music.

Moreover one of the chief conditions of artistic creation is the complete freedom of the artist from every kind of preconceived demand. And the necessity of adjusting his musical work to a work from another realm of art is a preconceived demand of such a kind as to destroy all possibility of creative power; and therefore adjusted works of this kind are and must be (as has always happened) not works of art but only imitations of art, like the music of a melodrama, titles to pictures, illustrations to books, and librettos to operas.

And such Wagner's productions are. A confirmation of this is to be seen in the fact that Wagner's new music lacks the chief characteristic of every true work of art, namely, such entirety and completeness that the smallest alteration in its form would disturb the meaning of the whole work. In a true work of art— poem, drama, picture, song, or symphony—it is impossible to extract one line, one scene, one figure, or one bar from its place and put it in another, without infringing the significance of the whole work, just as it is impossible without infringing the life of an organic being to extract an organ from one place and insert it somewhere else. But in the music of Wagner's last period, with the exception of certain parts of little importance which have an independent musical meaning, it is possible to make all kinds of transpositions, putting what was in front behind and *vice versa*, without altering the musical sense. And the reason why these transpositions do not alter the sense of Wagner's music is because the sense lies in the words and not in the music.

The musical score of Wagner's later operas is like what would result should one of those versifiers—of whom there are now many, with tongues so broken that they can, on any theme to any rhymes in any rhythm, write verses which sound as if they had a meaning—conceive the idea of illustrating by his verses some symphony or sonata of Beethoven, or some *ballade* of Chopin, in the following manner: To the first bars of one character, he writes verses corresponding in his opinion to those first bars. Next come some bars of a different character, and he also writes verses corresponding in his opinion to them, but with no internal connexion with the first verses and moreover without rhymes and without rhythm. Such a production without the music, would be exactly parallel in poetry to what Wagner's operas are in music, if heard without the words.

But Wagner is not only a musician—he is also a poet, or both together; and therefore, to judge of Wagner one must know his poetry also—that same poetry which the music has to subserve. The chief poetical production of Wagner is the *Nibelungen Ring*. This work has attained such enormous importance in our time and has such influence on all that now professes to be art, that it is necessary for every one to-day to have some idea of it. I have carefully read through the four booklets which contain this work and have drawn up a brief summary of it, which I give in Appendix III. I would strongly advise the reader (if he has not perused the poem itself, which would be the best thing to do) at least to read my account of it, so as to have an idea of this extraordinary work. It is a model work of counterfeit art so gross as to be even ridiculous.

But we are told that it is impossible to judge of Wagner's works without seeing them on the stage. The Second Day of this drama, which as I was told is the best part of the whole work, was given in Moscow last winter and I went to see the performance.

When I arrived, the enormous theatre was already filled from top to bottom. There were Grand-Dukes, and the flower of the aristocracy, of the merchant class, of the learned, and of the middle-class official public. Most of them held the libretto, fathoming its meaning. Musicians—some of them elderly, grey-haired men—followed the music score in hand. Evidently the performance of this work was an event of importance.

I was rather late, but I was told that the short prelude with which the act begins was of slight importance and that it did not matter having missed it. When I arrived, an actor sat on the stage amid decorations intended to represent a cave and before something which was meant to represent a smith's forge. He was dressed in tricot tights, with a cloak of skins, wore a wig and an artificial beard, and with white, weak, genteel hands (his easy movements and especially the shape of his stomach and his lack of muscle revealed the actor) beat an impossible sword with an unnatural hammer in a way in which no one ever uses a hammer; and at the same time, opening his mouth in a strange way, he sang something incomprehensible. The music of various instruments accompanied the strange sounds which he emitted. From the libretto one was able to gather that the actor had to represent a powerful dwarf who lived in the cave, and who was forging a sword for Siegfried, whom he had reared. One could tell he was a dwarf by the fact that the actor walked all the time bending the knees of his tricot-covered legs. This dwarf, still opening his mouth in the same strange way, long continued to sing or shout. The music meanwhile runs over something strange, like beginnings which are not continued and never get finished. From the libretto one could learn that the dwarf is telling himself about a ring a giant had obtained, and which the dwarf wishes to procure through Siegfried's aid, while Siegfried wants a good sword, on the forging of which the dwarf is occupied. After this conversation or singing to himself has gone on rather a long time, other sounds are heard in the orchestra, also like something beginning and not finishing, and another actor appears with a horn slung over his shoulder and accompanied by a man running on all fours dressed up as a bear, whom he sets at the smith-dwarf. The latter runs away without unbending the knees of his tricot-covered legs. This actor with the horn represented the hero, Siegfried. The sounds which were emitted in the orchestra on the entrance of this actor were intended to represent Siegfried's character and are called Siegfried's *leit-motiv*. And these sounds are repeated each time Siegfried appears. There is one fixed combination of sounds, or *leit-motiv*, for each character, and this *leit-motiv* is repeated every time the person whom it represents appears; and when any one is mentioned the *motiv* is heard which relates to that person. Moreover each article also has its own *leit-motiv* or chord. There is a *motiv* of the ring, a *motiv* of the helmet, a *motiv* of the apple, a *motiv* of fire, spear, sword, water, etc.; and as soon as the ring, helmet, or apple is mentioned, the *motiv* or chord of the ring, helmet, or apple, is heard. The actor with the horn opens his mouth as unnaturally as the dwarf, and long continues in a chanting voice to shout some words, and in a similar chant Mime (that is the dwarf's name) makes some reply to him. The meaning of this conversation can only be discovered from the libretto; and it is, that Siegfried was brought up by the dwarf and therefore, for some reason, hates him and always wishes to kill him. The dwarf has forged a sword for Siegfried, but Siegfried is dissatisfied with it. From a ten-page conversation (by the libretto), lasting half-an-hour and conducted with the same strange openings of the mouth and chantings, it appears that Siegfried's mother gave birth to him in the wood, and that concerning his father all that is known is that he had a sword which was broken, the pieces of which are in Mime's possession, and that Siegfried does not know fear and wishes to go out of the wood. Mime however does not want to let him go. During the conversation the music never omits, at the mention of father, sword, etc., to sound the *motiv* of these people and things. After these conversations fresh sounds are heard—those of the god Wotan—and a wanderer appears. This wanderer is the god Wotan. Also dressed up in a wig and also in tights, this god Wotan, standing in a stupid pose with a spear, thinks proper to recount what Mime must have known before, but what it is necessary to tell the audience. He does not tell it simply, but in the form of riddles which he orders himself to guess, staking his head (one does not know why) that he will guess right. Moreover, whenever the wanderer strikes his spear on the ground, fire comes out of the ground and in the orchestra the sounds of spear and of fire are heard. The orchestra accompanies the conversation, and the *motivs* of the people and things spoken of are always artfully intermingled. Besides this, the music expresses feelings in the most naïve manner: the terrible by sounds in the bass, the frivolous by rapid touches in the treble, and so forth.

The riddles have no meaning except to tell the audience what the *nibelungs* are, what the giants are, what the gods are, and what has happened before. This conversation also is chanted with strangely opened mouths, and continues for eight libretto pages and a correspondingly long time on the stage. After this the wanderer departs and Siegfried returns and talks with Mime for thirteen pages more. There is not a single melody the whole this time, but merely intertwinings of the *leit-motivs* of the people and things mentioned. The conversation shows that Mime wishes to teach Siegfried fear and that Siegfried does not know what fear is. Having finished this conversation, Siegfried seizes one of the pieces of what is meant to represent the broken sword, saws it up, puts it on what is meant to represent the forge, melts it, and then forges it and sings: 'Heiho! heiho! heiho! Ho! ho! Aha! oho! aha! Heiaho! heiaho! heiaho! Ho! ho! Hahei! hoho! hahei!' and Act I finishes.

Upon the question I had come to the theatre to decide, my mind was fully made up, as surely as on the question of the merits of my lady acquaintance's novel when she read me the scene between the loose-haired maiden in the white dress and the hero with two white dogs and a hat with a feather *à la Guillaume Tell*.

From an author who could compose such spurious scenes, outraging all æsthetic feeling, as those which I had witnessed, there was nothing to be hoped; it may safely be decided that all that such an author can write will be bad, because he evidently does not know what a true work of art is. I wished to leave, but the friends I was with asked me to remain, declaring that one could not form an opinion by that one act and that the second would be better. So I stopped for the second act.

Act II, night. Afterwards dawn. In general the whole piece is crammed with lights, clouds, moonlight, darkness, magic fires, thunder, etc.

The scene represents a wood and in the wood there

is a cave. At the entrance to the cave sits a fourth actor in tights, representing another dwarf. Dawn appears. Enter the god Wotan, again with a spear and again in the guise of a wanderer. Again his sounds, together with fresh sounds of the deepest bass that can be produced. These latter indicate that the dragon is speaking. Wotan awakens the dragon. The same bass sounds are repeated, growing yet deeper and deeper. First the dragon says, 'I want to sleep,' but afterwards he crawls out of the cave. The dragon is represented by two men: it is dressed in a green scaly skin, and waves a tail at one end while at the other it opens a kind of crocodile's jaw that is fastened on and from which flames appear. The dragon (who is meant to be dreadful and may seem so to five-year-old children) utters some words in a terribly bass voice. This is all so stupid, so like what is done in a booth at a fair, that it is surprising that people over seven years of age can witness it seriously; yet thousands of quasi-cultured people sit and attentively hear and see it, and are delighted.

Siegfried with his horn reappears, as does Mime also. In the orchestra the sounds denoting them are emitted, and they talk about whether Siegfried does or does not know fear. Mime goes away and a scene commences which is intended to be most poetic. Siegfried, in his tights, lies down in a would-be beautiful pose and alternately keeps silent and talks to himself. He ponders, listens to the singing of birds, and desires to imitate them. For this purpose he cuts a reed with his sword and makes a pipe. The dawn grows brighter and brighter; and birds sing. Siegfried tries to imitate the birds. In the orchestra is heard the imitation of birds, alternating with sounds corresponding to the words he speaks. But Siegfried does not succeed with his pipeplaying, so he plays on his horn instead. This scene is unendurable. Of music,

that is, of art serving as a means to transmit a state
of mind experienced by the author, there is not even
a suggestion. There is something that is absolutely
unintelligible musically. In a musical sense a hope
continually arises followed by disappointment, as if a
musical thought were commenced only to be broken
off. If there are something like musical beginnings,
these beginnings are so short, so encumbered with
complications of harmony and orchestration and with
effects of contrast, are so obscure and unfinished,
and what is happening on the stage meanwhile is so
abominably false, that it is difficult even to perceive
these musical snatches, let alone to be infected by
them. Above all, from the very beginning to the very
end and in each note, the author's purpose is so audible
and visible that one sees and hears neither Siegfried
nor the birds, but only a limited self-opinionated German of bad taste and bad style, who has a most false
conception of poetry and in the rudest and most primitive manner wishes to transmit to one these false and
mistaken conceptions of his.

Every one knows the feeling of distrust and resistance
always evoked by an author's evident predetermina-
tion. A narrator need only say in advance, 'Prepare
to cry,' or 'to laugh,' and you are sure neither to cry
nor to laugh. But when you see that an author pre-
scribes emotion at what is not touching, but only
laughable or disgusting, and when you see moreover
that the author is fully assured that he has captivated
you, a painfully tormenting feeling results, similar to
what you would feel if an old, deformed woman put
on a ball-dress and smilingly coquetted before you
confident of your approbation. This impression was
strengthened by the fact that around me I saw a
crowd of three thousand people, who not only patiently
witnessed all this absurd nonsense but even considered
it their duty to be delighted with it.

I somehow managed to sit out the next scene also, in which the monster appears to the accompaniment of his bass notes intermingled with the *motiv* of Siegfried; but after the fight with the monster, and all the roars, fires, and sword-wavings, I could stand no more of it and escaped from the theatre with a feeling of repulsion which even now I cannot forget.

Listening to this opera I involuntarily thought of a respected, wise, educated, country labourer—one, for instance, of the wise and truly religious men whom I know among the peasants—and I pictured to myself the terrible perplexity such a man would be in were he to witness what I was seeing that evening.

What would he think if he knew of all the labour spent on such a performance, and saw that audience, those great ones of the earth—old, bald-headed, grey-bearded men, whom he had been accustomed to respect—sitting silent and attentive, listening to and looking at all these stupidities for five hours on end? Not to speak of an adult labourer, one can hardly imagine even a child of over seven occupying himself with such a stupid, incoherent, fairy tale.

And yet an enormous audience, the cream of the cultured upper classes, sits out five hours of this insane performance, and goes away imagining that by paying tribute to this nonsense it has acquired a fresh right to esteem itself advanced and enlightened.

I speak of the Moscow public. But what is the Moscow public? It is but a hundredth part of that public which, while considering itself most highly enlightened, esteems it a merit so to have lost the capacity of being infected by art that not only can it witness this stupid sham without being revolted, but can even take delight in it.

In Bayreuth, where these performances were first given, people who considered themselves finely cultured assembled from the ends of the earth, spent, say, £100 each to see this performance, and for four days running went to see and hear this nonsensical rubbish, sitting it out for six hours each day.

But why did people go, and why do they still go, to these performances, and why do they admire them? The question naturally presents itself: How is the success of Wagner's works to be explained?

That success I explain to myself in this way: thanks to his exceptional position in having at his disposal the resources of a king, Wagner was able to command all the methods for counterfeiting art which have been developed by long usage, and employing these methods with great ability he produced a model work of counterfeit art. The reason why I have selected his work for my illustration is that in no other counterfeit of art known to me are all the methods by which art is counterfeited—viz., borrowing, imitations, dramatic effects, and interest—so ably and powerfully united.

From the subject borrowed from antiquity, to the clouds and the risings of the sun and moon, Wagner in this work has made use of all that is considered poetic. We have here the sleeping beauty, and nymphs, and subterranean fires, and dwarfs, and battles, and swords, and love, and incest, and a monster, and singing-birds: the whole arsenal of the poetic is brought into action.

Moreover everything is imitative: the decorations are imitated and the costumes are imitated. All is just as it would have been, according to the data supplied by archæology, in antiquity. The very sounds are imitative, for Wagner, who was not destitute of musical talent, invented just such sounds as imitate the strokes of a hammer, the hissing of molten iron, the singing of birds, etc.

Furthermore in this work everything is in the highest degree striking in its effects and its peculiarities: its monsters, its magic fires, and its scenes under water; the darkness in which the audience sit,

the invisibility of the orchestra, and the hitherto un-
employed combinations of harmony.

And besides, it is all interesting. The interest lies
not only in the question who will kill whom, and who
will marry whom, and who is whose son, and what
will happen next?—the interest lies also in the relation of the music to the text. The rolling waves of the
Rhine—now how is that to be expressed in music? An
evil dwarf appears—how is the music to express an
evil dwarf?—and how is it to express the sensuality
of this dwarf? How will bravery, fire, or apples, be
expressed in music? How are the *leit-motivs* of the
people speaking to be interwoven with the *leit-motivs*
of the people and objects about whom they speak?
And the music has a further interest. It diverges from
all formerly accepted laws, and most unexpected and
totally new modulations crop up (as is not only possible but even easy in music having no inner law of its
being); the dissonances are new and are allowed in a
new way—and this, too, is interesting.

And it is this poeticality, imitativeness, effectiveness,
and interestingness which, thanks to the peculiarities
of Wagner's talent and to the advantageous position
in which he was placed, are in these productions
carried to the highest pitch of perfection, which so act
on the spectator, hypnotizing him as one would be
hypnotized who listened for several consecutive hours
to maniacal ravings pronounced with great oratorical
power.

People say, 'You cannot judge without having seen
Wagner performed at Bayreuth: in the dark, where
the orchestra is out of sight, concealed under the stage,
and where the performance is brought to the highest
perfection.' And this just proves that we have here no
question of art, but one of hypnotism. It is just what
the spiritualists say. To convince you of the reality
of their apparitions they usually say, 'You cannot

judge; you must try it, be present at several séances,'
that is, come and sit silent in the dark for hours
together in the same room with semi-sane people and
repeat this some ten times over, and you shall see all
that we see.

Yes, naturally! Only place yourself in such conditions and you may see what you will. But this can be
still more quickly attained by getting drunk or smok-
ing opium. It is the same when listening to an opera
of Wagner's. Sit in the dark for four days in company
with people who are not quite normal, and through
the auditory nerves subject your brain to the strongest
action of the sounds best adapted to excite it, and you
will no doubt be reduced to an abnormal condition
and be enchanted by absurdities. But to attain this
end you do not even need four days; the five hours
during which one 'day' is enacted, as in Moscow, are
quite enough. Nor are five hours needed; even one
hour is enough for people who have no clear conception of what art should be and who have concluded
in advance that what they are going to see is excellent,
and that indifference or dissatisfaction with this work
will serve as a proof of their inferiority and lack of
culture.

I observed the audience present at this representation.
The people who led the whole audience and gave the
tone to it were those who had previously been hypnotized and who again succumbed to the hypnotic influence to which they were accustomed. These hypnotized people being in an abnormal condition were
perfectly enraptured. Moreover all the art critics, who
lack the capacity to be infected by art and therefore
always especially prize works like Wagner's opera
where it is all an affair of the intellect, also with much
profundity expressed their approval of a work affording such ample material for ratiocination. And following these two groups went that large city crowd

(indifferent to art, with their capacity to be infected by it perverted and partly atrophied), headed by the princes, millionaires, and art patrons, who like sorry harriers keep close to those who most loudly and decidedly express their opinion.

'Oh yes, certainly! What poetry! Marvellous! Especially the birds!' 'Yes, yes! I am quite captivated', exclaim these people, repeating in various tones what they have just heard from men whose opinion appears to them authoritative.

If some people do feel insulted by the absurdity and spuriousness of the whole thing, they are timidly silent as sober men are timid and silent when surrounded by tipsy people.

And thus, thanks to the masterly skill with which it counterfeits art while having nothing in common with it, a meaningless, coarse, spurious production finds acceptance all over the world, costs millions of rubles to produce, and assists more and more to pervert the taste of people of the upper classes and their conception of art.

CHAPTER XIV

Truths fatal to preconceived views not readily recognized.
Proportion of works of art to counterfeits. Perversion of
taste, and incapacity to recognize art. Examples.

I KNOW that most men—not only those considered
clever, but even those who are very clever and capable of understanding most difficult scientific, mathe-
matical, or philosophic, problems—can seldom dis-
cern even the simplest and most obvious truth if it be
such as obliges them to admit the falsity of conclusions
they have formed, perhaps with much difficulty—
conclusions of which they are proud, which they have
taught to others, and on which they have built their
lives. And therefore I have little hope that what I
adduce as to the perversion of art and taste in our
society will be accepted or even seriously considered.
Nevertheless I must state fully the inevitable conclusion to which my investigation into the question of art
has brought me. This investigation has brought me
to the conviction that almost all that our society considers to be art, good art, and the whole of art, far from
being real and good art and the whole of art, is not
even art at all but only a counterfeit of it. This position I know will seem very strange and paradoxical,
but if we once acknowledge art to be a human activity
by means of which some people transmit their feelings
to others (and not a service of Beauty, or a manifestation of the Idea, and so forth), we shall inevitably have
to admit this further conclusion also. If it is true that
art is an activity by means of which one man having
experienced a feeling intentionally transmits it to
others, then we have inevitably to admit further that
of all that among us is termed art (the art of the upper

classes)—of all those novels, stories, dramas, comedies, pictures, sculptures, symphonies, operas, operettas, ballets, etc., which profess to be works of art, scarcely one in a hundred thousand proceeds from an emotion felt by its author, all the rest being but manufactured counterfeits of art in which borrowing, imitation, effects, and interest, replace the contagion of feeling. That the proportion of real productions of art is to the counterfeits as one to some hundreds of thousands or even more, may be seen by the following calculation: I have read somewhere that the artist painters in Paris alone number 30,000; there will probably be as many in England, as many in Germany, and as many in Russia, Italy, and the smaller states combined. So that in all there will be in Europe, say, 120,000 painters; and there are probably as many musicians and as many literary artists. If these 360,000 individuals produce three works a year each (and many of them produce ten or more), then each year yields over a million so-called works of art. How many then must have been produced in the last ten years, and how many in the whole time since upper-class art broke off from the art of the whole people? Evidently millions. Yet who of all the connoisseurs of art has received impressions from all these pseudo works of art? Not to mention the labouring classes who have no conception of these productions, even people of the upper classes cannot know one in a thousand of them all, and cannot remember those they have known. These works all appear under the guise of art, produce no impression on any one (except when they serve as pastimes for an idle crowd of rich people), and vanish utterly.

In reply to this it is usually said that without this enormous number of unsuccessful attempts we should not have the real works of art. But such reasoning is as though a baker, in reply to a reproach that his bread was bad, were to say that if it were not for the

hundreds of spoiled loaves there would not be any well-
baked ones. It is true that where there is gold there
is also much sand, but that cannot serve as a reason for
talking a lot of nonsense in order to say something wise.

We are surrounded by productions considered
artistic. Thousands of verses, thousands of poems,
thousands of novels, thousands of dramas, thousands
of pictures, thousands of musical pieces, follow one
after another. All the verses describe love, or nature,
or the author's state of mind, and in all of them
rhyme and rhythm are observed. The dramas and
comedies are all splendidly staged and are performed
by admirably trained actors. All the novels are
divided into chapters; all of them describe love, contain effective situations, and correctly describe the
details of life. All the symphonies contain *allegro*,
andante, *scherzo*, and *finale*; all consist of modulations
and chords and are played by highly-trained musicians. All the pictures, in gold frames, saliently depict
faces and sundry accessories. But among these productions in the various branches of art there is in each
branch one among hundreds of thousands not only
somewhat better than the rest, but differing from them
as a diamond differs from paste. The one is priceless,
the others not only have no value, but are worse than
valueless for they deceive and pervert taste. And yet
externally they are, to a man of perverted or atrophied artistic perception, precisely alike.

In our society the difficulty of recognizing real
works of art is further increased by the fact that the
external quality of the work in false productions is not
only no worse, but often better, than in real ones; the
counterfeit is often more effective than the real, and
its subject more interesting. How is one to discriminate? How is one to find a production in no way
distinguished in externals from hundreds of thousands
of others intentionally made precisely to imitate it?

For a country peasant of unperverted taste this is as easy as it is for an animal of unspoilt scent to follow the trace he needs among a thousand others in wood or forest. The animal unerringly finds what he needs. So also the man, if only his natural qualities have not been perverted, will without fail select from among thousands of objects the real work of art he requires— that which infects him with the feeling experienced by the artist. But it is not so with those whose taste has been perverted by their education and life. The receptive feeling of these people is atrophied, and in valuing artistic productions they must be guided by discussion and study, which discussion and study completely confuse them. So that most people in our society are quite unable to distinguish a work of art from the grossest counterfeits. People sit for whole hours in concert-rooms and theatres listening to the new composers, consider it a duty to read the novels of the famous modern novelists, and to look at pictures representing either something incomprehensible or just the very things they see much better in real life; and above all they consider it incumbent on them to be enraptured by all this, imagining it all to be art, while at the same time they will pass real works of art by, not only without attention but even with contempt, merely because in their circle these works are not included in the list of works of art.

A few days ago I was returning home from a walk feeling depressed, as sometimes happens. On nearing the house I heard the loud singing of a large choir of peasant women. They were welcoming my daughter, celebrating her return home after her marriage. In this singing, with its cries and clanging of scythes, such a definite feeling of joy, cheerfulness, and energy, was expressed, that without noticing how it infected me I continued my way towards the house in a better mood and reached home smiling and quite in good spirits.

That same evening a visitor, an admirable musician, famed for his execution of classical music and particularly of Beethoven, played us Beethoven's sonata, Opus 101. For the benefit of those who might otherwise attribute my judgment of that sonata of Beethoven to non-comprehension of it, I should mention that whatever other people understand of that sonata and of other productions of Beethoven's later period, I, being very susceptible to music, understand equally. For a long time I used to attune myself to delight in those shapeless improvizations which form the subject-matter of the works of Beethoven's later period, but I had only to consider the question of art seriously, and to compare the impression I received from Beethoven's later works, with those pleasant, clear, and strong, musical impressions which are transmitted, for instance, by the melodies of Bach (his arias), Haydn, Mozart, Chopin (when his melodies are not overloaded with complications and ornamentation), of Beethoven himself in his earlier period, and above all, with the impressions produced by folk-songs,— Italian, Norwegian, or Russian,—by the Hungarian *csárdás*, and other such simple, clear, and powerful music, for the obscure, almost unhealthy, excitement from Beethoven's later pieces, which I had artificially evoked in myself, to be immediately destroyed.

On the completion of the performance (though it was noticeable that every one had become dull) those present warmly praised Beethoven's profound production in the accepted manner, and did not forget to add that formerly they had not been able to understand that last period of his, but that they now saw he was really then at his very best. And when I ventured to compare the impression made on me by the singing of the peasant women—an impression which had been shared by all who heard it—with the effect of this sonata, the admirers of Beethoven only smiled contemptuously, not considering it necessary to reply to such strange remarks.

But for all that, the song of the peasant women was real art transmitting a definite and strong feeling, while the 101st sonata of Beethoven was only an unsuccessful attempt at art containing no definite feeling and therefore not infectious.

For my work on art I have this winter read diligently, though with great effort, the celebrated novels and stories praised by all Europe, written by Zola, Bourget, Huysmans, and Kipling. At the same time I chanced on a story in a child's magazine, by a quite unknown writer, which told of the Easter preparations in a poor widow's family. The story tells how the mother managed with difficulty to obtain some wheat-flour, which she poured on the table ready to knead. She then went out to procure some yeast, telling the children not to leave the hut and to take care of the flour. When the mother had gone, some other children ran shouting near the window calling those in the hut to come to play. The children forgot their mother's warning, ran into the street, and were soon engrossed in the game. The mother on her return with the yeast finds a hen on the table throwing the last of the flour to her chickens, who were busily picking it out of the dust of the earthen floor. The mother, in despair, scolds the children, who cry bitterly. And the mother begins to feel pity for them—but the white flour has all gone. So to mend matters she decides to make the Easter cake with sifted rye-flour, brushing it over with white of egg and surrounding it with eggs. 'Rye-bread we bake is as good as a cake,' says the mother, using a rhyming proverb to console the children for not having an Easter cake of white flour, and the children, quickly passing from despair to rapture, repeat the proverb and await the Easter cake more merrily even than before.

Well! the reading of the novels and stories by Zola, Bourget, Huysmans, Kipling, and others, handling the most harrowing subjects, did not touch me for one moment, and I was provoked with the authors all the while as one is provoked with a man who considers you so naïve that he does not even conceal the trick by which he intends to take you in. From the first lines one sees the intention with which the book is written, the details all become superfluous, and one feels dull. Above all, one knows that the author had no other feeling all the time than a desire to write a story or a novel, and so one receives no artistic impression. On the other hand I could not tear myself away from the unknown author's tale of the children and the chickens, because I was at once infected by the feeling the author had evidently experienced, re-evoked in himself, and transmitted.

Vasnetsóv is one of our Russian painters. He has painted ecclesiastical pictures in Kíev Cathedral and every one praises him as the founder of some new, elevated, kind of Christian art. He worked at those pictures for ten years, was paid tens of thousands of rubles for them, and they are all simply bad imitations of imitations of imitations, destitute of any spark of feeling. And this same Vasnetsóv once drew a picture for Turgénev's story 'The Quail' (in which it is told how a son pitied a quail he had seen his father kill) showing the boy asleep with pouting upper lip, and above him, as a dream, the quail. And this picture is a true work of art.

In the English Academy of 1897 two pictures were exhibited together; one of these, by J. C. Dollman, was the temptation of St. Anthony. The Saint is on his knees praying. Behind him stands a naked woman and animals of some kind. It is apparent that the naked woman pleased the artist very much, but that Anthony did not concern him at all, and that so far from the temptation being terrible to him (the artist) it is highly agreeable. Therefore if there be any art in this picture, it is very nasty and false. Next in the same book of academy pictures comes a picture by Langley, showing a stray beggar boy, who has evidently been called in by a woman who has taken pity on him. The boy, pitifully drawing his bare feet under the bench, is eating; the woman is looking on, probably considering whether he will not want some more; and a girl of about seven, leaning on her arm, is carefully and seriously looking on, not taking her eyes from the hungry boy and evidently understanding for the first time what poverty is and what inequality among people is, and asking herself why she has everything provided for her while this boy goes barefoot and hungry? She feels sorry and yet pleased, and she loves both the boy and goodness. . . . One feels that the artist loved this girl and that she too loves. And this picture, by an artist who, I think, is not very widely known, is an admirable and true work of art.

I remember seeing a performance of *Hamlet* by Rossi. Both the tragedy itself and the performer who took the chief part are considered by our critics to represent the climax of supreme dramatic art. And yet, both from the subject-matter of the drama and from the performance, I experienced all the time that peculiar suffering which is caused by false imitations of works of art. But I lately read of a theatrical performance among a savage tribe—the Voguls. A spectator describes the play. A big Vogul and a little one, both dressed in reindeer skins, represent a reindeer-doe and its young. A third Vogul with a bow represents a huntsman on snow-shoes, and a fourth imitates with his voice a bird that warns the reindeer of their danger. The play is that the huntsman follows the track the doe with its young one has travelled. The deer run off the scene and again reappear. (Such performances take place in a small tent-house.) The huntsman gains more and more on the pursued. The little deer is tired and presses against its mother; the doe stops to draw breath. The hunter comes up with them and draws his bow. But just then the bird sounds its note warning the deer of their danger. They escape. Again there is a chase and again the hunter gains on them, catches them, and lets fly his arrow. The arrow strikes the young deer. Unable to run, the little one presses against its mother. The mother licks its wound. The hunter draws another arrow. The audience, as the eye-witness describes them, are paralysed with suspense; deep groans and even weeping are heard among them. And from the mere description I felt that this was a true work of art.

What I am saying will be considered irrational paradox at which one can only be amazed, but for all that I must say what I think, namely, that people of our circle, of whom some compose verses, stories, novels, operas, symphonies, and sonatas, paint all kinds of pictures, and make statues, while others hear and look at these things, and others again appraise and criticize them all: discuss, condemn, triumph, and generation after generation raise monuments to one another—that all these people with very few exceptions, artists, and public, and critics, have never (except in childhood and earliest youth before hearing any discussions on art) experienced that simple feeling familiar to the plainest man and even to a child, that sense of infection with another's feeling—compelling us to rejoice in another's gladness, to sorrow at another's grief and to mingle souls with another—which is the very essence of art. And therefore these people not only cannot distinguish true works of art from counterfeits, but continually mistake for real art the worst and most artificial, while they do not even perceive works of real art, because the counterfeits are always more ornate, while true art is modest.

CHAPTER XV

THE QUALITY OF ART (WHICH DEPENDS ON ITS FORM) CONSIDERED APART FROM ITS SUBJECT-MATTER—The sign of art: infectiousness. Art is incomprehensible to those whose taste is perverted. Conditions of infection: Individuality, Clearness, and Sincerity of the feeling conveyed.

ART in our society has become so perverted that not only has bad art come to be considered good, but even the very perception of what art really is has been lost. In order to be able to speak about the art of our society it is, therefore, first of all necessary to distinguish art from counterfeit art.

There is one indubitable sign distinguishing real art from its counterfeit—namely, the infectiousness of art. If a man without exercising effort and without altering his standpoint, on reading, hearing, or seeing another man's work experiences a mental condition which unites him with that man and with others who are also affected by that work, then the object evoking that condition is a work of art. And however poetic, realistic, striking, or interesting, a work may be, it is not a work of art if it does not evoke that feeling (quite distinct from all other feelings) of joy and of spiritual union with another (the author) and with others (those who are also infected by it).

It is true that this indication is an *internal* one and that there are people who, having forgotten what the action of real art is, expect something else from art (in our society the great majority are in this state), and that therefore such people may mistake for this æsthetic feeling the feeling of diversion and a certain excitement which they receive from counterfeits of art. But though it is impossible to undeceive these people, just as it may be impossible to convince a man suffering from colour-blindness that green is not red, yet for all that, this indication remains perfectly definite to those whose feeling for art is neither perverted nor atrophied, and it clearly distinguishes the feeling produced by art from all other feelings.

The chief peculiarity of this feeling is that the recipient of a truly artistic impression is so united to the artist that he feels as if the work were his own and not some one else's—as if what it expresses were just what he had long been wishing to express. A real work of art destroys in the consciousness of the recipient the separation between himself and the artist, and not that alone, but also between himself and all whose minds receive this work of art. In this freeing of our personality from its separation and isolation, in this uniting of it with others, lies the chief characteristic and the great attractive force of art.

If a man is infected by the author's condition of soul, if he feels this emotion and this union with others, then the object which has effected this is art; but if there be no such infection, if there be not this union with the author and with others who are moved by the same work—then it is not art. And not only is infection a sure sign of art, but the degree of infectiousness is also the sole measure of excellence in art.

The stronger the infection the better is the art, as art, speaking of it now apart from its subject-matter—that is, not considering the value of the feelings it transmits.

And the degree of the infectiousness of art depends on three conditions:—

(1) On the greater or lesser individuality of the feeling transmitted; (2) on the greater or lesser clearness with which the feeling is transmitted; (3) on the sincerity of the artist, that is, on the greater or lesser force with which the artist himself feels the emotion he transmits.

The more individual the feeling transmitted the more strongly does it act on the recipient; the more individual the state of soul into which he is transferred the more pleasure does the recipient obtain and therefore the more readily and strongly does he join in it.

Clearness of expression assists infection because the recipient who mingles in consciousness with the author is the better satisfied the more clearly that feeling is transmitted which, as it seems to him, he has long known and felt and for which he has only now found expression.

But most of all is the degree of infectiousness of art increased by the degree of sincerity in the artist. As soon as the spectator, hearer, or reader, feels that the artist is infected by his own production and writes, sings, or plays, for himself, and not merely to act on others, this mental condition of the artist infects the recipient; and, on the contrary, as soon as the spectator, reader, or hearer, feels that the author is not writing, singing, or playing, for his own satisfaction—does not himself feel what he wishes to express, but is doing it for him, the recipient—resistance immediately springs up, and the most individual and the newest feelings and the cleverest technique not only fail to produce any infection but actually repel.

I have mentioned three conditions of contagion in art, but they may all be summed up into one, the last, sincerity; that is, that the artist should be impelled by an inner need to express his feeling. That condition includes the first; for if the artist is sincere he will express the feeling as he experienced it. And as each man is different from every one else, his feeling will be individual for every one else; and the more individual it is—the more the artist has drawn it from the depths of his nature—the more sympathetic and sincere will it be. And this same sincerity will impel the artist to find clear expression for the feeling which he wishes to transmit.

Therefore this third condition—sincerity—is the most important of the three. It is always complied with in peasant art, and this explains why such art always acts so powerfully; but it is a condition almost entirely absent from our upper-class art, which is continually produced by artists actuated by personal aims of covetousness or vanity.

Such are the three conditions which divide art from its counterfeits, and which also decide the quality of every work of art considered apart from its subject-matter.

The absence of any one of these conditions excludes a work from the category of art and relegates it to that of art's counterfeits. If the work does not transmit the artist's peculiarity of feeling and is therefore not individual, if it is unintelligibly expressed, or if it has not proceeded from the author's inner need for expression—it is not a work of art. If all these conditions are present even in the smallest degree, then the work even if a weak one is yet a work of art.

The presence in various degrees of these three conditions: individuality, clearness, and sincerity, decides the merit of a work of art as art, apart from subject-matter. All works of art take order of merit according to the degree in which they fulfil the first, the second, and the third, of these conditions. In one the individuality of the feeling transmitted may predominate; in another, clearness of expression; in a third, sincerity; while a fourth may have sincerity and individuality but be deficient in clearness; a fifth, individuality and clearness, but less sincerity; and so forth, in all possible degrees and combinations.

Thus is art divided from what is not art, and thus is the quality of art, as art, decided, independently of its subject-matter, that is to say, apart from whether the feelings it transmits are good or bad.

But how are we to define good and bad art with reference to its content or subject-matter?

CHAPTER XVI

Having recognized certain productions as being works of art, since their excellence of form renders them infectious, consider now THE QUALITY OF THE FEELINGS WHICH FORM THE SUBJECT MATTER OF THESE WORKS. The better the feeling the better the art. The cultured crowd. The religious perception of our age. New ideals place fresh demands on art. Art unites. Religious art. Universal art. Both co-operate to one result. The new appraisement of art. Bad art. Examples. Beauty, though it can supply no *standard* of art, has its legitimate place in art. Beethoven's Ninth Symphony.

HOW in the subject-matter of art are we to decide what is good and what is bad?

Art like speech is a means of communication and therefore of progress, that is, of the movement of humanity forward towards perfection. Speech renders accessible to men of the latest generations all the knowledge discovered by the experience and reflection both of preceding generations and of the best and foremost men of their own times; art renders accessible to men of the latest generations all the feelings experienced by their predecessors and also those felt by their best and foremost contemporaries. And as the evolution of knowledge proceeds by truer and more necessary knowledge dislodging and replacing what was mistaken and unnecessary, so the evolution of feeling proceeds by means of art—feelings less kind and less necessary for the well-being of mankind being replaced by others kinder and more needful for that end. That is the purpose of art. And speaking now of the feelings which are its subject-matter, the more art fulfils that purpose the better the art, and the less it fulfils it the worse the art.

The appraisement of feelings (that is, the recognition of one or other set of feelings as more or less good, more or less necessary for the well-being of mankind) is effected by the religious perception of the age.

In every period of history and in every human society there exists an understanding of the meaning of life, which represents the highest level to which men of that society have attained—an understanding indicating the highest good at which that society aims. This understanding is the religious perception of the given time and society. And this religious perception is always clearly expressed by a few advanced men and more or less vividly perceived by members of the society generally. Such a religious perception and its corresponding expression always exists in every society. If it appears to us that there is no religious perception in our society, this is not because there really is none, but only because we do not wish to see it. And we often wish not to see it because it exposes the fact that our life is inconsistent with that religious perception.

Religious perception in a society is like the direction of a flowing river. If the river flows at all it must have a direction. If a society lives, there must be a religious perception indicating the direction in which, more or less consciously, all its members tend.

And so there always has been, and is, a religious perception in every society. And it is by the standard of this religious perception that the feelings transmitted by art have always been appraised. It has always been only on the basis of this religious perception of their age, that men have chosen from amid the endlessly varied spheres of art that art which transmitted feelings making religious perception operative in actual life. And such art has always been highly valued and encouraged, while art transmitting feelings already outlived, flowing from the antiquated religious perceptions of a former age, has always been condemned and despised. All the rest of art transmitting those most diverse feelings by means of which people commune with one another was not condemned and was tolerated if only it did not transmit feelings contrary to religious perception. Thus for instance among the Greeks, art transmitting feelings of beauty, strength, and courage (Hesiod, Homer, Phidias) was chosen, approved, and encouraged, while art transmitting feelings of rude sensuality, despondency, and effeminacy, was condemned and despised. Among the Jews, art transmitting feelings of devotion and submission to the God of the Hebrews and to His will (the epic of Genesis, the prophets, the Psalms) was chosen and encouraged, while art transmitting feelings of idolatry (the Golden Calf) was condemned and despised. All the rest of art—stories, songs, dances, ornamentation of houses, of utensils, and of clothes—which was not contrary to religious perception, was neither distinguished nor discussed. Thus as regards its subject-matter has art always and everywhere been appraised and thus it should be appraised, for this attitude towards art proceeds from the fundamental characteristics of human nature, and those characteristics do not change.

I know that according to an opinion current in our times religion is a superstition humanity has outgrown, and it is therefore assumed that no such thing exists as a religious perception common to us all by which art in our time can be appraised. I know that this is the opinion current in the pseudo-cultured circles of to-day. People who do not acknowledge Christianity in its true meaning because it undermines their social privileges, and who therefore invent all kinds of philosophic and æsthetic theories to hide from themselves the meaninglessness and wrongfulness of their lives, cannot think otherwise. These people intentionally, or sometimes unintentionally, confuse the notion of a religious cult with the notion of religious perception, and think that by denying the cult they get rid of the perception. But even the very attacks on religion and the attempts to establish an idea of life contrary to the religious perception of our times, most clearly demonstrate the existence of a religious perception condemning the lives that are not in harmony with it.

If humanity progresses, that is, moves forward, there must inevitably be a guide to the direction of that movement. And religions have always furnished that guide. All history shows that the progress of humanity is accomplished no otherwise than under the guidance of religion. But if the race cannot progress without the guidance of religion,—and progress is always going on, and consequently goes on also in our own times,—then there must be a religion of our times. So that whether it pleases or displeases the so-called cultured people of to-day, they must admit the existence of religion—not of a religious cult, Catholic, Protestant, or another, but of religious perception—which even in our times is the guide always present where there is any progress. And if a religious perception exists amongst us, then the feelings dealt with by our art should be appraised on the basis of that religious perception; and as has been the case always and everywhere, art transmitting feelings flowing from the religious perception of our time should be chosen from amid all the indifferent art, should be acknowledged, highly valued, and encouraged, while art running counter to that perception should be condemned and despised, and all the remaining, indifferent, art should neither be distinguished nor encouraged.

The religious perception of our time in its widest and most practical application is the consciousness that our well-being, both material and spiritual, individual and collective, temporal and eternal, lies in the growth of brotherhood among men—in their loving harmony with one another. This perception is not only expressed by Christ and all the best men of past ages, it is not only repeated in most varied forms and from most diverse sides by the best men of our times, but it already serves as a clue to all the complex labour of humanity, consisting as this labour does on the one hand in the destruction of physical and moral obstacles to the union of men, and on the other hand in establishing the principles common to all men which can and should unite them in one universal brotherhood. And it is on the basis of this perception that we should appraise all the phenomena of our life and among the rest our art also: choosing from all its realms and highly prizing and encouraging whatever transmits feelings flowing from this religious perception, rejecting whatever is contrary to it, and not attributing to the rest of art an importance that does not properly belong to it.

The chief mistake made by people of the upper classes at the time of the so-called Renaissance,—a mistake we still perpetuate,—was not that they ceased to value and attach importance to religious art (people of that period could not attach importance to it because, like our own upper classes, they could not believe in what the majority considered to be religion), but their mistake was that they set up in place of the religious art that was lacking, an insignificant art which aimed merely at giving pleasure, that is, they began to choose, to value, and to encourage, in place of religious art, something which in any case did not deserve such esteem and encouragement.

One of the Fathers of the Church said that the great evil is not that men do not know God, but that they have set up instead of God, that which is not God.

So also with art. The great misfortune of the people of the upper classes of our time is not so much that they are without a religious art as that, instead of a supreme religious art chosen from all the rest as being specially important and valuable, they have chosen a most insignificant and, usually, harmful art, which aims at pleasing certain people and which therefore, if only by its exclusive nature, stands in contradiction to that Christian principle of universal union which forms the religious perception of our time. Instead of religious art, an empty and often vicious art is set up, and this hides from men's notice the need of that true religious art which should be present in life to improve it.

It is true that art which satisfies the demands of the religious perception of our time is quite unlike former art, but notwithstanding this dissimilarity, to a man who does not intentionally hide the truth from himself, what forms the religious art of our age is very clear and definite. In former times when the highest religious perception united only some people (who even if they formed a large society were yet but one society among others—Jews, or Athenian or Roman citizens), the feelings transmitted by the art of that time flowed from a desire for the might, greatness, glory, and prosperity, of that society, and the heroes of art might be people who contributed to that prosperity by strength, by craft, by fraud, or by cruelty (Ulysses, Jacob, David, Samson, Hercules, and all the heroes). But the religious perception of our times does not select any one society of men; on the contrary it demands the union of all—absolutely of all people without exception—and above every other virtue it sets brotherly love of all men. And therefore the feelings transmitted by the art of our time not only cannot coincide with the feelings transmitted by former art, but must run counter to them.

Christian, truly Christian, art has been so long in

establishing itself, and has not yet established itself, just because the Christian religious perception was not one of those small steps by which humanity advances regularly, but was an enormous revolution which, if it has not already altered, must inevitably alter the entire conception of life of mankind, and consequently the whole internal organization of that life. It is true that the life of humanity, like that of an individual, moves regularly; but in that regular movement come, as it were, turning-points which sharply divide the preceding from the subsequent life. Christianity was such a turning-point; such at least it must appear to us who live by the Christian perception of life. Christian perception gave another, a new, direction to all human feelings, and therefore completely altered both the content and the significance of art. The Greeks could make use of Persian art and the Romans could use Greek art, or, similarly, the Jews could use Egyptian art—the fundamental ideals were one and the same. Now the ideal was the greatness and prosperity of the Persians, now the greatness and prosperity of the Greeks, now that of the Romans. The same art was transferred to other conditions and served new nations. But the Christian ideal changed and reversed everything, so that, as the Gospel puts it, 'That which was exalted among men has become an abomination in the sight of God.' The ideal is no longer the greatness of Pharaoh or of a Roman emperor, not the beauty of a Greek nor the wealth of Phœnicia, but humility, purity, compassion, love. The hero is no longer Dives, but Lazarus the beggar; not Mary Magdalene in the day of her beauty but in the day of her repentance; not those who acquire wealth but those who have abandoned it; not those who dwell in palaces but those who dwell in catacombs and huts; not those who rule over others, but those who acknowledge no authority but God's. And the greatest

I

work of art is no longer a cathedral of victory [1] with statues of conquerors, but the representation of a human soul so transformed by love that a man who is tormented and murdered, yet pities and loves his persecutors.

And the change is so great that men of the Christian world find it difficult to resist the inertia of the heathen art to which they have been accustomed all their lives. The subject-matter of Christian religious art is so new to them, so unlike the subject-matter of former art, that it seems to them as though Christian art were a denial of art, and they cling desperately to the old art. But this old art, having no longer in our day any source in religious perception, has lost its meaning, and we shall have to abandon it whether we wish to or not.

The essence of the Christian perception consists in the recognition by every man of his sonship to God and of the consequent union of men with God and with one another, as is said in the Gospel (John xvii. 21 [2]). Therefore the subject-matter of Christian art is of a kind that feeling can unite men with God and with one another.

The expression *unite men with God and with one another* may seem obscure to people accustomed to the misuse of these words that is so customary, but the words have a perfectly clear meaning nevertheless. They indicate that the Christian union of man (in contradiction to the partial, exclusive, union of only certain men) is that which unites all without exception.

Art, all art, has this characteristic, that it unites people. Every art causes those to whom the artist's feeling is transmitted to unite in soul with the artist

---

[1] There is in Moscow a magnificent 'Cathedral of our Saviour,' erected to commemorate the defeat of the French in the war of 1812.—A. M.

[2] 'That they may all be one; even as thou, Father, art in me, and I in Thee, that they also may be in us.'

and also with all who receive the same impression. But non-Christian art while uniting some people, makes that very union a cause of separation between these united people and others; so that union of this kind is often a source not merely of division but even of enmity towards others. Such is all patriotic art, with its anthems, poems, and monuments; such is all Church art, that is, the art of certain cults, with their images, statues, processions, and other local ceremonies. Such art is belated and non-Christian, uniting the people of one cult only to separate them yet more sharply from the members of other cults, and even to place them in relations of hostility to one another. Christian art is such only as tends to unite all without exception, either by evoking in them the perception that each man and all men stand in a like relation towards God and towards their neighbour, or by evoking in them identical feelings, which may even be the very simplest, provided that they are not repugnant to Christianity and are natural to every one without exception.

Good Christian art of our time may be unintelligible to people because of imperfections in its form or because men are inattentive to it, but it must be such that all men can experience the feelings it transmits. It must be the art not of some one group of people, or of one class, or of one nationality, or of one religious cult; that is, it must not transmit feelings accessible only to a man educated in a certain way, or only to an aristocrat, or a merchant, or only to a Russian, or a native of Japan, or a Roman Catholic, or a Buddhist, and so on, but it must transmit feelings accessible to every one. Only art of this kind can in our time be acknowledged to be good art, worthy of being chosen out from all the rest of art and encouraged.

Christian art, that is, the art of our time, should be catholic in the original meaning of the word, that is, universal, and therefore it should unite all men. And only two kinds of feeling unite all men: first, feelings flowing from a perception of our sonship to God and of the brotherhood of man; and next, the simple feelings of common life accessible to every one without exception—such as feelings of merriment, of pity, of cheerfulness, of tranquillity, and so forth. Only these two kinds of feelings can now supply material for art good in its subject-matter.

And the action of these two kinds of art apparently so dissimilar, is one and the same. The feelings flowing from the perception of our sonship to God and the brotherhood of man—such as a feeling of sureness in truth, devotion to the will of God, self-sacrifice, respect for and love of man—evoked by Christian religious perception; and the simplest feelings, such as a softened or a merry mood caused by a song or an amusing jest intelligible to every one, or by a touching story, or a drawing, or a little doll: both alike produce one and the same effect—the loving union of man with man. Sometimes people who are together, if not hostile to one another, are at least estranged in mood and feeling, till perhaps a story, a performance, a picture, or even a building, but oftenest of all music, unites them all as by an electric flash, and in place of their former isolation or even enmity they are conscious of union and mutual love. Each is glad that another feels what he feels; glad of the communion established not only between him and all present, but also with all now living who will yet share the same impression; and, more than that, he feels the mysterious gladness of a communion which, reaching beyond the grave, unites us with all men of the past who have been moved by the same feelings and with all men of the future who will yet be touched by them. And this effect is produced both by religious art which transmits feelings of love of God and one's neighbour, and by universal art transmitting the very simplest feelings common to all men.

The art of our time should be appraised differently from former art chiefly in this, that the art of our time, that is, Christian art (basing itself on a religious perception which demands the union of man), excludes from the domain of art good in its subject-matter, everything transmitting exclusive feelings which do not unite men but divide them. It relegates such work to the category of art that is bad in its subject-matter; while on the other hand it includes in the category of art that is good in subject-matter a section not formerly admitted as deserving of selection and respect, namely, universal art transmitting even the most trifling and simple feelings if only they are accessible to all men without exception, and therefore unite them. Such art cannot but be esteemed good in our time, for it attains the end which Christianity, the religious perception of our time, sets before humanity.

Christian art either evokes in men feelings which through love of God and of one's neighbour draw them to closer and ever closer union and make them ready for, and capable of, such union; or evokes in them feelings which show them that they are already united in the joys and sorrows of life. And therefore the Christian art of our time can be and is of two kinds: first, art transmitting feelings flowing from a religious perception of man's position in the world in relation to God and to his neighbour—religious art in the limited meaning of the term; and secondly, art transmitting the simplest feelings of common life, but such always as are accessible to all men in the whole world—the art of common life—the art of the people—universal art. Only these two kinds of art can be considered good art in our time.

The first, religious art—transmitting both positive

feelings of love of God and one's neighbour, and negative feelings of indignation and horror at the violation of love—manifests itself chiefly in the form of words, and to some extent also in painting and sculpture: the second kind, universal art, transmitting feelings accessible to all, manifests itself in words, in painting, in sculpture, in dances, in architecture, and most of all in music.

If I were asked to give modern examples of each of these kinds of art, then as examples of the highest art flowing from love of God and man (both of the higher, positive, and of the lower, negative kind), in literature I should name *The Robbers* by Schiller; Victor Hugo's *Les Pauvres Gens* and *Les Misérables*; the novels and stories of Dickens—*The Tale of Two Cities, The Christmas Carol, The Chimes*, and others—*Uncle Tom's Cabin*; Dostoévski's works—especially his *Memoirs from the House of Death*—and *Adam Bede* by George Eliot.

In modern painting, strange to say, works of this kind, directly transmitting the Christian feeling of love of God and of one's neighbour, are hardly to be found, especially among the works of the celebrated painters. There are plenty of pictures treating of the Gospel stories; these however, while depicting historical events with great wealth of detail, do not and cannot transmit religious feelings not possessed by their painters. There are many pictures treating of the personal feelings of various people, but of pictures representing great deeds of self-sacrifice and Christian love there are very few, and what there are are principally by artists who are not celebrated, and they are for the most part not pictures but merely sketches. Such for instance is the drawing by Kramskóy (worth many of his finished pictures), showing a drawing-room with a balcony past which troops are marching in triumph on their return from the war. On the balcony stands a wet-nurse holding a baby, and a boy.

They are admiring the procession of the troops, but the mother, covering her face with a handkerchief, has fallen back on the sofa sobbing. Such also is the picture by Walter Langley to which I have already referred, and such again is a picture by the French artist Morlon, depicting a lifeboat hastening in a heavy storm to the relief of a steamer that is being wrecked. Approaching these in kind are pictures which represent the hard-working peasant with respect and love. Such are the pictures by Millet and particularly his drawing, 'The Man with the Hoe,' also pictures in this style by Jules Breton, Lhermitte, Defregger, and others. As examples of pictures evoking indignation and horror at the violation of love of God and man, Gay's picture 'Judgment' may serve, and also Leizen-Mayer's 'Signing the Death Warrant.' But there are very few of this kind also. Anxiety about the technique and the beauty of the picture for the most part obscures the feeling. For instance, Gérôme's 'Pollice Verso' expresses, not so much horror at what is being perpetrated as attraction by the beauty of the spectacle.[1]

To give examples from the modern art of our upper classes, of art of the second kind: good universal art, or even of the art of a whole people, is yet more difficult, especially in literature and music. If there are some works which by their inner contents might be assigned to this class (such as *Don Quixote*, Molière's comedies, *David Copperfield* and *The Pickwick Papers* by Dickens, Gógol's and Púshkin's tales, and some things of Maupassant's), these works for the most part—owing to the exceptional nature of the feelings they transmit, and the superfluity of special details of time and locality, and above all on account of the poverty of their

---

[1] In this picture the spectators in the Roman Amphitheatre are turning down their thumbs to show that they wish the vanquished gladiator to be killed.—A. M.

subject-matter in comparison with examples of universal ancient art (such, for instance, as the story of Joseph)—are comprehensible only to people of their own circle. That Joseph's brethren, being jealous of his father's affection, sell him to the merchants; that Potiphar's wife wishes to tempt the youth; that having attained to highest station he takes pity on his brothers, including Benjamin the favourite—these and all the rest are feelings accessible alike to a Russian peasant, a Chinese, an African, a child, or an old man, educated or uneducated; and it is all written with such restraint, is so free from any superfluous detail, that the story may be told to any circle and will be equally comprehensible and touching to everyone. But not such are the feelings of Don Quixote or of Molière's heroes (though Molière is perhaps the most universal, and therefore the most excellent, artist of modern times), nor of Pickwick and his friends. These feelings are not common to all men but very exceptional, and therefore to make them contagious the authors have surrounded them with abundant details of time and place. And this abundance of detail makes the stories difficult of comprehension to all who do not live within reach of the conditions described by the author.

The author of the novel of Joseph did not need to describe in detail, as would be done nowadays, the blood-stained coat of Joseph, the dwelling and dress of Jacob, the pose and attire of Potiphar's wife, and how adjusting the bracelet on her left arm she said, 'Come to me,' and so on, because the content of feeling in this novel is so strong that all details except the most essential—such as that Joseph went out into another room to weep—are superfluous and would only hinder the transmission of emotion. And therefore this novel is accessible to all men, touches people of all nations and classes young and old, and has lasted to our times and will yet last for thousands of years to come. But strip the best novels of our time of their details and what will remain?

It is therefore impossible in modern literature to indicate works fully satisfying the demands of universality. Such works as exist are to a great extent spoilt by what is usually called 'realism', but would be better termed 'provincialism', in art.

In music the same occurs as in verbal art, and for similar reasons. In consequence of the poorness of the feeling they contain, the melodies of the modern composers are amazingly empty and insignificant. And to strengthen the impression produced by these empty melodies the new musicians pile complex modulations on each trivial melody, not only in their own national manner, but also in the way characteristic of their own exclusive circle and particular musical school. Melody—every melody—is free and may be understood of all men; but as soon as it is bound up with a particular harmony, it ceases to be accessible except to people trained to such harmony, and it becomes strange, not only to common men of another nationality, but to all who do not belong to the circle whose members have accustomed themselves to certain forms of harmonization. So that music, like poetry, travels in a vicious circle. Trivial and exclusive melodies, in order to make them attractive, are laden with harmonic, rhythmic, and orchestral complications and thus become yet more exclusive, and far from being universal are not even national, that is, they are not comprehensible to the whole people, but only to some people.

In music, besides marches and dances by various composers which satisfy the demands of universal art, one can indicate very few works of this class: Bach's famous violin *aria*, Chopin's nocturne in E flat major, and perhaps a dozen bits (not whole pieces, but parts) selected from the works of Haydn, Mozart, Schubert, Beethoven, and Chopin.[1]

Although in painting the same thing is repeated as in poetry and in music—namely, that in order to make them more interesting, works weak in conception are surrounded by minutely studied accessories of time and place which give them a temporary and local interest but make them less universal—still in painting more than in other spheres of art may be found works satisfying the demands of universal Christian art; that is to say, there are more works expressing feelings in which all men may participate.

In the arts of painting and sculpture, all pictures and statues in so-called genre style, representations of animals, landscapes, and caricatures with subjects comprehensible to every one, and also all kinds of ornaments, are universal in subject-matter. Such productions in painting and sculpture are very numerous (for instance, china dolls), but for the most part such objects (for instance, ornaments of all kinds) are either not considered to be art or are considered to be

---

[1] While offering as examples of art those that seem to me best, I attach no special importance to my selection; for, besides being insufficiently informed in all branches of art, I belong to the class of people whose taste has been perverted by false training. And therefore my old, inured habits may cause me to err, and I may mistake for absolute merit the impression a work produced on me in my youth. My only purpose in mentioning examples of works of this or that class is to make my meaning clearer and to show how, with my present views, I understand excellence in art in relation to its subject-matter. I must moreover mention that I consign my own artistic productions to the category of bad art, excepting the story *God sees the Truth but Waits*, which seeks a place in the first class, and *A Prisoner of the Caucasus*, which belongs to the second.—L. T.

(Both the stories mentioned are included in *Twenty-Three Tales* in the 'World's Classics' Tolstóy series.—A. M.)

art of a low quality. In reality all such objects if only they transmit a true feeling experienced by the artist and comprehensible to every one (however insignificant it may seem to us to be), are works of real, good, Christian, art.

I fear it will here be urged against me that having denied that the conception of beauty can supply a standard for works of art, I contradict myself by acknowledging ornaments to be works of good art. The reproach is unjust, for the subject-matter of all kinds of ornamentation consists not in the beauty but in the feeling (of admiration at, and delight in, the combination of lines and colours) which the artist has experienced and with which he infects the spectator. Art remains what it was and what it must be: nothing but the infection by one man of another or of others with the feelings experienced by the artist. Among these feelings is the feeling of delight at what pleases the sight. Objects pleasing the sight may be such as please a small or a large number of people, or such as please all men—and ornaments for the most part are of the latter kind. A landscape representing a very unusual view, or a genre picture of a special subject, may not please every one, but ornaments, from Yakútsk ornaments to Greek ones, are intelligible to every one and evoke a similar feeling of admiration in all, and therefore this despised kind of art should in Christian society be esteemed far above exceptional, pretentious, pictures and sculptures.

So that in relation to feelings conveyed, there are only two kinds of good Christian art, all the rest of art not comprised in these two divisions should be acknowledged to be bad art, deserving not to be encouraged but to be driven out, denied, and despised, as being art not uniting but dividing people. Such in literary art are all novels and poems which transmit ecclesiastical or patriotic feelings, and also exclusive feelings pertaining only to the class of the idle rich: such as aristocratic honour, satiety, spleen, pessimism, and refined and vicious feelings flowing from sex-love —quite incomprehensible to the great majority of mankind.

In painting we must similarly place in the class of bad art all ecclesiastical, patriotic, and exclusive pictures; all pictures representing the amusements and allurements of a rich and idle life; all so-called symbolic pictures in which the very meaning of the symbol is comprehensible only to those of a certain circle; and above all pictures with voluptuous subjects—all that odious female nudity which fills all the exhibitions and galleries. And to this class belongs almost all the chamber and opera music of our times,—beginning especially with Beethoven (Schumann, Berlioz, Liszt, Wagner),—by its subject-matter devoted to the expression of feelings accessible only to people who have developed in themselves an unhealthy nervous irritation evoked by this exclusive, artificial, and complex music.

'What! the *Ninth Symphony* not a good work of art!' I hear exclaimed by indignant voices.

And I reply: Most certainly it is not. All that I have written I have written with the sole purpose of finding a clear and reasonable criterion by which to judge the merits of works of art. And this criterion, coinciding with the indications of plain and sane sense, indubitably shows me that that symphony of Beethoven's is not a good work of art. Of course to people educated in the worship of certain productions and of their authors, to people whose taste has been perverted just by being educated in such a worship, the acknowledgment that such a celebrated work is bad, is amazing and strange. But how are we to escape the indications of reason and common sense?

Beethoven's *Ninth Symphony* is considered a great work of art. To verify its claim to be such I must first ask myself whether this work transmits the highest religious feeling? I reply in the negative, since music in itself cannot transmit those feelings; and therefore I ask myself next: Since this work does not belong to the highest kind of religious art, has it the other characteristic of the good art of our time—the quality of uniting all men in one common feeling—does it rank as Christian universal art? And again I have no option but to reply in the negative; for not only do I not see how the feelings transmitted by this work could unite people not specially trained to submit themselves to its complex hypnotism, but I am unable to imagine to myself a crowd of normal people who could understand anything of this long, confused, and artificial production, except short snatches which are lost in a sea of what is incomprehensible. And therefore, whether I like it or not, I am compelled to conclude that this work belongs to the rank of bad art. It is curious to note in this connexion, that attached to the end of this very symphony is a poem of Schiller's which (though somewhat obscurely) expresses this very thought, namely, that feeling (Schiller speaks only of the feeling of gladness) unites people and evokes love in them. But though this poem is sung at the end of the symphony, the music does not accord with the thought expressed in the verses; for the music is exclusive and does not unite all men, but unites only a few, dividing them off from the rest of mankind.

And just in this same way, in all branches of art, many and many works considered great by the upper classes of our society will have to be judged. By this one sure criterion we shall have to judge the celebrated *Divine Comedy* and *Jerusalem Delivered*, and a great part of Shakespeare's and Goethe's work, and in painting every representation of miracles, including Raphael's Transfiguration, etc.

Whatever the work may be and however it may have been extolled, we have first to ask whether this work is one of real art, or a counterfeit. Having acknowledged, on the basis of the indication of its infectiousness even to a small class of people, that a certain production belongs to the realm of art, it is necessary on this basis to decide the next question, Does this work belong to the category of bad exclusive art opposed to religious perception, or of Christian art uniting people? And having acknowledged a work to belong to real Christian art, we must then, according to whether it transmits feelings flowing from love of God and man, or merely the simple feelings uniting all men, assign it a place in the ranks of religious art, or in those of universal art.

Only on the basis of such verification shall we find it possible to select from the whole mass of what in our society claims to be art, those works which form real, important, necessary, spiritual food, and to separate them from all the harmful and useless art and from the counterfeits of art which surround us. Only on the basis of such verification shall we be able to rid ourselves of the pernicious results of harmful art and avail ourselves of that beneficent action which is the purpose of true and good art, and which is indispensable for the spiritual life of man and of humanity.

CHAPTER XVII

Results of absence of true art. Results of perversion of art:
labour and lives spent on what is useless and harmful. The
abnormal life of the rich. Perplexity of children and plain
folk. Confusion of right and wrong. Nietzsche and Redbeard. Superstition, Patriotism, and Sensuality.

ART is one of two organs of human progress. By
words man interchanges thoughts, by the forms of art
he interchanges feelings, and this with all men not
only of the present time but also of the past and the
future. It is natural to human beings to employ both
these organs of intercommunication, and therefore
the perversion of either of them must cause evil results
to the society in which it occurs. And these results
will be of two kinds: first, the absence in that society
of the work which should be performed by the organ,
and secondly, the harmful activity of the perverted
organ. And just these results have shown themselves
in our society. The organ of art has been perverted,
and therefore the upper classes of society have to a
great extent been deprived of the effect that it should
have produced. The diffusion in our society, on the
one hand, of enormous quantities of those counterfeits
of art which only serve to amuse and corrupt people,
and on the other hand, of works of insignificant exclusive art mistaken for the highest art, have perverted
most men's capacity to be infected by true works of
art and have thus deprived them of the possibility of
experiencing the highest feelings to which mankind
has attained, and which can only be transmitted from
man to man by art.

All the best that has been done in art by man remains strange to people who lack the capacity to be

infected by art, and is replaced either by spurious counterfeits of art, or by insignificant art which they mistake for real art. People of our time and of our society are delighted with Baudelaires, Verlaines, Moréases, Ibsens, and Maeterlincks, in poetry; with Monets, Manets, Puvis de Chavannes, Burne-Joneses, Stucks, and Böcklins, in painting; with Wagners, Liszts, Richard Strausses, in music; and they are no longer capable of comprehending either the highest or the simplest art.

In the upper classes, in consequence of this loss of capacity to be infected by works of art, people grow up, are educated, and live, lacking the fertilizing, improving, influence of art, and therefore not only do not advance towards perfection, do not become kinder, but on the contrary, possessing highly-developed external means of civilization, they yet tend to become continually more savage, more coarse, and more cruel.

Such is the result of the absence from our society of the activity of that essential organ—art. But the consequences of the perverted activity of that organ are yet more harmful, and they are numerous.

The first consequence, plain for all to see, is the enormous expenditure of the labour of working people on things which are not only useless, but are for the most part harmful; and more than that, the waste of priceless human lives on this unnecessary and harmful business. It is terrible to consider with what intensity and amid what privations millions of people—who lack time and opportunity to attend to what they and their families urgently require—labour for ten, twelve, or fourteen, hours on end, and even at night, setting the type for pseudo-artistic books which spread vice among mankind, or working for theatres, concerts, exhibitions, and picture galleries, which for the most part also serve vice; but it is yet more terrible to reflect that lively, kindly, children capable of all that is good, are devoted from their early years to such tasks as these: that for six, eight, or ten, hours a day, and for ten or fifteen years, some of them should play scales and exercises; others should twist their limbs, walk on their toes, and lift their legs above their heads; a third set should sing solfeggios; a fourth set, showing themselves off in all manner of ways, should recite verses; a fifth set should draw from busts or from nude models, and paint studies; a sixth set should write compositions according to the rules of certain periods; and that in these occupations unworthy of a human being, which are often continued long after full maturity, they should waste their physical and mental strength, and lose all perception of the meaning of life. It is often said that it is horrible and pitiful to see little acrobats putting their legs over their necks, but it is not less pitiful to see children of ten giving concerts, and it is still worse to see schoolboys of ten who as a preparation for literary work have learnt by heart the exceptions to the Latin grammar. These people not only grow physically and mentally, but also morally, deformed, and they become incapable of doing anything really needed by man. Occupying in society the rôle of amusers of the rich, they lose their sense of human dignity and develop in themselves such a passion for public applause that they are always a prey to an inflated and unsatisfied vanity, which grows in them to diseased dimensions, and they expend their mental strength in efforts to obtain satisfaction for this passion. And what is most tragic of all is that these people, who for the sake of art are spoilt for life, not only do not render service to this art, but on the contrary inflict great harm on it. They are taught in academies, schools, and conservatoires, how to counterfeit art, and by learning this they so pervert themselves that they quite lose the capacity to produce works of real art, and become purveyors of that counterfeit, or trivial, or depraved, art which floods our society. This is the first obvious consequence of the perversion of the organ of art.

The second consequence is that the productions of amusement-art, which are prepared in such terrific quantities by the armies of professional artists, enable the rich people of our times to live the lives they do, lives not only unnatural but in contradiction to the humane principles they themselves profess. To live as do the idle rich, especially the women, far from nature and from animals, in artificial conditions, with muscles atrophied or misdeveloped by gymnastics, and with enfeebled vital energy, would be impossible were it not for what is called art—for this occupation and amusement which hides from them the meaningless-ness of their lives and saves them from the dullness that oppresses them. Take from all these people the theatres, concerts, exhibitions, piano-playing, songs, and novels, with which they now fill their time, in full assurance that occupation with these things is a very refined, æsthetic, and therefore good, occupation; take from the patrons of art who buy pictures, assist musicians, and are acquainted with writers, their rôle of protectors of this important business of art, and they will not be able to continue such a life but will all be eaten up by ennui and spleen, and will become conscious of the meaninglessness and wrongfulness of their present mode of life. Only occupation with what among them is considered art, renders it possible for them to continue to live on, infringing all natural conditions, without perceiving the emptiness and cruelty of their lives. And this support afforded to the false manner of life pursued by the rich is the second consequence, and a serious one, of the perversion of art.

The third consequence of the perversion of art is the

perplexity produced in the minds of children and plain folk. Among people not perverted by the false theories of our society, among workers and children, there exists a very definite conception of why people should be respected and praised. In the minds of peasants and children the ground for praise or eulogy can only be either physical strength (Hercules, the heroes and conquerors) or moral, spiritual, strength (Sakya Muni giving up a beautiful wife and a kingdom to save mankind, Christ going to the cross for the truth he professed, and all the martyrs and the saints). Both are understood by peasants and children. They understand that physical strength must be respected, for it compels respect; and the moral strength of goodness an unperverted man cannot fail to respect, because his whole spiritual being draws him towards it. But these people, children and peasants, suddenly perceive that besides those praised, respected, and rewarded for physical or moral strength, there are others who are praised, extolled, and rewarded, much more than the heroes of strength and virtue, merely because they sing well, compose verses, or dance. They see that singers, composers, painters, ballet-dancers, earn millions of rubles and receive more honour than the saints do: and peasants and children are perplexed.

When fifty years had elapsed after Púshkin's death, and simultaneously the cheap editions of his works began to circulate among the people and a monument was erected to him in Moscow, I received more than a dozen letters from different peasants, asking why Púshkin was raised to such dignity? And only the other day a literate [1] man from Sarátov, who had evidently

---

[1] In Russian it is customary to make a distinction between literate and illiterate people, that is, between those who can and those who cannot read. *Literate* in this sense does not imply that the man would speak or write correctly. —A. M.

gone out of his mind over this very question called on me. He was on his way to Moscow to expose the clergy for having taken part in raising a monument to Mr. Púshkin.

Indeed one need only imagine to oneself what the state of mind of such a man of the people must be when he learns, from such rumours and newspapers as reach him, that the clergy, Government officials, and all the best people in Russia, are triumphantly unveiling a statue to a great man, the benefactor, the pride of Russia—Púshkin, of whom till then he had never heard. On all sides he reads or hears about this, and he naturally supposes that if such honours are rendered to any one, then without doubt he must have done something extraordinary—either some feat of strength or of goodness. He tries to learn who Púshkin was, and having discovered that Púshkin was neither a hero, nor a general, but a private person and a writer, he comes to the conclusion that Púshkin must have been a holy man and a teacher of goodness, and he hastens to read or to hear his life and works. But what must be his perplexity when he learns that Púshkin was a man of more than easy morals, who was killed in a duel when attempting to kill another man, and that all his service consisted in writing verses about love, which were often very indecent.

That a hero, or Alexander the Great, or Jenghiz Khan, or Napoleon, was great, he understands, because any one of them could have crushed him and a thousand like him; that Buddha, Socrates, and Christ, were great he also understands, for he knows and feels that he and all men should be such as they were; but why a man should be great because he wrote verses about the love of women he cannot make out.

A similar perplexity must trouble the brain of a Breton or Norman peasant who hears that a monument, *'une statue'* (as to the Madonna), is being erected to Baudelaire, and who reads, or is told, what the contents of his *Fleurs du Mal* are; or, more amazing still, to Verlaine, when he learns the story of that man's wretched, vicious life, and reads his verses. And what confusion it must cause in the brains of peasants when they learn that some Patti or Taglioni is paid £10,000 for a season, or that a painter gets as much for a picture, or that authors of novels describing love-scenes have received even more than that.

And it is the same with children. I remember how I passed through this stage of amazement and stupefaction, and only reconciled myself to this exaltation of artists to the level of heroes and saints by lowering in my own estimation the importance of moral excellence, and by attributing a false, unnatural, meaning to works of art. And a similar confusion must occur in the soul of each child and each man of the people when he learns of the strange honours and rewards that are lavished on artists. This is the third consequence of the false relation in which our society stands towards art.

The fourth consequence is that people of the upper classes, more and more frequently encountering the contradictions between beauty and goodness, put the ideal of beauty first, thus freeing themselves from the demands of morality. These people, reversing the rôles, instead of admitting, as is really the case, that the art they serve is an antiquated affair, allege that morality is an antiquated affair, which can have no importance for people on the high plane of development which they think that they occupy.

This result of the false relation to art showed itself in our society long ago; but recently, with its prophet Nietzsche and his adherents, and with the Decadents, and certain English æsthetes who agree with him, it is being expressed with especial impudence. The Decadents, and æsthetes of the type at one time represented by Oscar Wilde, select as a theme for their productions the denial of morality and the laudation of vice.

This art has partly generated and partly coincides with a similar philosophic theory. I recently received from America a book entitled *The Survival of the Fittest: Philosophy of Power*, 1896, by Ragner Redbeard, Chicago. The substance of this book, as it is expressed in the editor's preface, is that to measure right by the false philosophy of the Hebrew prophets and 'weepful Messiahs' is madness. Right is not the offspring of doctrine, but of power. All laws, commandments, or doctrines, as to not doing to another what you do not wish done to you, have no inherent authority whatever, but receive it only from the club, the gallows, and the sword. A man truly free is under no obligation to obey any injunction, human or divine. Obedience is the sign of the degenerate. Disobedience is the stamp of the hero. Men should not be bound by moral rules invented by their foes. The whole world is a slippery battlefield. Ideal justice demands that the vanquished should be exploited, emasculated, and scorned. The free and brave may seize the world. And therefore there should be eternal war for life, for land, for love, for women, for power, and for gold. (Something similar was said a few years ago by the celebrated and refined academician, de Vogüé.) The earth with its treasures is booty for the bold.

The author has evidently by himself, independently of Nietzsche, come to the same conclusions as are professed by the new artists.

Expressed in the form of a doctrine, these positions startle us. In reality they are implied in the ideal of art serving beauty. The art of our upper classes has educated people in this ideal of the superman—which is in reality the old ideal of Nero, Sténka Rázin,[1]

[1] Sténka Rázin was by origin a common Cossack. His brother was hanged for a breach of military discipline, and

Jenghiz Khan, Robert Macaire,[1] or Napoleon, and all their accomplices, assistants, and adulators—and it supports this ideal with all its might.

It is this supplanting of the ideal of what is right by the ideal of what is beautiful, that is, of what is pleasant, that is the fourth consequence, and a terrible one, of the perversion of art in our society. It is fearful to think of what would befall humanity were such art to spread among the masses of the people. And it is already beginning to spread.

Finally, the fifth and chief result is that the art which flourishes in the upper classes of European society has a directly vitiating influence, infecting people with the worst feelings, and with those most harmful to humanity—superstition, patriotism, and above all sensuality.

Look carefully into the causes of the ignorance of the masses, and you may see that the chief cause does not at all lie in the lack of schools and libraries as we are accustomed to suppose, but in those superstitions, both ecclesiastical and patriotic, with which the people are saturated, and which are unceasingly

---

to this event Sténka Rázin's hatred of the governing classes has been attributed. He formed a robber band and subsequently headed a formidable rebellion, declaring himself in favour of freedom for the serfs, religious toleration, and the abolition of taxes. Like the Government he opposed, he relied on force, and though he used it largely in defence of the poor against the rich, he still held to

'The good old rule, the simple plan,
    That they should take who have the power,
    And they should keep who can.'

Like Robin Hood he is favourably treated in popular legends.—A. M.

[1] Robert Macaire is a modern type of adroit and audacious rascality. He was the hero of a popular play produced in Paris in 1834, and of one written by R. L. Stevenson and W. E. Henley, 1897.—A. M.

generated by all the methods of art. Church superstitions are supported and produced by the poetry of
prayers, hymns, paintings, by the sculpture of images
and of statues, by singing, by organs, by music, by
architecture, and even by dramatic art in religious
ceremonies. Patriotic superstitions are supported and
produced by verses and stories (which are supplied
even in schools), by music, by songs, by triumphal
processions, by royal meetings, by martial pictures,
and by monuments.

Were it not for this continual activity in all depart-
ments of art, perpetuating the ecclesiastical and
patriotic intoxication and embitterment of the people,
the masses would long ere this have attained true
enlightenment.

But it is not only in Church matters and patriotic
matters that art depraves; it is art in our time that
serves as the chief cause of the perversion of people in
the most important question of social life—in their
sexual relations. We nearly all know by our own experience, and those who are fathers and mothers know
in the case of their grown-up children also, what fearful mental and physical suffering, what useless waste
of strength, people suffer merely as a consequence of
dissoluteness in sexual desire.

Since the world began, from the Trojan war which
sprang from that same sexual dissoluteness down to
and including the suicides and murders of lovers
described in almost every newspaper, a large proportion of the sufferings of the human race have come
from this source.

And what is art doing? All art real and counterfeit,
with very few exceptions, is devoted to describing,
depicting, and inflaming, sexual love in every shape
and form. If one remembers all those novels and their
lust-kindling descriptions of love, from the most refined to the grossest, with which the literature of our

society overflows; if one only remembers all those pictures and statues representing women's naked bodies and all sorts of abominations, which are reproduced in illustrations and advertisements; if one only remembers all the filthy operas and operettas, songs and ballads, with which our world teems, involuntarily it seems as though existing art had but one definite aim—to disseminate vice as widely as possible.

Such are the most direct, though not all, the consequences of the perversion of art which has occurred in our society. So that what in our society is called art, not only does not conduce to the progress of mankind but more than almost anything else hinders the attainment of goodness in our lives.

Therefore the question which involuntarily presents itself to every man free from artistic activity and not bound to existing art by self-interest, the question asked by me at the beginning of this work: Is it just that to what we call art, to a something possessed by but a small section of society, should be offered up such sacrifices of human labour, of human lives, and of goodness, as are now being offered up? receives the natural reply: No; it is unjust, and these things should not be! Such is also the answer of sound sense and unperverted moral feeling. Not only should these things not be, not only should no sacrifices be offered up to what among us is called art, but on the contrary the efforts of those who wish to live rightly should be directed towards the destruction of this art, for it is one of the most cruel of the evils that harass our section of humanity. So that were the question put: Would it be preferable for our Christian world to be deprived of *all* that is now esteemed to be art, and together with the false to lose *all* that is good in it? I think that every reasonable and moral man would again decide the question as Plato decided it for his *Republic*, and as all the early Church-Christian and

Mahommedan teachers of mankind decided it, that is, would say, Rather let there be no art at all than continue the depraving art or simulation of art, which now exists. Happily no one has to face this question and no one need adopt either solution. All that man can do, and that we—the so-called educated people who are so placed that it is possible for us to understand the meaning of the phenomena of our life—can and should do, is to understand the error we are involved in, and not harden our hearts in it but seek for a way of escape.

CHAPTER XVIII

The purpose of human life is the brotherly union of man.
Art must be guided by this perception.

THE cause of the lie into which the art of our society
has fallen was that people of the upper classes, having
ceased to believe in the Church teaching (called Christian), did not resolve to accept true Christian teaching
in its real and fundamental principles of sonship to
God and brotherhood to man, but continued to live
on without any belief, endeavouring to make up for
the absence of belief—some by hypocrisy, pretending
still to believe in the nonsense of the Church creeds;
others by boldly asserting their disbelief; others by
refined agnosticism; and others again by returning to
the Greek worship of beauty, proclaiming egotism to
be right, and elevating it to the rank of a religious
doctrine.

The cause of the malady was the non-acceptance of
Christ's teaching in its real, that is, its full, meaning.
And the only cure lies in acknowledging that teaching
in its full meaning. Such acknowledgement in our
time is not only possible but inevitable. Already to-
day a man standing on the height of the knowledge of
our age, whether he be nominally a Catholic or a
Protestant, cannot say that he really believes in the
dogmas of the Church: in God being a Trinity, in
Christ being God, in the Scheme of Redemption, and
so forth, nor can he satisfy himself by proclaiming his
unbelief or scepticism, nor by relapsing into the worship of beauty and egotism. Above all he can no
longer say that we do not know the real meaning of
Christ's teaching. That meaning has not only become
accessible to all men of our times, but the whole life

of man to-day is permeated by the spirit of that teaching and is, consciously or unconsciously, guided by it.

However differently in form people belonging to our Christian world may define the destiny of man: whether they see it in human progress (in whatever sense of the words), in the union of all men in a socialistic realm, or in the establishment of a commune; whether they look forward to the union of mankind under the guidance of one universal Church, or to the federation of the world—however various in form their definitions of the destination of human life may be, all men in our times already admit that the highest well-being attainable by men is to be reached by their union with one another.

However people of our upper classes (feeling that their ascendency can only be maintained as long as they separate themselves—the rich and learned—from the labourers—the poor and the unlearned) may seek to devise new conceptions of life by which their privileges may be perpetuated—now the ideal of returning to antiquity, now mysticism, now Hellenism, now the cult of the superior person (supermanism)—they have, willingly or unwillingly, to admit the truth which is becoming clear upon all sides, voluntarily and involuntarily, namely, that our welfare lies only in the union and brotherhood of man.

This truth is unconsciously confirmed by the construction of means of communication—telegraphs, telephones, the press, and the ever-increasing attainability of material well-being for every one—and it is consciously affirmed by the destruction of superstitions which divide men, by the diffusion of the truths of knowledge, and by the expression of the ideal of the brotherhood of man in the best works of art of our time.

Art is a spiritual organ of human life which cannot be destroyed, and therefore, notwithstanding all the efforts made by people of the upper classes to conceal the religious ideal by which humanity lives, that ideal is more and more clearly recognized by man, and even in our perverted society is more and more often partially expressed by science and by art. During the present century works of the higher kind of religious art, permeated by a truly Christian spirit, have appeared more and more frequently both in literature and in painting, as also works of the universal art of common life accessible to all. So that even art knows the true ideal of our times and tends towards it. On the one hand the best works of art of our time transmit religious feelings urging towards the union and brotherhood of man (such are the works of Dickens, Hugo, Dostoévski; and, in painting, of Millet, Bastien Lepage, Jules Breton, Lhermitte, and others); on the other hand they strive towards the transmission, not of feelings which are natural to people of the upper classes only, but of feelings that may unite every one without exception. There are as yet few such works, but the need of them is already acknowledged. In recent times we also meet more and more frequently with attempts at publications, pictures, concerts, and theatres, for the people. All this is still very far from accomplishing what should be done, but the direction in which good art instinctively presses forward to regain the path natural to it, can already be discerned.

The religious perception of our time—which consists in acknowledging that the aim of life (both collective and individual) is the union of mankind—is already so sufficiently distinct that people have now only to reject the false theory of beauty—according to which enjoyment is considered to be the purpose of art—and religious perception will naturally take its place as the guide of the art of our time.

And as soon as this religious perception, which already unconsciously directs the life of man, is consciously acknowledged, then immediately and naturally the division of art into art for the lower and art for the upper classes will disappear. There will be one common, brotherly, universal art; and then first, that art will naturally be rejected which transmits feelings incompatible with the religious perception of our time—feelings which do not unite, but divide men—and later, that insignificant, exclusive art to which an unmerited importance is now attributed will be rejected.

And as soon as this occurs art will immediately cease to be what it has been in recent times, a means of making people coarser and more vicious, and it will become what it always used to be and should be, a means by which humanity progresses towards union and blessedness.

Strange as the comparison may sound, what has happened to the art of our circle and time is what happens to a woman who sells her womanly attractiveness, intended for maternity, for the gratification of those who desire such pleasures.

The art of our time and of our circle has become a prostitute. And this comparison holds good even in minute details. Like her it is not limited to certain times, like her it is always adorned, like her it is always saleable, and like her it is enticing and ruinous.

A real work of art can only arise in the soul of an artist occasionally, as the fruit of the life he has lived, just as a child is conceived by its mother. But counterfeit art is produced by artisans and handicraftsmen continually, if only consumers can be found.

Real art, like the wife of an affectionate husband, needs no ornaments. But counterfeit art, like a prostitute, must always be decked out.

The cause of the production of real art is the artist's inner need to express a feeling that has accumulated, just as for a mother the cause of sexual conception was love. The cause of counterfeit art, as of prostitution, is gain.

The consequence of true art is the introduction of a new feeling into the intercourse of life, as the consequence of a wife's love is the birth of a new man into life.

The consequences of counterfeit art are the perversion of man, pleasure which never satisfies, and the weakening of man's spiritual strength.

And this is what people of our day and of our circle should understand, in order to avoid the filthy torrent of depraved and prostituted art with which we are deluged.

CHAPTER XIX

The art of the future not the possession of a select minority but a means towards perfection and unity.

PEOPLE talk of the art of the future, meaning by art of the future some especially refined new art which they imagine will be developed out of that exclusive art of one class which is now considered the highest art. But no such new art of the future can or will be found. Our exclusive art, that of the upper classes of Christendom, has found its way into a blind alley. The direction in which it has been going leads nowhere. Having once lost hold of that which is most essential to art (namely, the guidance given by religious perception), this art has become ever more and more exclusive and therefore ever more and more perverted, until finally it has come to nothing. The art of the future, that which is really coming, will not be a development of present-day art, but will arise on quite other and new foundations having nothing in common with those by which our present art of the upper classes is guided.

Art of the future, that is to say, such part of art as will be chosen from among all the art diffused among mankind, will consist not in transmitting feelings accessible only to members of the rich classes, as is the case to-day, but in transmitting feelings embodying the highest religious perception of our times. Only those productions will be esteemed art which transmit feelings drawing men together in brotherly union, or such universal feelings as can unite all men. Only such art will be chosen, tolerated, approved, and diffused. But art transmitting feelings flowing from antiquated, outworn, religious teaching; ecclesiastical art, patriotic art, voluptuous art; transmitting feelings of superstitious fear, of pride, of vanity, of ecstatic admiration of national heroes; art exciting exclusive love of one's own people, or sensuality, will be considered bad, harmful art, and will be censured and despised by public opinion. All the rest of art, transmitting feelings accessible only to a section of people, will be considered unimportant, and will be neither blamed nor praised. And the appraisement of art in general will devolve not as is now the case on a separate class of rich people, but on the whole people; so that for a work to be thought good and to be approved and diffused, it will have to satisfy the demands not of a few people living under similar and often unnatural conditions, but of all those great masses of people who undergo the natural conditions of laborious life.

Nor will the artists producing the art be as now merely a few people selected from a small section of the nation, members of the upper classes or their hangers-on, but they will consist of all those gifted members of the whole people who prove capable of, and have an inclination towards, artistic activity.

Artistic activity will then be accessible to all men. It will become accessible to the whole people because (in the first place) in the art of the future not only will that complex technique which deforms the productions of the art of to-day, and requires so great an effort and expenditure of time, not be demanded, but on the contrary the demand will be for clearness, simplicity, and brevity—conditions brought about not by mechanical methods but through the education of taste. And secondly, artistic activity will become accessible to all men of the people because, instead of the present professional schools which only some can enter, all will learn music and graphic art (singing and drawing) equally with letters, in the elementary schools, in such a way that every man, having

K

received the first principles of drawing and music and
feeling a capacity for and a call to one or other of the
arts, will be able to perfect himself in it.

People think that if there are no special art-schools
the technique of art will deteriorate. Undoubtedly
it will deteriorate if by technique we understand
those *complexities* of art which are now considered an
excellence; but if by technique is understood clearness, beauty, simplicity, and compression, in works of
art, then even if the elements of drawing and music
were not to be taught in the national schools, not only
will the technique not deteriorate but, as shown by all
peasant art, it will be a hundred times better. It will
be improved because all the artists of genius now
hidden among the masses will become producers of
art and supply models of excellence which (as has
always been the case) will be the best schools of technique for their successors. For even now every
true artist chiefly learns his technique not in the
schools but in life, from the examples of the great
masters, and then—when art is produced by the best
artists of the whole nation and there are more such
examples and they are more accessible—such part of
school training as the future artist may lose will be
a hundredfold compensated for by the training he
will receive from the numerous examples of good art
diffused in society.

Such will be one difference between present and
future art. Another difference will be that art will not
be produced by professional artists receiving payment
for their work and engaged on nothing else besides
their art. The art of the future will be produced by all
the members of the community who feel need of such
activity, but they will occupy themselves with art only
when they feel such need.

In our society people think that an artist will work
better and produce more if he has a secured mainten-

ance; and this opinion once more would prove quite clearly, were such proof still needed, that what among us is considered to be art is not art but only a counterfeit. It is quite true that for the production of boots or loaves division of labour is very advantageous, and that the bootmaker or baker who need not prepare his own dinner or fetch his own fuel will make more boots or loaves than if he had to busy himself with those matters. But art is not a handicraft, it is the transmission of feeling the artist has experienced. And sound feeling can only be engendered in a man when he is living a life in all respects natural and proper to man. Therefore security of maintenance is a condition most harmful to an artist's true productiveness, since it removes him from the condition natural to all men—that of struggle with nature for the maintenance both of his own life and the lives of others—and thus deprives him of the opportunity and possibility of experiencing the most important and most natural feelings of man. There is no position more injurious to an artist's productiveness than the position of complete security and luxury in which in our society artists usually live.

The artist of the future will live the common life of man, earning his subsistence by some kind of labour. The fruits of the highest spiritual strength that passes through him he will try to share with the greatest possible number of people, for in such transmission to others of the feelings that have arisen in him he will find his happiness and reward. The artist of the future will be unable to understand how an artist, whose chief delight is in the wide diffusion of his works, could give them only in exchange for a certain payment.

Until the dealers are driven out, the temple of art will not be a temple. But the art of the future will drive them out.

And therefore the subject-matter of the art of the future, as I imagine it to myself, will be totally unlike that of to-day. It will consist, not in the expression of exclusive feelings: pride, spleen, satiety, and all possible forms of voluptuousness, available and interesting only to people who have freed themselves by force from the labour natural to human beings; but in the expression of feelings flowing from the religious perception of our times, or open to all men without exception and experienced by a man living a life natural to all men.

To people of our circle who do not know, and cannot or will not understand, the feelings which will form the subject-matter of the art of the future, such subject-matter appears very poor in comparison with those subtleties of exclusive art with which they are now occupied. 'What is there fresh to be said about the Christian feeling of love to one's fellow-man?' 'The feelings common to every one are so insignificant and monotonous,' think they. And yet in our time the really fresh feelings can only be religious, Christian, feelings, and such as are open and accessible to all. The feelings flowing from the religious perception of our times, Christian feelings, are infinitely new and varied, only not in the way some people imagine,—not because they can be evoked by depicting Christ and Gospel episodes, or by repeating in new forms the Christian truths of unity, brotherhood, equality, and love,—but because all the oldest, commonest, and most hackneyed, phenomena of life evoke the newest, most unexpected and poignant emotions as soon as a man regards them from the Christian point of view.

What can be older than the relations of married couples, of parents to children, of children to parents; the relations of men to their fellow-countrymen and to foreigners, to an invasion, to defence, to property, to the land, or to animals? But as soon as a man regards these matters from the Christian point of view, endlessly varied, fresh, complex, and strong, emotions immediately arise.

And in the same way, that realm of subject-matter for the art of the future which relates to the simplest feelings of common life open to all will not be narrowed but widened. In our former art only the expression of feelings natural to people of a certain exceptional position was considered worthy of being transmitted by art, and even then only on condition that those feelings were transmitted in a most refined manner, incomprehensible to the majority of men; all the immense realm of folk-art and children's art—jests, proverbs, riddles, songs, dances, children's games, and mimicry—was not esteemed a domain worthy of art.

The artist of the future will understand that to compose a fairy-tale, a touching little song, a lullaby, an entertaining riddle, an amusing jest, or to draw a sketch which will delight dozens of generations or millions of children and adults, is incomparably more important and more fruitful than to compose a novel or a symphony, or paint a picture, which will divert some members of the wealthy classes for a short time and then for ever be forgotten. The region of this art of the simple feelings accessible to all is enormous and it is as yet almost untouched.

The art of the future, therefore, will not be poorer but infinitely richer in subject-matter. And the form of the art of the future will also not be inferior to the present forms but infinitely superior; superior, not in the sense of having a refined and complex technique, but in the sense of the capacity briefly, simply, and clearly to transmit, without any superfluities, the feeling the artist has experienced and wishes to convey.

I remember once speaking to a famous astronomer who had given public lectures on the spectrum analysis

of the stars of the Milky Way, and saying it would be
a good thing if, with his knowledge and masterly
delivery, he would give a lecture merely on the forma-
tion and movements of the earth, for certainly there
were many people at his lectures on the spectrum
analysis of the stars of the Milky Way, especially among
the women, who did not well know why night follows
day and summer follows winter. The wise astronomer smiled as he answered, 'Yes, it would be a good
thing, but it would be very difficult. To lecture on
the spectrum analysis of the Milky Way is far easier.'

And so it is in art. To write a rhymed poem dealing
with the times of Cleopatra, or paint a picture of Nero
burning Rome, or compose a symphony in the manner
of Brahms or Richard Strauss, or an opera like Wagner's, is far easier than to tell a simple story without
any unnecessary details yet so that it shall transmit
the feelings of the narrator, or to draw a pencil-sketch
which shall touch or amuse the beholder, or to
compose four bars of clear and simple melody without
any accompaniment, which shall convey an impression and be remembered by those who hear it.

'It is impossible for us, with our culture, to return to
a primitive state,' say the artists of our time. 'It is
impossible for us now to write such stories as that of
Joseph or the Odyssey, to produce such statues as the
Venus of Milo, or to compose such music as the folk-
songs.'

And indeed for the artists of our society and day it
is impossible, but not for the future artist who will be
free from all the perversion of technical improvements
concealing the absence of subject-matter, and who,
not being a professional artist, and receiving no payment for his activity, will only produce art when he
feels impelled to do so by an irresistible inner impulse.

The art of the future will thus be completely distinct both in subject-matter and in form from what is

now called art. The only subject-matter of the art of the future will be either feelings drawing men towards union, or such as already unite them; and the forms of art will be such as will be open to every one. And therefore the ideal of excellence in the future will not be exclusiveness of feeling, accessible only to some, but, on the contrary, its universality; and not bulkiness, obscurity, and complexity of form, which are now valued, but on the contrary, brevity, clearness, and simplicity of expression. Only when art has attained to that, will it neither divert nor deprave men as it does now, calling on them to expend their best strength on it, but be what it should be—a vehicle wherewith to transmit religious, Christian, perception from the realm of reason and intellect into that of feeling, and really drawing people in actual life nearer to the perfection and union indicated to them by their religious perception.

CHAPTER XX

The connexion between science and art. The mendacious sciences; the trivial sciences. Science should deal with the great problems of human life and serve as a basis for art.

CONCLUSION

I HAVE accomplished to the best of my ability this work which has occupied me for fifteen years, on a subject near to me—that of art. By saying that this subject has occupied me for fifteen years I do not mean that I have been writing this book fifteen years, but only that I began to write on art fifteen years ago thinking that when once I undertook the task I should be able to accomplish it without a break. It proved however that my views on the matter then were so far from clear that I could not arrange them in a way that satisfied me. From that time I have never ceased to think on the subject, and I have recommenced writing on it six or seven times; but each time after writing a considerable part of it I have found myself unable to bring the work to a satisfactory conclusion and have had to put it aside. Now I have finished it; and however badly I may have performed the task, my hope is that my fundamental thought on the false direction the art of our society has taken and is following, on the reasons of this, and on the real destination of art, is correct, and that therefore my work will not be without avail. But that this should come to pass and that art should really abandon its false path and take the new direction, it is necessary that another equally important spiritual human activity—science—in intimate dependence on which art always rests, should abandon the false path which it too, like art, is following.

Science and art are as closely bound together as the lungs and the heart, so that if the one organ is vitiated the other cannot act rightly.

True science investigates and brings to human perception such truths and such knowledge as the people of a given time and society consider most important. Art transmits these truths from the region of perception to the region of emotion. If therefore the path chosen by science be false, so also will be the path taken by art. Science and art are like a certain kind of barge with kedge-anchors, which used to ply on our rivers. Science, like the boats which took the anchors up-stream and made them secure, gives direction to the forward movement; while art, like the windlass worked on the barge to draw it towards the anchor, causes the actual progression. And thus a false activity of science inevitably causes a correspondingly false activity of art.

As art in general is the transmission of every kind of feeling, but in the limited sense of the word we call nothing art unless it transmits feelings acknowledged by us to be important, so also science in general is the transmission of all possible knowledge, but in the limited sense of the word we accord the name of science to that which transmits knowledge admitted by us to be important.

And the degree of importance both of the feelings transmitted by art and of the information transmitted by science, is decided by the religious perception of the given time and society, that is, by the common understanding of the purpose of their lives possessed by the people of that time or society.

What most of all contributes to the fulfilment of that purpose will be studied most; what contributes less will be studied less; what does not contribute at all to the fulfilment of the purpose of human life will be entirely neglected, or, if studied, such study will not be accounted science. So it always has been and so it should be now, for such is the nature of human knowledge and of human life. But the science of the upper classes of our time, which not only does not acknowledge any religion but considers every religion to be mere superstition, could not and cannot make such distinctions.

Scientists of our day affirm that they study *everything* impartially; but as everything is too much, is in fact an infinity of objects, and it is impossible to study all alike, this is only said in theory, while in practice not everything is studied and study is applied far from impartially—only that being studied which, on the one hand is most wanted by, and on the other hand is pleasantest to, those who occupy themselves with science. And what the members of the upper classes who are occupying themselves with science most want is the maintenance of the system under which they retain their privileges; and what is pleasantest are things that satisfy idle curiosity, do not demand great mental effort, and can be practically applied.

Therefore one side of science, including theology and philosophy adapted to the existing order, as also history and political economy of the same sort, is chiefly occupied in proving that the existing order is the very one which ought to endure; that it has come into existence and continues to exist by the operation of immutable laws not amenable to human will, and that all efforts to change it are therefore harmful and wrong. The other part, experimental science—including mathematics, astronomy, chemistry, physics, botany, and all the natural sciences—is exclusively occupied with things that have no direct relation to the purpose of human life: with what is curious, and with things of which practical application advantageous to people of the upper classes can be made. And to justify this selection of objects of study, which (in conformity with their own position) the men of science of our times have made, they have devised a theory of science for science's sake, quite similar to the theory of art for art's sake.

As by the theory of art for art's sake it appears that occupation with all those things that please us is art, so by the theory of science for science's sake, the study of that which interests us is science.

So that one side of science, instead of studying how people should live in order to fulfil their mission in life, demonstrates the righteousness and immutability of the bad and false arrangements of life which exist around us; while the other part, experimental science, occupies itself with questions of simple curiosity, or with technical improvements.

The first of these divisions of science is harmful, not only because it confuses people's perceptions and gives false decisions, but also by its mere existence, occupying the ground which should belong to true science. It does this harm, that every man in order to approach the study of the most important questions of life must first refute these erections of lies which have for ages been piled around each of the most essential questions of human life, and which are propped up by all the strength of human ingenuity.

The second division—the one of which modern science is so particularly proud, and which is considered by many people to be the only real science—is harmful in that it diverts attention from the really important subjects to insignificant subjects, and is also directly harmful in that under the evil system of society which the first division of science justifies and supports, a great part of the technical gains of science are turned not to the advantage, but to the injury, of mankind.

Indeed it is only to those who are devoting their lives to such study that it seems as if all the inventions which are made in the sphere of natural science were very important and useful things. And to these people it seems so only when they do not look around them and do not see what really is important. They only need tear themselves away from the psychological microscope under which they examine the objects of their study, and look about them, in order to see how insignificant is all that has afforded them such naïve pride, all that knowledge not only of n dimensional geometry, spectrum analysis of the Milky Way, the form of atoms, dimensions of human skulls of the Stone Age, and similar trifles, but even our knowledge of micro-organisms, x-rays, and so forth, in comparison with such knowledge as we have thrown aside and handed over to the perversions of the professors of theology, jurisprudence, political economy, financial science, etc. We need only look around us to perceive that the activity proper to real science is not the study of whatever happens to interest us, but the study of how man's life should be established,—the study of those questions of religion, morality, and social life, without the solution of which all our knowledge of nature will be harmful or insignificant.

We are highly delighted and very proud that our science renders it possible to utilize the energy of a waterfall and make it work in factories, or that we have pierced tunnels through mountains, and so forth; but the pity of it is that we make the force of the waterfall labour not for the benefit of the workmen, but to enrich capitalists who produce articles of luxury or weapons of man-destroying war. The same dynamite with which we blast the mountains to pierce tunnels, we use for wars, which latter we not only do not intend to abstain from, but consider inevitable and unceasingly prepare for.

If we are now able to inoculate preventively with diphtheritic microbes, to find a needle in a body by means of x-rays, to straighten a hunchback, cure syphilis, and perform wonderful operations, we should not be proud of these acquisitions (even were they all established beyond dispute) if we fully understood the true purpose of real science. If but one-tenth of the efforts now spent on objects of pure curiosity or of merely practical application were expended on real science organizing the life of man, more than half the people now sick would not have the illnesses from which a small minority of them get cured in hospitals. There would be no anæmic and deformed children growing up in factories, no death-rates, as now, of 50 per cent. among children, no deterioration of whole generations, no prostitution, no syphilis, and no murdering of hundreds of thousands in wars, nor those horrors of folly and misery which our present science considers a necessary condition of human life.

We have so perverted the conception of science that it seems strange to men of our day to allude to sciences which should prevent the mortality of children, prostitution, syphilis, the deterioration of whole generations, and the wholesale murder of men. It seems to us that science is only then real science when a man in a laboratory pours liquids from one jar into another, or analyses the spectrum, or cuts up frogs and porpoises, or weaves in a specialized scientific jargon an obscure network of conventional phrases—theological, philosophical, historical, juridical, or politico-economical—semi-intelligible to the man himself, and intended to demonstrate that what now is, is what should be.

But science, true science—such science as would really deserve the respect which is now claimed by the followers of one(the least important) part of science—is not at all of this kind: real science lies in knowing what we should and what we should not believe, in knowing how the associated life of man should, and should not, be constituted: how to treat sexual relations, how to educate children, how to use the land, how to cultivate it oneself without oppressing other people, how to treat foreigners, how to treat animals, and much more that is important for the life of man.

Such has true science ever been and such it should be. And such science is springing up in our times; but on the one hand, such true science is denied and refuted by all those scientific people who defend the existing order of society, and on the other hand, it is considered empty, unnecessary, unscientific science by those who are engrossed in experimental science.

For instance, books and sermons appear demonstrating the antiquatedness and absurdity of Church dogmas, as well as the necessity of making clear the reasonable religious perception suitable to our times, and all the theology that is held to be real science is engaged only in refuting these works, and in exercising human intelligence again and again on finding support and justification for superstitions long since outlived and which have now become quite meaningless. Or a sermon appears showing that land should not be an object of private possession and that the institution of private property in land is a chief cause of the poverty of the masses. Apparently science, real science, should welcome such a sermon and draw further deductions from this position. But the science of our times does nothing of the kind: on the contrary, political economy demonstrates the opposite position, namely, that landed property, like every other form of property, must be more and more concentrated in the hands of a small number of owners. Again, in the same way, one would suppose it to be the business of real science to demonstrate the irrationality, unprofitableness, and immorality, of war and of executions; or the inhumanity and harmfulness of prostitution; or the absurdity, harmfulness, and immorality of using narcotics or eating animals; or the irrationality, harmfulness, and obsolescence of patriotism. And such works exist, but are all considered unscientific; while works to prove that all these things ought to continue, and works intended to satisfy an idle thirst for knowledge lacking any relation to human life, are considered to be scientific.

The deviation of the science of our time from its true purpose is strikingly illustrated by the ideals which are put forward by some scientists, and are not denied but admitted by the majority of scientific men.

These ideals are expressed not only in stupid, fashionable, books describing the world as it will be a thousand or three thousand years hence, but also by sociologists who consider themselves to be serious men of science. These ideals are that food, instead of being obtained from the land by agriculture, will be prepared in laboratories by chemical means, and that human labour will be almost entirely superseded by the utilization of natural forces.

Man will not, as now, eat an egg laid by a hen he has kept, or bread grown in his field, or an apple from a tree he has reared, and which has blossomed and matured in his sight; but he will eat tasty, nutritious food prepared in laboratories by the conjoint labour of many people in which he will share to a small extent. Man will hardly need to labour, so that all men will be able to yield to idleness as the upper, ruling, classes now yield to it.

Nothing shows more plainly than these ideals, to what a degree the science of our times has deviated from the true path.

The great majority of men in our times lack good and sufficient food (as well as dwellings and clothes and all the first necessities of life). And this great majority of men is compelled, to the injury of its well-being, to labour continually beyond its strength. Both these evils can easily be removed by abolishing mutual strife, luxury, and the unrighteous distribution of wealth—in a word by the abolition of a false and harmful order and the establishment of a reasonable, human, manner of life. But science considers the existing order of things to be as immutable as the movements of the planets, and therefore assumes that the purpose of science is, not to elucidate the falseness of this order and arrange a new, reasonable way of life, but under the existing order of things to feed everybody and enable all to be as idle as the ruling classes, living depraved lives, now are.

And meanwhile it is forgotten that nourishment by corn, vegetables, and fruit, raised from the soil by one's own labour, is the pleasantest, healthiest, easiest, and most natural nourishment, and that the work of using one's muscles is as necessary a condition of life as is the oxidization of the blood by breathing.

To invent means whereby people, while continuing our false division of property and labour, might be well nourished by means of chemically-prepared food, and might make the forces of nature work for them, is like inventing means to pump oxygen into the lungs of a man kept in a closed chamber the air of which is bad, when all that is needed is for the man no longer to be confined in a closed chamber.

In the vegetable and animal kingdoms a laboratory has been arranged for the production of food such as can be surpassed by no professors, and to enjoy the fruits of this laboratory and to participate in it man has only to yield to that ever joyful impulse to labour without which his life is a torment. And lo and behold! the scientists of our times, instead of employing all their strength to abolish whatever hinders man from utilizing the good things prepared for him, acknowledge the conditions under which man is deprived of these blessings to be unalterable; and instead of arranging the life of man so that he may work joyfully and be fed from the soil, they devise methods which will cause him to become an artificial abortion. It is like not helping a man out of confinement into the fresh air, but devising means, instead, to pump into him the necessary quantity of oxygen, and arranging so that he may live in a stifling cellar instead of living at home.

Such false ideals could not exist if science were not on a false path.

And yet the feelings transmitted by art grow up on the bases supplied by science.

But what feelings can such misdirected science evoke? One side of this science evokes antiquated feelings which humanity has exhausted and which in our times are bad and exclusive. The other side, occupied with the study of subjects unrelated to the conduct of human life, by its very nature cannot serve as a basis for art.

So that art in our times, to be art, must either open up its own road independently of science, or must take its direction from unrecognized science which is denounced by the orthodox section of science. And this is what art, when it even partially fulfils its mission, is doing.

It is to be hoped that the work I have tried to perform concerning art will be performed also for science: that the falseness of the theory of science for science's sake will be demonstrated; that the necessity of acknowledging Christian teaching in its true meaning will be clearly shown, and on the basis of that teaching a re-appraisement be made of the knowledge we possess and of which we are so proud; that the secondariness and insignificance of experimental science, and the primacy and importance of religious, moral, and social, knowledge will be established; and that such knowledge will not, as now, be left to the guidance of the upper classes only, but will form a chief interest of all free, truth-loving men, such as those who, not by the help of the upper classes but in spite of them, have always forwarded the real science of life.

Astronomical, physical, chemical, and biological science, as also technical and medical science, will be studied only in so far as they can help to free mankind from religious, juridical, or social deceptions, or can serve to promote the well-being of all men and not of any single class.

Only then will science cease to be what it is now—on the one hand a system of sophistries needed for the maintenance of the existing worn-out order of society, and on the other hand a shapeless mass of miscellaneous knowledge, for the most part good for little or nothing—and become a shapely and organic whole having a definite and reasonable purpose comprehensible to all men, namely, that of bringing to the consciousness of men the truths that flow from the religious perception of our times.

And only then will art, which is always dependent on science, be what it might and should be, an organ co-equally important with science for the life and progress of mankind.

Art is not a pleasure, a solace, or an amusement; art is a great matter. Art is an organ of human life transmitting man's reasonable perception into feeling. In our age the common religious perception of men is the consciousness of the brotherhood of man—we know that the well-being of man lies in union with his fellow-men. True science should indicate the various methods of applying this consciousness to life. Art should transform this perception into feeling.

The task of art is enormous. Through the influence of real art, aided by science, guided by religion, that peaceful co-operation of man which is now maintained by external means,—by our law-courts, police, charitable institutions, factory inspection, and so forth,—should be obtained by man's free and joyous activity. Art should cause violence to be set aside.[1]

And it is only art that can accomplish this.

All that now, independently of the fear of violence and punishment, makes the social life of man possible (and already this is an enormous part of the order of our lives)—all this has been brought about by art. If by art it has been inculcated on people how they should treat religious objects, their parents, their children, their wives, their relations, strangers, foreigners; how to conduct themselves towards their elders, their superiors, towards those who suffer, towards their enemies, and towards animals; and if this has been obeyed through generations by millions of people, not only unenforced by any violence but so that the force of such customs can be shaken in no way but by means of art: then by art also other customs more in accord with the religious perception of our time may be evoked. If art has been able to convey the sentiment of reverence for images, for the Eucharist, and for the king's person; of shame at betraying a comrade, devotion to a flag, the necessity of revenge for an insult, the need to sacrifice one's labour for the erection and adornment of churches, the duty of defending one's honour, or the glory of one's native land,—then that same art can also evoke reverence for the dignity of every man and for the life of every animal; can make

---

[1] Tolstóy's doctrine of Non-Resistance to 'him that is evil' by any use of physical force has caused much perplexity, and is accepted in its completeness by but few people in the Western world. In this passage however he states it in a form to which it would be hard to raise any objection. Never before had the doctrine of Non-Resistance been put so briefly, persuasively, and attractively. —A. M.

men ashamed of luxury, of violence, of revenge, or of using for their own pleasure that of which others are in need; can compel people freely, gladly, and spontaneously, to sacrifice themselves in the service of man.

The task for art to accomplish is to make that feeling of brotherhood and love of one's neighbour, now attained only by the best members of society, the customary feeling and the instinct of all men. By evoking under imaginary conditions the feeling of brotherhood and love, religious art will train men to experience those same feelings under similar circumstances in actual life; it will lay in the souls of men the rails along which the actions of those whom art thus educates will naturally pass. And universal art, by uniting the most different people in one common feeling by destroying separation, will educate people to union and will show them, not by reason but by life itself, the joy of universal union reaching beyond the bounds set by life.

The destiny of art in our time is to transmit from the realm of reason to the realm of feeling the truth that well-being for men consists in their being united together, and to set up, in place of the existing reign of force, that kingdom of God—that is, of love—which we all recognize to be the highest aim of human life.

Possibly in the future science may reveal to art yet newer and higher ideals which art may realize; but in our time the destiny of art is clear and definite. The task of Christian art is to establish brotherly union among men.

APPENDICES

APPENDIX I

Translations of French poems and prose quoted in Chapter X.[1]

BAUDELAIRE's 'FLOWERS OF EVIL'

No. XXIV

I adore thee as much as the vaults of night,
O vessel of grief, taciturnity great,
And I love thee the more because of thy flight.
It seemeth, my night's beautifier, that you
Still heap up those leagues—yes! ironically heap!—
That divide from my arms the immensity blue.

I advance to attack, I climb to assault,
Like a choir of young worms at a corpse in the vault;
Thy coldness, oh cruel, implacable beast!
Yet heightens thy beauty, on which my eyes feast!

BAUDELAIRE's 'FLOWERS OF EVIL'

No. XXXVI

Duellum

Two warriors come running, to fight they begin,
With gleaming and blood they bespatter the air;
These games, and this clatter of arms, is the din
Of youth that's a prey to the raging of love.

---

[1] The translations in Appendices I, II, and III are by my wife, Louise Maude. The aim of these renderings has been to keep as close to the originals as the obscurity of meaning allowed. The sense (or absence of sense) has therefore been more considered than the form of the verses. —A. M.

The rapiers are broken! and so is our youth,
But the dagger's avenged, dear! and so is the sword,
By the nail that is steeled and the hardened tooth.
Oh! the fury of hearts aged and ulcered by love!
In the ditch, where the lynx and the pard have their lair,
Our heroes have rolled in an angry embrace;
Their skin blooms on brambles that erewhile were bare.
That ravine is a friend-inhabited hell!
Then let us roll in, oh woman inhuman,
To immortalize hatred that nothing can quell!

FROM BAUDELAIRE'S PROSE WORK ENTITLED 'LITTLE POEMS IN PROSE'

The Stranger

Whom dost thou love best? say, enigmatical man—thy father, thy mother, thy sister, or thy brother?

'I have neither father, nor mother, nor sister, nor brother.'

Thy friends?

'There you use an expression the meaning of which till now remains unknown to me.'

Thy country?

'I know not in what latitude it is situated.'

Beauty?

'I would gladly love her, goddess and immortal.'

Gold?

'I hate it, as you hate God.'

Then what do you love, extraordinary stranger?

'I love the clouds ... the clouds that pass ... there ... the marvellous clouds!'

The Soup and the Clouds

My beloved little stupid was giving me my dinner, and I was contemplating, through the open window of the dining-room, those moving architectures which God makes out of vapours, the marvellous constructions of the impalpable. And I said to myself, amid my contemplation, All these phantasmagoria are almost as beautiful as the eyes of my beautiful beloved, the monstrous little silly with the green eyes.

Suddenly I felt the violent blow of a fist on my back, and I heard a harsh, charming voice, an hysterical voice, as it were hoarse with brandy, the voice of my dear little well-beloved, saying, Are you going to eat your soup soon, you d——b——of a dealer in clouds?

The Gallant Marksman

As the carriage was passing through the forest he ordered it to be stopped near a shooting-gallery, saying that he wished to shoot off a few bullets to *kill* Time. To kill this monster, is it not the most ordinary and the most legitimate occupation of every one? And he gallantly offered his arm to his dear, delicious, and execrable wife—that mysterious woman to whom he owed so much pleasure, so much pain, and perhaps also a large part of his genius.

Several bullets struck far from the intended mark—one even penetrated the ceiling; and as the charming creature laughed wildly, mocking her husband's awkwardness, he turned abruptly towards her and said, Notice that doll there on the right with the haughty mien and her nose in the air; well, dear angel, *I imagine to myself that it is you!* And he closed his eyes and pulled the trigger. The doll was neatly decapitated.

Then, bowing towards his dear one, his delightful, execrable wife, his inevitable, pitiless muse, and kissing her hand respectfully, he added, Ah! my dear angel, how I thank you for my skill!

Verlaine's 'Forgotten Airs'

No. I

'The wind in the plain
Suspends its breath.'—FAVART.

'Tis ecstasy languishing,
Amorous fatigue,
Of woods all the shudderings
Embraced by the breeze,
'Tis the choir of small voice
Towards the grey trees.

Oh the frail and fresh murmuring!
The twitter and buzz,
The soft cry resembling
Breathed forth by the grass . . .
Oh, the roll of the pebbles
'Neath waters that pass!

Oh, this soul that is groaning
In sleepy complaint!
In us is it moaning?
In me and in you?
Low anthem exhaling
While soft falls the dew.

Verlaine's 'Forgotten Airs'

No. VIII

In the unending
Dullness of this land,
Uncertain the snow
Is gleaming like sand.

No kind of brightness
In copper-hued sky,
The moon you might see
Now live and now die.

Grey float the oak trees—
Cloudlike they seem—
Of neighbouring forests,
Mists in between.

Wolves hungry and lean,
And famishing crow,
What happens to you
When acrid winds blow?

In the unending
Dullness of this land,
Uncertain the snow
Is gleaming like sand.

Song by Maeterlinck

When he went away,
(Then I heard the door)
When he went away,
On her lips a smile there lay . . .

Back he came to her,
(Then I heard the lamp)
Back he came to her,
Some one else was there . . .

It was death I met,
(And I heard her soul)
It was death I met,
For her he's waiting yet . . .

Some one came to say,
(Child, I am afraid)
Some one came to say
That he would go away . . .

With my lamp alight,
(Child, I am afraid)
With my lamp alight,
Approached I in affright . . .

To one door I came,
(Child, I am afraid)
To one door I came,
A shudder shook the flame . . .

At the second door,
(Child, I am afraid)
At the second door
Words did the flame outpour . . .

To the third I came,
(Child, I am afraid)
To the third I came,
Then died the little flame . . .

Should he one day return,
And see you lying dead?
Say I longed for him
When on my dying bed . . .

Should he question more
Without knowing me?
Like a sister speak;
Suffering he may be ...

If he asks for you,
Say what answer then?
Give him my gold ring
And answer not a thing ...

Should he question why
Empty is the hall?
Show the gaping door,
The lamp alight no more ...

Should he question me
Concerning the last hour?
Say I smiled for fear
Lest he should shed a tear ...

APPENDIX II

This is the first page of Mallarmé's book *Divagations*, referred to in Chapter X, page 146.

Le Phénomène Futur

Un ciel pâle, sur le monde qui finit de décrépitude, va peut-être partir avec les nuages: les lambeaux de la pourpre usée des couchants déteignent dans une rivière dormant à l'horizon submergé de rayons et d'eau. Les arbres s'ennuient, et, sous leur feuillage blanchi (de la poussière du temps plutôt que celle des chemins), monte la maison en toile de Montreur de choses Passées: maint réverbère attend le crépuscule et ravive les visages d'une malheureuse foule, vaincue par la maladie immortelle et le péché des siècles, d'hommes près de leurs chétives complices enceintes des fruits misérables avec lesquels périra la terre. Dans le silence inquiet de tous les yeux suppliant là-bas le soleil qui, sous l'eau, s'enfonce avec le désespoir d'un cri, voici le simple boniment: 'Nulle enseigne ne vous régale du spectacle intérieur, car il n'est pas maintenant un peintre capable d'en donner une ombre triste. J'apporte, vivante (et préservée à travers les ans par la science souveraine), une Femme d'autrefois. Quelque folie, originelle et naïve, une extase d'or, je ne sais quoi! par elle nommée sa chevelure, se ploie avec la grâce des étoffes autour d'un visage qu'éclaire la nudité sanglante de ses lèvres. A la place du vêtement vain, elle a un corps; et les yeux, semblables aux pierres rares! ne valent pas ce regard qui sort de sa chair heureuse: des seins levés comme s'ils étaient pleins d'un lait éternel, la pointe vers le ciel, les jambes lisses qui gardent le sel de la mer première.'

Se rappelant leurs pauvres épouses, chauves, morbides et pleines d'horreur, les maris se pressent: elles aussi par curiosité, mélancoliques, veulent voir.

Quand tous auront contemplé la noble créature, vestige de quelque époque déjà maudite, les uns indifférents, car ils n'auront pas eu la force de comprendre, mais d'autres navrés et la paupière humide de larmes résignées, se regarderont; tandis que les poètes de ces temps, sentant se rallumer leurs yeux éteints, s'achemineront vers leur lampe, le cerveau ivre un instant d'une gloire confuse, hantés du Rythme et dans l'oubli d'exister à une époque qui survit à la beauté.

The Future Phenomenon—BY MALLARMÉ

A pale sky, above the world that is ending through decrepitude, about perhaps to pass away with the clouds: shreds of worn-out purple of the sunsets wash off their colour in a river sleeping on the horizon, submerged with rays and water. The trees are weary, and beneath their whitened foliage (whitened by the dust of time rather than of the roads) rises the canvas house of 'Showman of Things Past.' Many a lamp awaits the gloaming and brightens the faces of a miserable crowd vanquished by the everlasting sickness and sin of ages, of men by the sides of their puny accomplices pregnant with the miserable fruit through which the world will perish. In the anxious silence of all the eyes there supplicating the sun, which sinks under the water with the desperation of a cry, this is the plain announcement: 'No signboard regales you with the spectacle that is inside, for there is no painter now capable of giving even a sad shadow of it. I bring, living (and preserved by sovereign science through the years), a Woman of other days. Some kind of folly, naïve and original, an ecstasy of gold, I know not what! by her called her hair, clings with the grace of drapery round a face brightened by the blood-red nudity of her lips. In place of vain clothing, she has a body; and her eyes, resembling precious stones! are not worth that look which comes from her happy flesh: breasts raised as if full of eternal milk, the points towards the sky; the smooth legs, that keep the salt of the first sea.' Remembering their poor spouses, bald, morbid, and full of horrors, the husbands press forward: the women too, from curiosity, gloomily wish to see.

When all shall have contemplated the noble creature, vestige of some epoch already damned, they will look at each other, some indifferently, for they will not have had the strength to understand, but others broken-hearted and with eye-lids wet with tears of resignation, while the poets of those times, feeling their dim eyes rekindled, will make their way towards their lamp, their brain for an instant drunk with confused glory, haunted by Rhythm and forgetful that they exist at an epoch which has survived beauty.

APPENDIX III

Poems referred to in Chapter X, page 169.

No. 1

The following verse is by Henri de Régnier, from page 28 of a volume of his poems:—

L'accueil

Si tu veux que ce soir, à l'âtre, je t'accueille—
Jette d'abord la fleur, qui de ta main s'effeuille;
Son cher parfum ferait ma tristesse trop sombre;
Et ne regarde pas derrière toi vers l'ombre,
Car je te veux, ayant oublié la forêt
Et le vent, et l'écho et ce qui parlerait
Voix à ta solitude ou pleur à ton silence!
Et debout, avec ton ombre qui te devance,
Et hautaine sur mon seuil, et pâle, et venue
Comme si j'étais mort ou que tu fusses nue!

HENRI DE RÉGNIER: *Les jeux rustiques et devins;*

The Welcome

If you wish us to-night by my fireside to greet—
Drop the flower you hold that sheds petals so sweet;
Its dear scent would render my sadness too black;
And do not on the shadows behind you look back,
For I want you, forgetful of forest and wind,
Of echoes and all you'd recall to your mind
Giving voice to your silence, to solitude tears,
At my door, while before you your shadow appears,
And haughty and pale and erect you stand there—
Just as if I were dead, or that naked you were.

No. 2

The following verses are by Vielé-Griffin, from page 28 of a volume of his poems:—

Oiseau Bleu Couleur du Temps

1.

Sais-tu l'oubli
D'un vain doux rêve,
Oiseau moqueur
De la forêt?
Le jour pâlit,
La nuit se lève,
Et dans mon cœur
L'ombre a pleuré;

2.

O chante-moi
Ta folle gamme,
Car j'ai dormi
Ce jour durant;
Le lâche émoi
Où fut mon âme
Sanglote ennui
Le jour mourant . . .

3.

Sais-tu le chant
De sa parole
Et de sa voix,
Toi qui redis
Dans le couchant
Ton air frivole
Comme autrefois
Sous les midis?

4.

O, chante alors
La mélodie
De son amour,
Mon fol espoir,

Parmi les ors
Et l'incendie
Du vain doux jour
Qui meurt ce soir.

FRANCIS VIELÉ-GRIFFIN: *Poèmes et Poésies.*

Blue Bird Colour Of The Times

I.

Canst thou forget
In dreams so vain,
Oh, mocking bird
Of forest deep?
The day doth set,
Night comes again,
My heart has heard
The shadows weep;

2.

Thy tones let flow
In maddening scale;
For I have slept
The livelong day;
Emotions low
In me now wail,
My soul they've kept:
Light dies away . . .

3.

That music sweet,
Ah, do you know
Her voice and speech?
Your airs so light
You who repeat
In sunset's glow,
As you sang, each,
At noonday's height.

4.

Of my desire,
My hope so bold,
Her love—up, sing,
Sing 'neath this light,

This flaming fire,
And all the gold
The eve doth bring
Ere comes the night.

No. 3

And here are some verses by the esteemed young poet Verhaeren, which I also take from page 28 of his Works:—

Attirances

Lointainement, et si étrangement pareils,
De grands masques d'argent que la brume recule,
Vaguent, au jour tombant, autour des vieux soleils.

Les doux lointains!—et comme, au fond du crépuscule,
Ils nous fixent le cœur, immensément le cœur,
Avec les yeux défunts de leur visage d'âme.

C'est toujours du silence, à moins, dans la pâleur
Du soir, un jet de feu soudain, un cri de flamme,
Un départ de lumière inattendu vers Dieu.

On se laisse charmer et troubler de mystère,
Et l'on dirait des morts qui taisent un adieu
Trop mystique, pour être écouté par la terre!

Sont-ils le souvenir matériel et clair
Des éphèbes chrétiens couchés aux catacombes
Parmi les lys? Sont-ils leur regard et leur chair?

Ou seul, ce qui survit de merveilleux aux tombes
De ceux qui sont partis, vers leurs rêves, un soir,
Conquérir la folie à l'assaut des nuées?

Lointainement, combien nous les sentons vouloir
Un peu d'amour pour leurs œuvres destituées,
Pour leur errance et leur tristesse aux horizons.

Toujours! aux horizons du cœur et de pensées,
Alors que les vieux soirs éclatent en blasons
Soudains, pour les gloires noires et angoissées.

ÉMILE VERHAEREN,
Poèmes.

L

Attractions

Large masks of silver, by mists drawn away,
So strangely alike, yet so far apart,
Float round the old suns when faileth the day.

They transfix our hearts, so immensely our hearts,
Those distances mild, in the twilight deep,
Looking out of dead faces, with their spirit eyes.

All around is now silence, except when there leap
In the pallor of evening, with fiery cries,
Some fountains of flame that Godward do fly.

Mysterious trouble and charms us enfold,
You might think that the dead spoke a silent good-bye,
Oh! too mystical far on earth to be told!

Are they the memories, material and bright,
Of the Christian youths that in catacombs sleep
'Mid the lilies? Are they their flesh or their sight?

Or the marvel alone that survives, in the deep,
Of those that, one night, returned to their dreams
Of conquering folly by assaulting the skies?

For their destitute works—we feel it, it seems,
For a little love their longing cries
From horizons far—for their wanderings and pain,

In horizons ever of heart and thought,
While the evenings old in bright blaze wane
Suddenly, for black glories anguish fraught.

No. 4

And the following is a poem by Moréas, evidently
an admirer of Greek beauty. It is from page 28 of a
volume of his poems:—

Énone au Clair Visage

Énone, j'avais cru qu'en aimant ta beauté
Où l'âme avec le corps trouvent leur unité,
J'allais, m'affermissant et le cœur et l'esprit,
Monter jusqu'à cela, qui jamais ne périt,

N'ayant été créé, qui n'est froidure ou feu,
Qui n'est beau quelque part et laid en autre lieu;
Et me flattais encor d'une belle harmonie
Que j'eusse composé du meilleur et du pire,
Ainsi que le chanteur qui chérit Polymnie,
En accordant le grave avec l'aigu, retire
Un son bien élevé sur les nerfs de sa lyre.
Mais mon courage, hélas! se pâmant comme mort,
M'enseigna que le trait qui m'avait fait amant
Ne fut pas de cet arc que courbe sans effort
La Vénus qui naquit du mâle seulement,
Mais que j'avais souffert cette Vénus dernière,
Qui a le cœur couard, né d'une faible mère.
Et pourtant, ce mauvais garçon, chasseur habile,
Qui charge son carquois de sagette subtile,
Qui secoue en riant sa torche, pour un jour,
Qui ne pose jamais que sur de tendres fleurs,
C'est sur un teint charmant qu'il essuie les pleurs,
Et c'est encore un Dieu, Énone, cet Amour.
Mais, laisse, les oiseaux du printemps sont partis,
Et je vois les rayons du soleil amortis.
Énone, ma douleur, harmonieux visage,
Superbe humilité, doux-honnête langage,
Hier me remirant dans cet étang glacé
Qui au bout du jardin se couvre de feuillage,
Sur ma face je vis que les jours ont passé.

JEAN MORÉAS: *Le Pèlerin Passionné.*

Enone of the Clear Visage

Enone, in loving thy beauty I thought
(Where the soul and the body to union are brought)
I should mount, by strengthening my heart and my mind,
Till that which knows nothing of Death I should find:
Uncreated, which is not here ugly, there fair,
Nor cold in one part and on fire otherwhere.
I flattered myself that the better and worse
To a harmony perfect should move in my verse;
As the poet who serves Polyhymnia can bring
The grave and the piercing to concord, and ring

Notes loftier still from the nerves of his lyre.
But my courage which now does but faintly suspire,
Nigh to death, hath proclaimed that the arrow—ah, woe!—
Which pierced me, and first with this love made me moan,
Was no arrow dispatched from the easy-bent bow
By a Venus who sprang from a father alone.
But 'twas that other Venus who caused me to smart,
She, born of frail mother with cowardly heart.
Yet this naughty rascal, this hunter so bold,
Whose quiver does arrows of subtlety hold,
Who, laughing and shaking his torch (for a day!),
Never rests but upon tender flowers and gay,
And on a sweet skin dries his tears as they flow—
'Tis a God still, Enone, this Love that we know.
Let it pass, for the birds of the springtime are fled,
And I see the last rays of a sun that's nigh dead.
Enone, my grief, ah harmonious face,
Humility grand, words of virtue and grace,
I looked yestere'en in the pond frozen fast,
Strewn with leaves at the end of the garden's fair space,
And I read in my face that those days are now past.

No. 5

And this is also from page 28 of a thick book, full of similar poems, by M. Montesquiou.

Berceuse d'ombre

Des formes, des formes, des formes
Blanche, bleue, et rose, et d'or
Descendront du haut des ormes
Sur l'enfant qui se rendort.
Des formes!

Des plumes, des plumes, des plumes
Pour composer un doux nid.
Midi sonne: les enclumes
Cessent; la rumeur finit ...
Des plumes!

Des roses, des roses, des roses
Pour embaumer son sommeil,
Vos pétales sont moroses
Près du sourire vermeil.
    O roses!

Des ailes, des ailes, des ailes
Pour bourdonner à son front,
Abeilles et demoiselles,
Des rythmes qui berceront.
    Des ailes!

Des branches, des branches, des branches
Pour tresser un pavillon,
Par où des clartés moins franches
Descendront sur l'oisillon.
    Des branches!

Des songes, des songes, des songes,
Dans ses pensers entr'ouverts
Glissez un peu de mensonges
A voir la vie au travers.
    Des songes!

Des fées, des fées, des fées,
Pour filer leurs écheveaux
De mirages, de bouffées
Dans tous ces petits cerveaux.
    Des fées.

Des anges, des anges, des anges
Pour emporter dans l'éther
Les petits enfants étranges
Qui ne veulent pas rester . . .
    Nos anges!

      Comte Robert de Montesquiou-Fezensac,
              Les Hortensias Bleues.

The Shadow Lullaby

Forms, forms, forms
White, blue, and gold, and red
Descending from the elm trees,
On sleeping baby's head.
    Forms!

Feathers, feathers, feathers
To make a cosy nest.
Twelve striking: stops the clamour;
The anvils are at rest . . .
  Oh feathers!

Roses, roses, roses
To scent his sleep awhile,
Pale are your fragrant petals
Beside his ruby smile.
  Oh roses!

Wings, wings, wings
Of bees and dragon-flies,
To hum around his forehead,
And lull him with your sighs.
  Oh wings!

Branches, branches, branches
A shady bower to twine,
Through which, oh daylight, faintly
Descend on birdie mine.
  Branches !

Dreams, dreams, dreams
Into his opening mind,
Let in a little falsehood
With sights of life behind.
  Dreams!

Fairies, fairies, fairies,
To twine and twist their threads
With puffs of phantom visions
Into these little heads.
  Fairies!

Angels, angels, angels
To the ether far away,
Those children strange to carry
That here don't wish to stay . . .
  Our angels!

APPENDIX IV

These are the contents of the *Nibelungen Ring*:

The first part tells that the nymphs, the daughters of the Rhine, guard gold in the Rhine for some reason, and sing: Weia, Waga, Woge du Welle, Walle zur Wiege, Wagalaweia, Wallala, Weila, Weia, and so forth.

These singing nymphs are pursued by a dwarf (a nibelung) who desires to seize them. The dwarf cannot catch any of them. Then the nymphs guarding the gold tell the dwarf just what they ought to keep secret, namely, that whoever renounces love will be able to steal the gold they are guarding. And the dwarf renounces love and steals the gold. This ends the first scene.

In the second scene a god and a goddess lie in a field in sight of a castle which giants have built for them. Presently they wake up and are pleased with the castle, and they relate that in payment for this work they must give the goddess Freia to the giants. The giants come for their pay. But the god Wotan objects to parting with Freia. The giants grow angry. The gods hear that the dwarf has stolen the gold, and promise to confiscate it and to pay the giants with it. But the giants won't trust them, and seize the goddess Freia in pledge.

The third scene takes place under ground. Alberich, the dwarf who stole the gold, for some reason beats another dwarf, Mime, and takes from him a helmet which has the power both of making people invisible and of turning them into animals. The gods, Wotan and others, appear and quarrel with one another and with the dwarfs, and wish to take the gold, but Alberich won't give it up, and (like everybody all through the piece) behaves in a way to ensure his own ruin. He puts on the helmet, and becomes first a dragon and then a toad. The gods catch the toad, take the helmet off it, and carry Alberich away with them.

Scene IV. The gods bring Alberich to their home and order him to command his dwarfs to bring them all the gold. The dwarfs bring it. Alberich gives up the gold but keeps a magic ring. The gods take the ring. So Alberich curses the ring and says it is to bring misfortune on any one who has it. The giants appear; they bring the goddess Freia, and demand her ransom. They stick up staves of Freia's height, and gold is poured in between these staves: this is to be the ransom. There is not enough gold, so the helmet is thrown in, and they demand the ring also. Wotan refuses to give it up, but the goddess Erda appears and commands him to do so because it brings misfortune. Wotan gives it up. Freia is released. The giants, having received the ring, fight, and one of them kills the other. This ends the Prelude, and we come to the First Day.

The scene shows a house in a tree. Siegmund runs in tired, and lies down. Sieglinda, the mistress of the house (and wife of Hunding), gives him a drugged draught and they fall in love with each other. Sieglinda's husband comes home, learns that Siegmund belongs to a hostile race, and wishes to fight him next day; but Sieglinda drugs her husband and comes to Siegmund. Siegmund discovers that Sieglinda is his sister and that his father drove a sword into the tree so that no one can get it out. Siegmund pulls the sword out and commits incest with his sister.

Act II. Siegmund is to fight with Hunding. The gods discuss the question as to whom they shall award the victory. Wotan, approving of Siegmund's incest with his sister, wishes to spare him, but under pressure

from his wife, Fricka, he orders the Valkyrie Brünnhilda to kill Siegmund. Siegmund goes to fight.
Sieglinda faints. Brünnhilda appears and wishes to
slay Siegmund. Siegmund wishes to kill Sieglinda also,
but Brünnhilda does not allow it, and he fights with
Hunding. Brünnhilda defends Siegmund, but Wotan
defends Hunding. Siegmund's sword breaks and he
is killed. Sieglinda runs away.

Act III. The Valkyries (divine Amazons) are on
the stage. The Valkyrie Brünnhilda arrives on horse-
back, bringing Siegmund's body. She is flying from
Wotan who is chasing her for her disobedience. Wotan
catches her, and as a punishment dismisses her from
her post as a Valkyrie. He also casts a spell on her, so
that she has to go to sleep and continue asleep until
a man wakes her. When some one wakes her she will
fall in love with him. Wotan kisses her; she falls
asleep. He lets off fire, which surrounds her.

We now come to the Second Day. The dwarf
Mime forges a sword in a wood. Siegfried appears.
He is a son born from the incest of brother with sister
(Siegmund with Sieglinda), and has been brought up
in this wood by the dwarf. In general the motives for
the actions of everybody in this production are quite
unintelligible. Siegfried learns his origin, and that
the broken sword was his father's. He orders Mime to
re-forge it, and then goes off. Wotan comes in the
guise of a wanderer and relates what will happen:
that he who has not learnt to fear will forge the sword
and will defeat everybody. The dwarf conjectures
that this is Siegfried and wants to poison him. Siegfried returns, forges his father's sword, and runs off,
shouting, 'Heiho heiho heiho! Ho ho! Aha! oho!
aha! Heiaho! heiaho! heiaho! Ho! ho! Hahei! hoho!
hahei!'

And we get to Act II. Alberich sits guarding a
giant, who, in form of a dragon, guards the gold he

M

has received. Wotan appears, and for some unknown
reason foretells that Siegfried will come and kill the
dragon. Alberich wakes the dragon and asks him for
the ring, promising to defend him from Siegfried.
The dragon won't give up the ring. Exit Alberich.
Mime and Siegfried appear. Mime hopes the dragon
will teach Siegfried to fear. But Siegfried does not
fear. He drives Mime away and kills the dragon,
after which he puts his finger, smeared with the
dragon's blood, to his lips. This enables him to know
men's secret thoughts, as well as the language of birds.
The birds tell him where the treasure and the ring are,
and also that Mime wishes to poison him. Mime returns
and says out loud that he wishes to poison Siegfried.
This is meant to signify that Siegfried, having tasted
dragon's blood, understands people's secret thoughts.
Siegfried, having learnt Mime's intentions, kills him.
The birds tell Siegfried where Brünnhilda is and he
goes to find her.

Act III. Wotan calls up Erda. Erda prophesies to
Wotan and gives him advice. Siegfried appears,
quarrels with Wotan, and they fight. Suddenly Siegfried's sword breaks Wotan's spear, which had been
more powerful than anything else. Siegfried goes into
the fire to Brünnhilda and kisses her; she wakes up,
abandons her divinity, and throws herself into Siegfried's arms.

Third Day. Prelude. Three Norns plait a golden
rope and talk about the future. They go away.
Siegfried and Brünnhilda appear. Siegfried takes
leave of her, gives her the ring, and goes away.

Act I. By the Rhine. A king wants to get married
and also to give his sister in marriage. Hagen, the
king's wicked brother, advises him to marry Brünnhilda and to give his sister to Siegfried. Siegfried
appears; they give him a drugged draught which
makes him forget the past and fall in love with the

king's sister, Gutrune. So he rides off with Gunther, the king, to get Brünnhilda to be the king's bride. The scene changes. Brünnhilda sits with the ring. A Valkyrie comes to her and tells her that Wotan's spear is broken, and advises her to give the ring to the Rhine nymphs. Siegfried comes and by means of the magic helmet turns himself into Gunther, demands the ring from Brünnhilda, seizes it, and drags her off to sleep with him.

Act II. By the Rhine. Alberich and Hagen discuss how to get the ring. Siegfried comes, tells how he has obtained a bride for Gunther and how he spent the night with her, but put a sword between himself and her. Brünnhilda rides up, recognizes the ring on Siegfried's hand, and declares that it was he, and not Gunther, who was with her. Hagen stirs everybody up against Siegfried and decides to kill him next day when hunting.

Act III. Again the nymphs in the Rhine relate what has happened. Siegfried, who has lost his way, appears. The nymphs ask him for the ring but he won't give it up. Hunters appear. Siegfried tells the story of his life. Hagen then gives him a draught which causes his memory to return to him. Siegfried relates how he aroused and obtained Brünnhilda, and every one is astonished. Hagen stabs him in the back, and the scene is changed. Gutrune meets the corpse of Siegfried. Gunther and Hagen quarrel about the ring, and Hagen kills Gunther. Brünnhilda cries. Hagen wishes to take the ring from Siegfried's hand, but the hand of the corpse raises itself threateningly. Brünnhilda takes the ring from Siegfried's hand, and when Siegfried's corpse is carried to the pyre she gets on to a horse and leaps into the fire. The Rhine rises, and the waves reach the pyre. In the river are three nymphs. Hagen throws himself into the fire to get the ring, but the nymphs seize him and carry him off.

One of them holds the ring; and that is the end of the matter.

The impression obtainable from my recapitulation is of course incomplete. But however incomplete it may be, it is certainly infinitely more favourable than the impression which results from reading the four booklets in which the work is printed.

PART IX

PREFACE TO VON POLENZ'S NOVEL 'DER BÜTTNERBAUER'[1]

'For you will find, if you think deeply of it, that the chief of all the curses of this unhappy age is the universal gabble of its fools, and of the flocks that follow them, rendering the quiet voices of the wise men of all past time inaudible. This is, first, the result of the invention of printing, and of the easy power and extreme pleasure to vain persons of seeing themselves in print. When it took a twelvemonth's hard work to make a single volume legible, men considered a little the difference between one book and another; but now, when not only anybody can get themselves made legible through any quantity of volumes, in a week, but the doing so becomes a means of living to them, and they can fill their stomachs with the foolish foam of their lips, the universal pestilence of falsehood fills the mind of the world as cicadas do olive-leaves, and the first necessity for our mental government is to extricate from among the insectile noise, the few books and words that are Divine.'—Ruskin, in *Fors Clavigera*, Letter 81.

Last year a friend of mine in whose taste I have confidence gave me a German novel, *Der Büttnerbauer*, by von Polenz, to read. I read it and was astonished that such a work, which appeared a couple of years ago, was hardly known by any one.

This novel is not one of those works of imitation-art

---

[1] W. VON POLENZ was born in 1861 and died in 1903. His novels, *Der Pfarrer von Breitendorf* (1893), and *Der Büttnerbauer* (1895), are descriptions of village life. His *Grabenhäger*, *Thekla Lüdekind*, and *Liebe ist ewig* (1900) describe the life of the landowning and town classes. *Wurzellocker* (1902) treats of a literary society.

that are produced in such enormous quantities in our time, but is a really artistic production. It is not one of those descriptions of events and of people, destitute of all interest, which are artificially put together merely because the author, having learned the technique of artistic descriptions, wants to write a new novel; nor is it one of those dissertations on a given theme set in the form of a drama or novel, which also in our day pass as artistic productions: nor does it belong to the class of works called 'decadent', which particularly please the modern public just because, resembling the ravings of a madman, they present something of the nature of rebuses the guessing of which forms a pleasant occupation besides being considered a sign of refinement.

This novel belongs neither to the first, nor to the second, nor to the third, of these categories, but is a real work of art, in which the author says what he feels he must say because he loves what he is speaking about, and says it not by reflections or hazy allegories, but in the one manner by which artistic content can be conveyed, by poetic images, not fantastic, extraordinary, unintelligible images with no essential inner connexion one with another, but by the presentation of the most ordinary, simple, persons and events, united one with another by an inner artistic necessity.

But not only is this novel a genuine work of art, it is also an admirable work of art, uniting in a high degree the three chief conditions of really good artistic production.

In the first place its content is important, relating as it does to the life of the peasantry—that is, to the majority of mankind who stand at the basis of every social structure, and in our day, not only in Germany but in all European countries, are enduring trying alterations of their ancient, age-long condition. (It is remarkable that almost simultaneously with *Der*

Büttnerbauer there has appeared a French novel, René Bazin's *La Terre qui meurt*, which is not at all bad, though far less artistic).

In the second place, this novel is written with great mastery in admirable German, particularly forcible when the author makes his characters speak the coarse peasant-labourer's *Plattdeutsch*.

In the third place this novel is thoroughly indued with love of the people whom the author sets before us.

In one of the chapters, for instance, there is a description of how after a night passed in drunkenness with his comrades, the husband when it is already morning returns home and knocks at the door. The wife looks out of the window and recognizes him; she loads him with abuse and is purposely slow about letting him in. When at last she opens the door for him, the husband tumbles in and wants to go into the large living-room, but the wife does not let him, lest the children should see their father drunk, and she pushes him back. But he catches hold of the lintel of the door and struggles with her. Usually a mild man, he suddenly becomes terribly exasperated (the cause of his exasperation is that the day before she had taken out of his pocket some money his master had given him, and had hidden it) and in his rage he flings himself upon her, seizes her by the hair, and demands his money.

'I won't give it up, I won't give it up for anything!' says she in reply to his demands, trying to free herself from him.

Then he, forgetting himself in his anger, strikes her where and as he can.

'I'll die before I'll give it up!' says she.

'You won't give it up!' he answers, knocking her off her feet and falling on her himself, while continuing to demand his money. Not receiving a reply, in his mad drunken anger he tries to throttle her. But the sight of blood which trickles from under her hair and flows over her forehead and nose, causes him to stop. He becomes frightened at what he has done, and letting go of her, staggers and falls down on his bed.

The scene is truthful and terrible. But the author loves his protagonists and adds one small detail which suddenly illumines everything with such a vivid ray as compels the reader not only to pity but also to love these people, despite their coarseness and cruelty. The wife who has been beaten comes to herself, rises from the floor, wipes her bleeding head with the hem of her skirt, feels her limbs, and opening the door leading to the crying children quiets them, and then seeks her husband with her eyes. He is lying on the bed as he had fallen, but his head has slipped from the pillow. The wife walks over to him, carefully raises his head on the pillow, and after that adjusts her dress and picks off some of her hair that had been pulled out.

Dozens of pages of dialogue would not have said all that is said by this detail. Here at once the reader is shown the consciousness of conjugal duty educated by tradition, and the triumph of a decision maintained—not to give up the money, needed, not for herself but for the family—here also is the offence, forgiveness of the beating, and pity, and if not love, at least the memory of love for her husband, the father of her children. Nor is that all. Such a detail, illuminating the inner life of this woman and this man, lights up for the reader the inner life of millions of such husbands and wives, who have lived or are now living, and not only teaches respect and love for these people who are crushed by toil, but compels us to consider why and wherefore they, strong in soul and body, with such possibilities in them of good, loving life, are so neglected, crushed, and ignorant.

And such truly artistic traits, which are revealed to an author only by love of what he is describing, are met with in every chapter of this novel.

It is undoubtedly a beautiful work of art, as all who read it will agree. And yet it appeared three years ago, and though translated into Russian in the *Messenger of Europe*, has passed unnoticed both in Russia and in Germany. I have asked several literary Germans whom I have met recently about this novel—they had heard von Polenz's name, but had not read his book, though they had all read the last novels of Zola, the last stories by Kipling, and the plays of Ibsen, d'Annunzio, and even of Maeterlinck.

Some twenty years ago Matthew Arnold wrote an admirable article on the purpose of criticism.[1] In his opinion the purpose of criticism is to find among all that has been written, whenever and wherever it may be, that which is most important and good, and to direct the attention of readers to this that is important and good.

In our time, when readers are deluged with newspapers, periodicals, books, and by the profusion of advertisements, not only does such criticism seem to me essential, but the whole future culture of the educated class of our European world depends on whether such criticism appears and acquires authority.

The over-production of any kind of article is harmful; but the over-production of articles which are not an aim but a means, is particularly harmful when people consider this means to be an aim.

Horses and carriages as means of conveyance, clothing and houses as means of protection against changes of weather, good food to maintain the strength of one's organism, are very useful. But as soon as men begin to regard the possession of means as an end in itself, considering it good to have as many horses, clothes, and houses, and as much food, as possible, such articles become not only useless but simply harmful. And this has come about with book-pro-

---

[1] *The Function of Criticism at the Present Time*, in his *Essays in Criticism*.

duction among the well-to-do circle of people of our European society. Printing, which is undoubtedly useful for the great masses of uneducated people, among well-to-do people has long ago become the chief organ for the dissemination of ignorance, and not of enlightenment.

It is easy to convince oneself of this. Books, periodicals, and especially newspapers, have become in our time great financial undertakings for the success of which the largest possible number of purchasers is required. But the interests and tastes of the largest number of purchasers are always low and vulgar, and so for the success of the productions of the press it is necessary that these productions should correspond to the demands of this great mass of purchasers, that is, that they should treat of mean interests and correspond to vulgar tastes. And the press fully satisfies these demands, having ample opportunity to do so, since among those who work for the press there are many more with the same mean interests and coarse tastes as the public, than there are men with lofty interests and refined taste. And since with the diffusion of printing, and the commercial methods applied to newspapers, periodicals, and books, these people receive good pay for matter they supply corresponding to the demands of the masses, there appears that terrible, ever and ever increasing deluge of printed paper, which by its quantity alone, not to speak of the harmfulness of its contents, forms a vast obstacle to enlightenment.

If in our day a clever young man of the people wishing to educate himself, is given access to all books, periodicals, and newspapers, and the choice of his reading is left to himself, he will, if he reads for ten years assiduously every day, in all probability read nothing but stupid and immoral books. It is as improbable that he will strike on a good book, as it would be that he should find a marked pea in a bushel of peas. What is worst of all is that, continually reading bad books, he will more and more pervert his understanding and his taste, so that when he does come on a good work he will either be quite unable to understand it or will understand it perversely.

Besides this, thanks to accident or to masterly advertisement, some bad works, such, for instance, as *The Christian* by Hall Caine, a novel false in its content and inartistic, which has been sold to the extent of a million copies, obtain, without the proper merit, as great a notoriety as Odol or Pears' Soap. And this great publicity causes an ever growing number of people to read such books, and the fame of an insignificant, or often harmful, book grows and grows like a snowball, and in the heads of the great majority of men an ever and ever greater confusion of ideas is formed, also like a snowball, involving complete incapacity to understand the qualities of literary productions. Therefore in proportion to the greater and greater diffusion of newspapers, periodicals, books, and printing in general, the level of the quality of what is printed falls lower and lower, and the great mass of the so-called educated public is ever more and more immersed in the most hopeless, self-satisfied, and therefore incurable, ignorance.

Within my own memory, during the last fifty years, this striking debasement of the taste and common sense of the reading public has occurred. One may trace this debasement in all branches of literature, but I will indicate only a few notable instances best known to me. In Russian poetry, for instance, after Púshkin and Lérmontov (Tyúchev is generally forgotten) poetic fame passes first to the very doubtful poets, Máykov, Polónski, and Fet, then to Nekrásov, who was quite destitute of the poetic gift, then to the artificial and prosaic versifier, Alexéy Tolstóy, then to the monotonous and weak Nádson, then to the quite ungifted Apúkhtin, and after that everything becomes confused, and versifiers appear whose name is legion—who do not even know what poetry is, or the meaning of what they write, or why they write.

Another astonishing example is that of the English prose writers. From the great Dickens we descend, first to George Eliot, then to Thackeray, from Thackeray to Trollope, and then there already begin the indifferent fabrications of Kipling, Hall Caine, Rider Haggard, and so forth. The same thing is yet more striking in American literature. After the great galaxy of Emerson, Thoreau, Lowell, Whittier, and others, suddenly everything crumbles, and there appear beautiful publications with beautiful illustrations, but with stories and novels it is impossible to read because of their lack of any content.

In our time the ignorance of the educated crowd has reached such a pass that all the really great thinkers, poets, and prose writers, both of ancient times and of the nineteenth century, are considered obsolete and no longer satisfy the lofty and refined demands of the new men; it is all regarded with contempt or with a smile of condescension. The immoral, coarse, inflated, disconnected, babble of Nietzsche is recognized as the last word of the philosophy of our day, and the senseless artificial arrangements of words in various decadent poems united by measure and rhythm, is regarded as poetry of the highest order. In all the theatres plays are produced the meaning of which is unknown to any one, even to the authors, and novels that have no content and no artistic merit are printed and circulated by millions under the guise of artistic productions.

'What shall I read to supplement my education?' asks a young man or girl who has finished his or her studies at the high-school.

The same question is put by a man of the people who has learned to read and to understand what he reads, and is seeking true enlightenment.

To answer such questions the naïve attempts made to interrogate prominent men as to which they consider to be the best hundred books is of course insufficient.

Nor is the matter helped by the classification existing in our European society and tacitly accepted by all, which divides writers into first, second, and third class, and so on—into those of genius, those who are very talented, and those simply good. Such a division, far from helping a true understanding of the excellences of literature and the search for what is good amid the sea of what is bad, still more confuses this aim. To say nothing of the fact that this division into classes is often incorrect, and is maintained only because it was made long ago and is accepted by everybody, such a division is harmful because writers acknowledged to be first-class have written some very bad things, and writers of the lowest class have produced some excellent things. So that a man who believes in the division of writers into classes, and thinks everything by first-class writers to be admirable and everything by writers of the lower class, or those quite unknown, to be weak, will only become confused and deprive himself of much that is useful and truly enlightening.

Only real criticism can reply to that most important question of our day, put by the youth of the educated class who seeks education and by the man of the people who seeks enlightenment—not such criticism as now exists, which sets itself the task of praising such works as have obtained notoriety and devising foggy philosophic æsthetic theories to justify them; and not criticism that makes it its task more or less wittily to ridicule bad works, or works proceeding from a different camp; still less such criticism as has functioned and still functions in Russia, and sets itself the task of deducing the direction of the movement of our whole society from some types depicted by certain writers, or in general of finding opportunities to express particular economic and political opinions under guise of discussing literary productions.

To that enormously important question, 'What, of all that has been written, is one to read?' only real criticism can furnish a reply: criticism which, as Matthew Arnold says, sets itself the task of bringing to the front and pointing out to people all that is best, both in former and in contemporary writers.

On whether such disinterested criticism, which understands and loves art and is independent of any party, makes its appearance or not, and on whether its authority becomes sufficiently established for it to be stronger than mercenary advertisement, depends, in my opinion, the decision of the question whether the last rays of enlightenment are to perish in our so-called educated European society without having reached the masses of the people, or whether they will revive, as they did in the Middle Ages, and reach the great mass of the people who are now without any enlightenment.

The fact that the mass of the public do not know of this admirable novel of von Polenz's, any more than they do of many other admirable works which are drowned in the sea of printed rubbish, while senseless, insignificant, and even simply nasty, literary productions are discussed from every aspect, invariably praised, and sold by millions of copies, has evoked in me these thoughts, and I avail myself of the opportunity, which will hardly present itself to me again, of expressing them, though it be but briefly.

PART X

AN AFTERWORD, BY TOLSTÓY, TO CHÉKHOV'S STORY, 'DARLING'

THERE is profound meaning in the story in the Book of Numbers, which tells how Balak, king of the Moabites, sent for Balaam to curse the people of Israel who had come to his borders. Balak promised Balaam many gifts for his service; and Balaam being tempted went to Balak, but was stopped on the way by an angel, who was seen by his ass but whom Balaam did not see. In spite of this, Balaam went on to Balak and went with him up a mountain, where an altar had been prepared with calves and lambs slaughtered in readiness for the imprecation. Balak waited for the curse to be pronounced, but instead of cursing them Balaam blessed the people of Israel.

Ch. XXIII, v. 11. 'And Balak said unto Balaam, What hast thou done unto me? I took thee to curse mine enemies, and, behold, thou hast blessed them altogether.

v. 12. 'And he answered and said, Must I not take heed to speak that which the Lord putteth in my mouth?

v. 13. 'And Balak said unto him, Come with me unto another place . . . and curse me them from thence.'

And he took him to another place, where also altars had been prepared.

But again Balaam, instead of cursing, blessed them.

And so it was a third time.

Chapter XXIV, v. 10. 'And Balak's anger was kindled against Balaam, and he smote his hands together; and Balak said unto Balaam, I called thee to curse mine enemies, and thou hast blessed them these three times. Therefore now flee thou to thy place: I thought to promote thee unto great honour; and, lo, the Lord hath kept thee back from honour.' And so Balaam departed without receiving the gifts, because instead of cursing Balak's enemies he had blessed them.

What happened to Balaam very often happens to true poets and artists. Tempted by Balak's promises of popularity, or by false views suggested to them, the poet does not even see the angel that bars his way, whom the ass sees, and he wishes to curse but yet he blesses.

This is just what happened with the true poet and artist Chékhov when he wrote his charming story, *Darling*.

The author evidently wanted to laugh at this pitiful creature—as he judged her with his intellect, not with his heart—this 'Darling', who, after sharing Kúkin's troubles about his theatre, and then immersing herself in the interests of the timber business, under the influence of the veterinary surgeon considers the struggle against bovine tuberculosis to be the most important matter in the world, and is finally absorbed in questions of grammar and the interests of the little school-boy in the big cap. Kúkin's name is ridiculous, and so even is his illness and the telegram announcing his death. The timber-dealer with his sedateness is ridiculous, and the veterinary surgeon and the boy are ridiculous; but the soul of 'Darling', with her capacity for devoting herself with her whole being to the one she loves, is not ridiculous but wonderful and holy.

I think that in the mind, though not in the heart, of the author when he wrote *Darling*, there was a dim idea of the new woman, of her equality of rights with

man; of woman, developed, learned, working independently, and as well as man if not better, for the
benefit of society; of the woman who has raised, and
insists upon, the woman question; and in beginning
to write *Darling* he wanted to show what woman
ought not to be. The Balak of public opinion invited
Chékhov to curse the weak, submissive, undeveloped
woman devoted to man, and Chékhov ascended the
mountain and the calves and sheep were laid upon
the altar, but when he began to speak, the author
blessed what he had meant to curse. Despite the
wonderful gay humour of the whole work, I, at any
rate, cannot read without tears some passages of this
beautiful story. I am touched by the description of the
complete devotion with which she loved Kúkin and all
that he cared for, and also the timber-dealer, and also
the veterinary surgeon, and yet more by her sufferings
when she was left alone and had no one to love, and
by the account of how finally, with all the strength of
her womanly and motherly feeling (which she had
never had the opportunity to expend on children of
her own), she devoted her unbounded love to the
future man, the school-boy in the big cap.

The author makes her love the ridiculous Kúkin,
the insignificant timber-dealer, and the unpleasant
veterinary surgeon; but love is not less sacred whether
its object be a Kúkin or a Spinoza, a Pascal or a
Schiller, whether its object changes as rapidly as in the
case of *Darling*, or remains the same for a whole life-
time.

I happened not long ago to read in the *Nóvoe
Vrémya* an excellent feuilleton by M. Ata about
women. In this feuilleton the author expressed a
remarkably wise and profound thought. 'Women',
he says, 'try to prove to us that they can do everything we men can do. I not only do not dispute this,
but am ready to agree that women can do all that

men do and perhaps even do it better, but the trouble is that men cannot do anything even approximately approaching what women can accomplish.'

Yes, that is certainly so, and it is true not only of the bearing, nursing, and early education of children, but men cannot do what is loftiest, best, and brings man nearest to God—the work of loving, of complete devotion to the beloved, which has been so well and naturally done, and is done and will be done, by good women. What would become of the world, what would become of us men, if women had not that faculty and did not exercise it? Without women doctors, women telegraphists, women lawyers and scientists and authoresses, we might get on, but without mothers, helpers, friends, comforters, who love in man all that is best in him—without such women it would be hard to live in the world. Christ would be without Mary or Magdalene, Francis of Assisi would have lacked Claire, there would have been no wives of the Decembrists in their exile, nor would the Dukhobors have had their wives, who did not restrain their husbands but supported them in their martyrdom for truth. There would not have been those thousands and thousands of unknown women—the very best (as the unknown generally are)—comforters of the drunken, the weak, and the dissolute, who more than any one else need the consolation of love. In that love, whether directed to Kúkin or to Christ, is the chief, grand, strength of women, irreplaceable by anything else.

What a wonderful misconception is the whole so-called woman's question, which has obsessed (as is natural with every empty idea) the majority of women and even of men!

'Woman wants to improve herself!' What can be more legitimate or more just than that?

But the business of a woman, by her very vocation, is different from that of a man. And therefore the ideal of perfection for a woman cannot be the same as the ideal for a man. Let us grant that we do not know in what that ideal consists, but in any case it is certainly not the ideal of perfection for a man. And yet to the attainment of that masculine ideal all the absurd and unwholesome activity of the fashionable woman's movement, which now so confuses women, is directed.

I am afraid that Chékhov when writing *Darling* was under the influence of this misunderstanding.

He, like Balaam, intended to curse, but the God of poetry forbade him to do so and commanded him to bless, and he blessed, and involuntarily clothed that sweet creature in such a wonderful radiance that she will always remain a type of what woman can be in order to be happy herself and to cause the happiness of those with whom her fate is united.

This story is so excellent because its effect was unintentional.

I learned to ride a bicycle in the great Moscow riding-school in which army-divisions are reviewed. At the other end of the riding-school a lady was learning to ride. I thought of how to avoid incommoding that lady and began looking at her. And, looking at her, I began involuntarily to draw nearer and nearer to her, and although she, noticing the danger, hastened to get out of the way, I rode against her and upset her, that is to say, I did exactly the opposite of what I wished to do, simply because I had concentrated my attention upon her.

The same thing has happened with Chékhov but in an inverse sense: he wanted to knock down 'Darling', and directing the close attention of a poet upon her he has exalted her.

INDEX

The figures in heavier type refer to pages of What is Art? *which is the principal article in this volume.*